"In *Gluten-Free Baking at Home*, Jeffrey succeeds in making gluten-free baking both accessible and nuanced. He refuses a one-mix-fits-all approach—a gift to those seeking flaky biscuits, tender breads, and chewy cookies, all of which deserve a unique set of ingredients and a thoughtfulness in regard to method. Jeffrey is both an artist and a perfectionist, two virtues that shine in each recipe in this book, but most notably in the Chocolate Chip Cookies—a cookie that is as beautiful as it is irresistible."

—ALEXANDRA STAFFORD, author of *Bread Toast Crumbs*

"*Gluten-Free Baking at Home* is a beautiful book, complete with mouthwatering photography and a wide variety of spectacular foolproof recipes for those who want to bake without gluten. Jeffrey's curiosity and baking skill make him the ultimate teacher who gently guides the reader toward success with every morsel of yum down to the last crumb. Superb!"

—REBECCA KATZ, author of *Clean Soups*

GLUTEN-FREE
baking at home

GLUTEN-FREE
baking at home

102 Foolproof Recipes for Delicious Breads, Cakes, Cookies, and More

JEFFREY LARSEN

photographs by KELLY PULEIO

TEN SPEED PRESS
California | New York

I dedicate this book to my Grandma Blake, my mother, Phyllis, and all of you who have also lived on the outside looking in.

My grandmother, Louise Blake, was married to my grandfather, William Blake, for seventy-one years. She had three children, eight grandchildren, five great-grandchildren, and three great-great-grandchildren. She was my best friend growing up. Her quiet strength, her playful spirit, and her creativity will forever be an inspiration to me.

contents

introduction

MY STORY

I was such an oddball kid. I really didn't fit in with other kids my own age, always feeling a little on the outside looking in, even within my family. I was introverted, shy, and extremely sensitive, but also very creative and good with my hands. I was happiest in the kitchen with my grandma, Louise Blake. It was there that I could contribute, and everything else melted away. I don't know if I was actually much help, especially at five years old. The important thing was that my grandmother made me feel vital to the workings of her kitchen.

My earliest memory of learning how to bake is of me wearing an apron and standing on a chair in front of Grandma's long kitchen counter. Grandma Blake's kitchen was always full of cooking and baking projects, and it seemed like she was continuously rolling out dough or pasta, or both. Instead of letting me play under her feet, Grandma would give me a small hunk of dough and a kid-size rolling pin, and I happily followed along with whatever she was making at the time.

Louise Blake was a stay-at-home mom, like many women of her time, but she was also an artist who used cooking as an outlet for her creativity. She seemed to relish baking and always brought a sense of play to the work. I was born with the soul of an artist, too, and Grandma Blake understood that that part of my creative spirit needed to be nourished. Teaching me how to cook not only gave her permission to be a kid again but also, more importantly, gave me permission to bring a spirit of playfulness to both my cooking and my life.

My evolution into a recipe developer and food stylist has been full of twists and turns—my résumé is pretty eclectic—but the common thread throughout my career has been that sense of passion and creativity that Grandma instilled in me.

I was always interested in food and cooking. My whole family was. (I often joke about how we would plan the next meal while sitting down to the current meal!) In the late 1960s, my mom and Grandma belonged to a ladies' club where they learned how to make ravioli, wontons, and Indian curries. It was their monthly "Home Demonstration" meetings that gave me an expansive appreciation for the cuisines of the world, long before there was an ethnic foods aisle in every grocery store and a good Thai or Vietnamese restaurant in every city across America. What an amazing gift these women gave me!

And cooking wasn't only women's work. On my mother's side of the family, my uncles and my grandfather were often involved in the preparation of meals for the holidays and other special occasions. I especially loved how Grandpa Blake put himself in charge of making turkey noodle soup using the leftovers from Thanksgiving. Grandpa took such pride in that soup. The night after Thanksgiving, we would reassemble at Grandma and Grandpa's for leftovers. This was without a doubt my favorite meal of the year. It was less formal, and the kids were allowed to eat from TV trays while sitting in front of some holiday special airing on television. Grandpa's soup with Grandma's hand-cut noodles was the highlight for me. I am still a sucker for a bowl of good soup.

Throughout high school, I was involved in the theater department. This was where I discovered a new outlet for my creativity and also found a community of like-minded people. I loved that time in my life. I challenged myself to get over being painfully shy and allowed myself to be out front, to be seen. When it came time to go off to college, I didn't know what I wanted to pursue; I just knew that I wanted to be with my friends and continue to explore my artistic side. I enrolled in dance, painting, and drawing classes. In 1981, I found myself in the theater department at the University of Montana in Missoula. I started out as a performance major but soon discovered that I did not have the fortitude for the auditioning and constant judgment that actors have to face.

In my second year of college, an insightful professor asked me to design costumes for the dance department's annual showcase. I completely immersed myself in that project and discovered that I really liked being away from the glare of the spotlight. The following semester, I changed my major to costume and set design. This was a great time in my life. I loved collaborating with other creative people. I also loved the process of bringing something unique into the world. I found that I was better suited for the backstage, and my college degree ended up being a BFA with an emphasis in theater design.

Starting in 1982, I spent three summers working for the Wells Fargo Restaurant in Virginia City, Montana, as a sous chef. The chef de cuisine liked to—how do I put this—drink, drank, drunk. Every morning he would stumble in, give me a list and a stack of recipes, and then go away and sleep off his hangover. I was left to do both the prep and the cooking. The chef would come back in the afternoon and go over what I had done, and then we would work the dinner service together. The days were long, but I remember loving being in the kitchen, working through my list. I learned the fundamentals of cooking, doing everything from preparing scalloped potatoes to cooking steak. The experience was trial by fire, but I was a tenacious kid with a strong work ethic, and I was determined not to let the chef down. In turn, he was firm but kind and became my first professional mentor in food.

After college, I was given many opportunities to hone my craft at designing and constructing costumes for community theater and dance productions, including a touring show for the Montana Repertory Theater. I eventually interviewed with the American Conservatory Theater, located in San Francisco, and was thrilled when I was chosen out of hundreds of young applicants to work in their costume shop. It was a dream come true. In fall 1988, I moved to San Francisco to pursue my professional career. It was hard to say goodbye to my family, but I fell in love with San Francisco immediately. I was completely enchanted by the fog, the distinctly different neighborhoods, and the creative inspiration I found there.

Throughout the 1990s, I continued to work as a costumer for theater and dance companies all over the Bay Area. I loved my career in the theater. However, by 2000, I felt like it was time for a significant change. I had grown weary of the financial struggles and the long hours in the theater, but I still wanted an outlet for my creativity and my passion. By this point, I had created a family of close friends in San Francisco, and I was tired of missing everyone's birthday and the holidays because my theater obligations required me to work most nights and weekends. I wasn't sure what I wanted to do next, but I had an inkling that it would have something to do with hospitality. I loved to bring people together with food and celebration.

My epiphany came in 2001. I was working on a commercial shoot for an ad campaign that involved food, and I was in charge of the wardrobe for the models. Once the models had been dressed, I had nothing else to do until the shoot was over, so I hung out in the studio kitchen with the food stylist and her assistant. I didn't even know that this was an actual job! A light bulb went off that day: I could do this! I knew how to cook—not everything, of course—but I knew more than most, and because I also had the design background, I saw how much food styling was like theater. There was a stage, props, lighting, and a director (the photographer) but all on a smaller scale, much more appropriate for my personality. I had never felt that I had a big enough personality for the grandeur of the theater. I tended to gravitate toward more intimate modern theater and dance. I liked to focus on the little details that really mattered for those disciplines. Food styling is also about the tiniest details—plus a little bit of storytelling. In that moment I turned all of my efforts toward becoming a food stylist.

I started by contacting food photographers, food stylists, and art directors in advertising. Joyce Oudkerk Pool, an accomplished food photographer, reached out to me and asked me to meet her for an interview. She paired me up with the food stylist Pouk'e on several projects. I seemed to have an innate sense of how to be helpful, how to be precise, and how to be focused, and most important, I could be trusted to work unsupervised. Suddenly, it was clear that everything I had done earlier in my life had led me to this point. I still had much to learn, but now I could learn while getting paid to do it. I will be forever thankful to Joyce and Pouk'e for giving me my first chance.

During this period, I met many food stylists, but one collaboration in particular turned out to be the most important mentorship of my career. In 2001 I began assisting Karen Shinto. Karen was a recent transplant from Los Angeles and a very accomplished food stylist. She taught me so much. For example, baking recipes can be especially daunting. It is not enough to simply bake your way through a recipe. You need to make sure that the recipe makes sense. Karen taught me how to weigh flours and not rely on measuring cups, which are terribly clumsy and not precise at all. We all measure flour so differently. I got used to looking up generalized baking ratios before I started anything major. I was becoming a recipe developer without even knowing it.

As I continued my career in food styling, something else began to emerge. My mother, Phyllis Wesche, and I have always suffered with digestive issues, yet our love of food and cooking overshadowed the intestinal conflict. In 2002, my mother decided to remove gluten and dairy from her diet. Because she didn't have community support or products to make her gluten-free diet easier, I decided to step in and help her as best I could. After all, my mother had always been so supportive of my creative endeavors.

This project kept us close even though we are many miles apart: she lives in Montana and I live in San Francisco. Mom and I traded gluten-free recipes and tested things out long-distance. I threw myself into reading about the science of baking and ingredient ratios and researching allergen-free alternatives. I used all that I had learned from Grandma Blake, from cookbooks, from my mom, and from my colleagues in food styling. I thought I was simply helping my mother, but it started to change my life in ways I could never have foreseen.

I began to develop my own gluten-free recipes and discovered that I had a knack for it. I just kept baking and baking. At first, much of what I devised went right into the compost bin, but I just kept trying. My baking eventually got better, and I finally resigned myself to joining my mother in removing gluten and dairy from my own diet. I was very passionate about this new hobby. I watched as my mother's health improved and mine as well.

It was around this time that we began to lose Grandma Blake to Alzheimer's. As she slipped a little further away each day, slowly wandering off to another plane of existence, I got stronger and more determined to embody her spirit. I couldn't let her slip from this world without allowing the full impact of her life be apparent in mine. She died three days before my birthday, on October 12, 2011. She was eighty-nine years old.

As I have mentioned, I was very shy and introverted as a child. My time as a performance major in the theater had already taught me that I wasn't comfortable in front of people. I never could have predicted that I would want to teach. But in 2011, I was convinced otherwise by a charismatic lady named Topher Delaney. A landscape architect by trade, Topher felt strongly about feeding people well, and she saw an opportunity to begin something unique in the Bay Area by starting the Gluten-Free Grocery Store out of her warehouse/home workspace. I heard about her shop from some colleagues and made a beeline there to meet her. We hit it off immediately. She is a self-starter who has a knack for progressive thinking and inspiring others to think outside the box. She saw something in me that I never saw in myself. She shoved an electric bread maker into my hands and told me she wanted me to teach a class in her store on making gluten-free bread in the bread machine.

I still find it funny to think about: me, teach? But I took it as a challenge. I went home and started researching gluten-free bread. It was so frustrating in the beginning—I threw out so much food. Up to this point, I had developed cookies and quick breads for my mom and me, but this was uncharted territory. I liken that time to being on a treasure hunt. The learning curve was steep, but I never gave up. I started to love the thrill of inventing something new and delicious.

I finally had a breakthrough after a month of experimenting. I was so scared, but I taught that class at the Gluten-Free Grocery Store. My shyness melted away, and I found that I could speak eloquently about this new passion of mine. The other benefit was that I could see that I was helping others. I, myself, have been the guy at the birthday party who is resigned to watching everyone else eat cake, so I knew the frustration my students felt. I understood how hard it is to be allergic to certain foods and how isolating that feels. I also understood that food is about so much more than sustenance—it is wrapped up in community, social engagement, and even love. So I decided to start teaching along with being a food stylist, as a way of helping others. It's been a tremendously rewarding process.

In 2012, I had heard about a new inn in Napa, California, that was going to be completely gluten-free. The first time I visited the Inn on Randolph, it was a construction zone. At the center of this mess was the dynamic Karen Lynch. She and I had an instant connection, and she asked me to lead my first gluten-free weekend for her guests shortly after the inn was scheduled to open. The full-weekend format allowed me to really go deep with the students. At the end of each weekend, I felt gratified to see the students leave feeling empowered. I led a total of six weekend retreats over the course of several years and met many wonderful people from all over the world.

Teaching had become so fulfilling for me, and I felt called upon to stay on this mission. But I wasn't content to teach just a few things—I wanted each student to take home a binder full of recipes. It was an exciting time of experimentation and I was extremely productive. The bulk of the recipes in this book come from that period.

These days I continue to work as a food stylist in a variety of disciplines—advertising, magazines, online, product packaging, and cookbooks. I develop products and recipes for a very diverse group of clients. I also teach professional classes at the San Francisco Cooking School. It is such a privilege to teach each new crop of pastry students about allergen-free baking. I am thankful for the progressive thinking of Jodi Liano and her team of instructors at the school. I know all of my students are going out into the hospitality industry and making life better for people with food allergies. It is such a different landscape than the one my mother and I started out in. There are so many great products and great resources out there, and there's a better understanding among chefs, bakers, and restaurant staff about food allergy sensitivity.

I really didn't see myself writing a book. I knew that I could devise a solid recipe, but writing a book is a whole other beast. I had a three-inch, three-ring binder full of recipes, but that was it. However, not only do I really understand this subject, but I also know from experience the isolation that comes with food allergies. When you are told that you can't have certain foods, it is emotionally challenging. There is nothing like witnessing the tears of joy in someone's eyes when I say to them, "Yes, this cake is for you," "this cookie is for you," or "this muffin, scone, or pie is for you." It has been my mission through the years to normalize these situations.

However, I don't want my food to be seen as a compromise for those who *don't* have allergy issues. I can't count how many times I've heard someone say, "gluten-free food—yuck!" before they even taste the food. This is what prompted me to write this book—a deep need to bring people together through cooking (the way my family did), while placing allergy issues in the background and great-tasting food in the foreground. I want my recipes to be sumptuous feasts for the eyes. I want the food in this cookbook to be approachable yet decadent, elegant yet easy to make. My greatest wish is for those of you reading this book to be able to bring *everyone* you love around your kitchen table to enjoy the process of both making and eating a great meal together, just as my grandmother did.

I dedicate this book to all of you who have also lived on the outside looking in.

MY PHILOSOPHY OF ALLERGEN-FREE BAKING

When I first began my journey of becoming a gluten-free baker, I had already been a baker, experienced in experimenting with gluten flours for many years. I had assimilated the visual cues of what wheat flour looked like as dough and what wheat-based batters looked and felt like. What was most striking when I turned to gluten-free baking was how different the process was and how different the doughs and batters sometimes looked. I struggled with this for a long time. I discovered that I couldn't rely on the instincts that I had internalized over my years of cooking and baking with wheat flour.

Thinking outside the box brought me to a place of success in my gluten-free baking. Sometimes it was a matter of blending techniques and sometimes it was a matter of finding new ways of handling the dough or batter. For instance, I borrowed an age-old technique for building structure in a cake and brought it to my cookie baking—creaming the butter and sugar together and adding the eggs one at a time.

The other striking thing was how wildly the end results varied. I was an experienced baker and yet I was having so many failures. In instances like this, it is easy to give up and stop baking. The ingredients are expensive, and your time is valuable. It is no fun having to throw a baked good out or, worse, having to suffer through eating a subpar sweet because you don't want to waste anything.

Somewhere along the line, I got frustrated enough to start weighing my ingredients and tracking my experience. It was about this time that I was working as a recipe tester for a gluten-free baking book, and all of the measurements were in cups. I discovered that the only good way to track my results was to weigh all the flours. I was working long-distance with the author, and I wanted her to be able to see exactly what I was doing. She began to weigh the flours as well, and eventually we found a more precise way of handling the testing process. The recipes began to work for both of us.

The other thing that is worth noting here is that the weights in this book are based on the way I was trained to weigh flours: using a spoon, lightly add the flour to the measuring cup, then level off the cup with a straight edge. For every flour in this book, I weighed each flour seven times, totaled the cumulative weight, and divided by seven to get an average. Once I created this standard, I stuck to it through all of my recipe development and testing. I also expected my testers to use the weights that I came up with. This is why my weights will not match the standardized weights that you see on the internet or anywhere else. If you are not going to use the weights in this book, I would suggest that you measure as I do—by measuring the flour lightly (not in packed cups). All of those standardized weights on the internet are based on how someone weighs flour, and we all do it very differently.

Weighing ingredients is a time-honored tradition with all professional bakers, and it is standard in countries that use the metric system. Throughout most of the world, nobody would bake without weighing the ingredients. I started writing all of my recipes only by weighing the ingredients. I developed the recipes in this book with my mother, working long-distance between Montana and San Francisco. I wanted my mother to have the same results that I was having, so I bought her a scale and taught her how to use it. She soon started to love this way of baking: measuring all of the dry ingredients into one bowl. We both agreed it was so much easier and more precise than using cup measures.

My key to successful gluten-free baking is this: buy a scale and weigh your ingredients. I have included the customary units of measure, but I would strongly urge you to weigh the dry ingredients if you want the best results and consistency. Gluten-free baking requires multiple flours, so the chance for error goes up incrementally with each consecutive dry ingredient. Take a look at the tutorial on the opposite page for how to use a scale properly for baking. After getting comfortable with it, you may never go back to the American way of measuring. All of your flours can be weighed in the same bowl simply by hitting the tare button between each flour. Tare weight is the true weight of the ingredients minus the weight of the bowl. You should always place your mixing bowl on the scale first and hit the tare button.

You might wonder why I adhere to customary units of measure when it comes to the smaller amounts: teaspoons and tablespoons. My belief is that most of the inexpensive kitchen scales on the market are not very accurate at measuring weights under 10 grams. More expensive, top-of-the-line scales are great at weighing small quantities, but not everyone needs or wants an expensive scale (see pages 30 and 265 for some recommendations). But remember: the smaller measurements need care as well. The best way to measure a teaspoon or tablespoon is to overfill the measurement, then level it off with an offset spatula, the back of a butter knife, or some other straightedge. Careful measuring is key to making these recipes work.

A note on mix-ins: Although I strongly urge you to weigh the ingredients for a recipe, I don't provide weights for mix-ins like chocolate, nuts, seeds, and other additions. These types of ingredients affect the recipe's integrity less than flour does, so it's okay if your mix-ins are not weighed to precise measurements. Use your regular dry measuring cup and fill it level with the sides.

I learned that the problems could be solved, but I also knew that I had to create a new vocabulary of visual cues for this book. Therefore, I photographed a series of visual tutorials of the important processes, and they are presented throughout the book. The first one is about weighing flour.

1. Place the mixing bowl on the scale and zero out the weight of the bowl by pressing the tare button.

2. Add your first dry ingredient to the weight stipulated in the recipe. Be careful to keep the ingredient in a concise lump in one part of the bowl.

3. Press the tare button again to zero out the scale and add your second dry ingredient into another part of the bowl. (Keeping the dry ingredients separate inside the bowl allows you to remove some if you accidentally add too much.)

4. The photo at left shows what the final bowl of weighed ingredients will look like.

HOW TO USE THIS BOOK

This book has been meticulously tested and carefully written for clarity, readability, and ease of use. It is my sincere wish that this book makes alternative baking easy and rewarding for all of you who purchase it.

As I have described above, it has not always been easy for me. Baking can be such a frustration for all of us—the way we each measure ingredients is so vastly different, our ovens are calibrated differently, and we live in different places with humidity, altitude, and availability of ingredients varying. I see this book as an immersive class in gluten-free and sometimes vegan baking. Here is how you begin on your own road to success.

BUY A SCALE AND USE THE RECIPES ACCORDING TO THE WEIGHTS GIVEN. I cannot overstate this enough. Inaccurate measuring is the single biggest factor in recipe failure. Use a scale to measure the flours in one bowl, following the how-to on page 13. This is more than half the battle. Baking requires focus and attention while you are measuring, but the fun of sharing the goodies makes it all worthwhile.

BUY A FREESTANDING THERMOMETER FOR YOUR OVEN. Use it to check how your oven dial may differ from the actual temperature inside the oven. The thermometer will not lie; the dial on your oven will. Set your oven for 350°F and see what your thermometer reads. Most ovens are off by 25° to 30°F. This is a significant amount and should not be taken lightly. Learn how to set your oven so that the temperature matches what is called for in the recipe.

CHOOSE THE BEST INGREDIENTS. I chose to place Bob's Red Mill products at the core of this book. With a few exceptions, Bob's Red Mill carries everything that you need to bake these recipes. The products are easy to find for most of us. If you don't have the ingredients near you, they all can be ordered online. If you are a beginner, use the products from Bob's until you are comfortable making substitutions. Another brand that I am very comfortable recommending is Authentic Foods. You can buy all of their flours at many natural food stores, including Whole Foods, as well as online. See Resources on page 259 for my other favorite ingredients.

Successful gluten-free baking is this simple: weigh your flours, watch your oven temperature, and buy the recommended products. If you are a novice, I suggest that you start with the cookie chapter or the quick breads and muffins chapter. Work your way up to breads and pies. I also believe the how-to photos will offer a lot of insight. I know for myself that a picture really is worth a thousand words.

A couple of side notes: You'll notice that I suggest freezing some baked goods before baking. Freezing cookies, scones, and biscuits before baking allows for a more gradual bake and thus less spread and a higher rise. If the butter in each of these items is frozen, it takes longer for the butter to melt. I also freeze all of my prebaked piecrusts for the same reason. The outer edge will hold the definition of the crimp through the par-baking if the shell is frozen when it goes into the oven. I use plastic cafeteria trays for placing all of my baked goods in the freezer; see page 35 for more about these trays.

You may notice that I don't rely on egg whites as a way of building structure in this book–they are not very reliable. Even as experienced as I am, I will bypass a recipe that involves folding in egg whites. Pastry chefs spend countless hours learning the various ways to use egg whites in classic French baking. It is my goal to keep this book approachable and foolproof. Allergen-free baking is already complex enough with all of the new ingredients and techniques. That said, there *is* one recipe that includes egg whites in this book and that is the lemon meringue pie.

You will find that success is built into all of the recipes throughout this book. I have done the research and development. All you have to do is follow the instructions. I do recommend that you read the corresponding chapter opener for each recipe you choose to make, and take a look at the tutorial photos that may also exist in that chapter.

KEY PLAYERS IN GLUTEN-FREE BAKING SUCCESS

It takes multiple flours to do the work of regular wheat flour. Wheat flour has a particular set of properties that really are quite glorious on so many levels. All of us who like to bake know the stretchy beauty of gluten that has been stimulated. Bubbles are held between the elastic layers. When yeast or leavening is added, a wondrous partnership is formed. The heat of the oven binds these ingredients into the heavenly goodies we all know and love.

When we take gluten out of the equation, we have a different animal altogether. As bakers, we are faced with finding a new combination of ingredients that can do the heavy lifting of gluten. Here is the good news: using multiple flours, all selected for their specific properties, allows you to bake without gluten. This entire book is dedicated to that endeavor: uncovering the truth of these alternative ingredients and using them in ways that suit the end product.

There are so many whole grains that don't contain gluten—sorghum, oat, and teff flours, to name a few. They are flavorful and powerful in their nutrition and flavor. Here is a big secret: throughout time, indigenous people have used the grains that they could find locally. Not all of these grains contained gluten. Ancient people used these grains until they fell out of favor when wheat flour took over the world.

There seems to be an endless array of flours made from alternative grains. Protein is crucial in creating structure in baked goods, so it seemed natural to try these flours. For a while, my pantry was packed with alternative flours. These products are expensive, and I soon discovered that I didn't like a lot of them. I needed to keep it simple. For instance, bean flours are full of protein. However, they are bitter and taste like beans. No, thanks! The same goes for quinoa flour: it is high in nutrition and protein, but I find that it is bitter. I have chosen to use whole grains that are sweet and neutral in flavor. Sorghum and oat flour are my favorites. They are high in protein without being bitter.

This brings me to a few words about rice flour and brown rice flour. You are not going to find much of them in this book. Rice flour is a terrific ingredient. It is neutral in flavor and works well in gluten-free baking. Most commercial baking mixes are made with rice flour. However, there is a property of rice that nobody talks about: rice plants are very talented at sucking substances out of the surrounding soil and storing them—in fact, scientists estimate they are about ten times better at it than all other grain plants. Consider that natural talent in light of all the artificial industrial contaminants and pesticides farmers use and have used for many years in rice-paddy fields, and you can see the problem. Those of us on gluten-free diets have far more exposure to pollutants than the general public. So much of our food is polluted due to the practices of modern agriculture. I decided that when it came to my own baking at home, I was going to stick to flours other than rice flour and brown rice flour. The other grains and flours in this book do not contain the level of heavy metals that rice flour does, especially if you buy organic. I do use some sweet rice flour in this book. It is important to note that I buy Japanese or Korean brands because the level of pesticide use is much lower and the farming practices are more responsible. See Resources on page 259 for my favorite brands.

I also made it my mission throughout this book to increase the percentages of whole grain in most of my recipes. The simple white starches such as potato starch and tapioca starch do not have the nutritional value of the flours made from whole grains, but they are necessary and valid for the reasons I describe below. Each recipe has different requirements for texture and structure. Because I do not use a generalized mix, I can be diligent about using more whole grain if the recipe can support it. My breads don't rise as high as others, but they are more nutritionally sound because I chose to emphasize the percentage of whole grain in those recipes.

On the following page is a short list of my favorite grains. All of them are crucial to the success of my baking.

ALMOND FLOUR. Almond flour is usually made with blanched almonds (no skin), whereas almond meal can be made with whole or blanched almonds. The consistency of almond flour is more like corn meal than wheat flour. It adds moistness and a rich, nutty taste to baked goods. It is high in calories. I like to use it in recipes that I develop that are lactose-free. Almond flour adds richness to baked goods in the absence of butter. I also use almond flour and almond meal interchangeably. When I call for almond flour, you can use either almond meal or almond flour. You can also substitute in any other nut flour that appeals to you; if you do so, keep in mind that it is best to sub it in by weight, not measure.

BUCKWHEAT FLOUR. Buckwheat is a fruit seed related to rhubarb; it is technically not a grain. Buckwheat flour is one of the best sources of protein in the plant kingdom. It has a unique, nutty, assertive flavor. I use it in very small amounts. Buckwheat flour is high in magnesium and manganese as well as in dietary fiber.

CORN FLOUR. Some people have trouble with corn. I love the sweetness and crunch that it imparts to baked goods. Corn flour that is ground fine blends better with other flours and doesn't create a gritty texture. Corn flour is high in magnesium and potassium.

MILLET FLOUR. The natural alkalinity of millet flour makes it easy to digest, so it is beneficial for people with ulcers and digestive problems. I also love millet flour for gluten-free baking. It imparts a roasted nut flavor. However, in an effort to simplify the pantry, I stuck with sorghum on most everything (see below). Millet flour is high in iron, magnesium, calcium, phosphorus, manganese, zinc, B vitamins, and fiber. You can substitute millet flour for sorghum flour anywhere in this book, but keep in mind that it has a slightly more assertive flavor with a bit of bitterness. I think it works best in the bread recipes, with the exception of my brioche.

GLUTEN-FREE OAT FLOUR. Oats are particularly beneficial to people who have high cholesterol and type 2 diabetes. They contain a special kind of soluble fiber known as beta-glucan that can help lower blood cholesterol and stabilize blood sugar. I like to use a small amount of this flour in cookies. It provides a chewy texture in the center and a crunch on the outside. Oat flour is high in fiber, manganese, the B vitamins thiamin and riboflavin, vitamin E, and protein.

SORGHUM FLOUR. Nutritionally, sorghum flour is similar to corn flour, but it has a higher concentration of protein. An ancient cereal grain, sorghum has a slight sweetness that appeals to my palate. Sorghum flour is high in calcium, iron, and potassium. This is hands-down my favorite flour!

SWEET RICE FLOUR. Sweet rice flour is ground from short-grain glutinous rice, aka "sticky rice." The fact that it's called glutinous rice does not mean that it contains gluten. Rather, this rice has a higher starch content than other kinds of rice, making it an extremely efficient thickening agent for sauces and binder for piecrust. It really has no nutritional value. The only reasons I keep it around are for making my piecrusts and gluten-free béchamel. See Resources on page 259 for my favorite brand.

TEFF FLOUR. Because the teff grain is so small, there is no way to remove the husk, bran, and germ, which means none of the nutrients are lost when the grain is ground into flour. Teff is expensive, but a little goes a long way. I like to use it in my breads because it boosts the protein levels closer to those in wheat flour. It is also very flavorful and adds depth and nuttiness. I use it in both its whole-grain and flour forms. Teff flour is high in calcium, iron, magnesium, zinc, thiamin, and fiber.

WHAT ABOUT GLUTEN-FREE FLOUR MIXES?

When I first started baking gluten-free in 2001, a lot of the cookbooks instructed you to mix together the flour blend first and then keep that blend on your shelf or in your refrigerator to grab, as needed, to use in recipes. This made sense at the time because it was easier to organize those cookbooks around one or two baking mixes. The recipes were shorter, more like conventional recipes. Then I subscribed to *Living Without* magazine (now called *Gluten-Free and More*). The magazine had four or five flour blends to use in combination with the recipes. I was also buying the gluten-free mixes that I could find in the markets. My refrigerator was full of bits of this and that. It was so confusing, and I kept losing track of what each one was. So much just ended up getting thrown out.

The other thing about mixes is that they are standardized. Each mix is devised to work for a variety of baked goods that are as diverse as breadsticks and crepes. This system usually means that the baked goods in the middle of the spectrum work best—the cakes, loaf cakes, muffins, and cookies—and the baked goods on the extreme ends usually don't have enough structure or have too much structure.

I decided to simplify this whole crazy system. I started to devise my recipes around the individual flours. That way, I could look after the requirements of each baked good. Breads require more tapioca starch because it imparts more crunch and chew. Cakes require more potato starch because it imparts more moisture and gives that silky mouth-feel that we all expect. I could also control the xanthan gum or the psyllium husk powder and use it in the most optimal way. Learning how to control these ingredients is how you become a better gluten-free baker.

SUPPORTING PLAYERS IN GLUTEN-FREE BAKING SUCCESS

Starches are crucial in gluten-free baking. You cannot simply sub in a whole-grain flour for wheat flour. Each of these ingredients adds an essential element to the baking process.

POTATO STARCH. A flourlike, gluten-free substance produced from only the white of the potato (not the skin), potato starch is a very fine powder that can be used in conjunction with flour for baking. It is my favorite supporting player. It contributes moisture and that silky mouthfeel that we expect a baked good to have. Just think about the silky smoothness of mashed potatoes—this is the beautiful property of this ingredient. Potato starch is often confused with potato flour, but potato flour is ground from the entire dried potato and is much heavier and denser.

TAPIOCA STARCH. This starchy ingredient is derived from the bitter variety of the cassava plant, also known as yucca, it is called manioc flour throughout Latin America. Tapioca adds a pleasantly crisp texture to the crust of gluten-free breads and body to their interior. This is my secret weapon for adding chew and crunch. If you think about the texture of tapioca pearls, you will get the idea of this ingredient's properties. That slightly chewy texture is its strength. Tapioca also has a binding capacity that is akin to that of gluten, but it cannot do all of the work of gluten.

XANTHAN GUM. Without getting too scientific, xanthan gum is a carbohydrate created through fermentation. During fermentation, a strain of bacteria (*Xanthomonas campestris*) is added to glucose or sucrose (such as corn sugar). This turns the sucrose into a gum, or viscous substance, that works as a colorless and tasteless thickener, stabilizer, and emulsifier. Without gluten, you do not have the key factor of pliability that allows the dough to come together and stay together after it is baked. Xanthan gum adds the elasticity that is much needed without gluten. This is by far the best substitute for gluten. Those who are hypersensitive to corn (xanthan gum is often derived from a corn base) might try using guar gum. Guar gum is legume-derived, so those who are sensitive to beans, soy, or legumes may react to it. Even if you are not allergic to legumes, guar gum may act as a laxative in sensitive individuals. I do not use guar gum i n this book, but you can sub it in wherever you see xanthan gum.

PSYLLIUM HUSK POWDER. Psyllium husk is a key component of laxatives and fiber supplements. As a stabilizer, it's very different from xanthan gum. It seems to work best in baked goods that have high density like breads, pizza crust, dinner rolls, breadsticks, and other yeasted dough. Psyllium husk powder is very high in fiber, and it will require more water and longer baking times. It will keep indefinitely on your pantry shelf. It is a good practice to keep your psyllium husk powder and your xanthan gum in labeled containers that are different in color and shape, so that you never confuse the two ingredients.

NUTS. I use a lot of nuts in my baking. They add so much flavor and textural complexity. If you suffer from a nut allergy, just omit the mixed-in nuts. If the recipe calls for a nut flour, I will generally provide an alternative for it. I chop all of the nuts by hand because I feel I do a better job of creating a coarse or fine texture. I generally call for a coarse texture, as I like the presentation it makes. If you sift the nuts in a colander or a sieve with slightly bigger holes, you can get rid of the nut dust or flour. This is something that I learned as a food stylist. Ingredients need to be distinct for the camera but also for the palate. I generally don't use a food processor to chop nuts, but it will not affect the recipe if you do.

CITRUS ZEST. Never underestimate the power of citrus zest. Zest adds a lightness and tingle to all baked goods. Using a Microplane zester, I go over the entire rind, being careful not to zest the pith, or white part, of the citrus. I measure zest lightly into the tablespoon or teaspoon. It should not be packed down.

DAIRY ALLERGEN SUBSTITUTIONS

BUTTER. There are some great-tasting vegan butter substitutes out there. Some feature olive oil or flax oil. For baking and frostings, I use Earth Balance Vegan Buttery Sticks.

I also really like raw organic coconut oil. It has lovely aroma, taste, and texture. Sometimes the coconut flavor can come through, so I use it only when I feel it might accentuate the flavor.

My favorite butter substitute is clarified butter, aka ghee. Clarified butter is naturally lactose- and casein-free. These are the two big allergens that usually cause an aversion to dairy. Clarified butter is the cornerstone of my baking practices. It gives a rich, buttery flavor. It is miraculous in cookies because it keeps them from spreading as they bake. Be sure to use a good amount of cheesecloth to filter out the milk solids (see the tutorial on the opposite page). I have a hard time with lactose, but clarified butter is never a problem for me.

MILK. It is my feeling that milk makes a small offering in most baked goods. Milk contributes to browning but beyond that, it really is just liquid. My favorite substitute is bubbly water. It boosts the rise of baked goods. Any brand will work; it doesn't need to be expensive. I also like to use gluten-free beer or gluten-free hard cider—they are really great in bread and dinner rolls.

1. Place unsalted butter in a heavy saucepan or Dutch oven and heat it slowly on the stove top until it melts. Do not stir.

2. Keep the heat at a low simmer. The butter will bubble and foam and the milk solids will begin to brown and sink to the bottom (picture 1). This usually takes 20 to 25 minutes. Keep your eye on it, making sure the milk solids do not burn. The liquid portion should be a deep amber color (picture 2).

3. Put 2 to 3 layers of cheesecloth/muslin into a sieve over a bowl (or use a coffee filter). Pour in the golden liquid to drain. Do not squeeze out the filtered solids. The lactose is stored inside the milk solids you just removed.

4. Store the clarified butter in a covered glass jar in the refrigerator. (I never worry about the clarified butter going bad in the refrigerator, as the removed milk solids are what make it volatile.) All of my recipes will require that you melt the clarified butter first and then measure it. Simply remove the lid and place the glass jar in the microwave for several minutes at high power and then measure out the clarified butter in a liquid measuring cup. Let it cool slightly before adding it in with the other ingredients, especially eggs.

MILK, CONTINUED. If I do use a nondairy milk substitute in allergen-free baking, I like organic coconut milk, almond milk, or rice milk. I always use an unsweetened, unflavored milk substitute. Check and compare labels, as too much guar gum, a common additive in coconut milk, can act as a laxative for sensitive individuals. The other notable thing with canned coconut milk is that you should use it well blended. When you first open the can, the coconut cream has risen to the top of the can. I usually dump the contents in a small bowl or saucepan and heat it up for several minutes in the microwave or over a very low temperature on the stove top. Blend it well with a wire whisk and let it cool before using it.

I typically don't use soy milk. If you do use soy milk, make sure it is non-GMO and contains no carrageenan. Carrageenan is a common food additive that is extracted from red seaweed. It can be highly inflammatory in some individuals.

It's important to note that any time I call for milk in my recipes, it can be replaced with an equal quantity of any type of dairy-free milk or sparkling water. If you are opting for cow's milk, please use whole milk.

BUTTERMILK

Several recipes call for buttermilk. If you don't have buttermilk on hand or would prefer to use a dairy-free replacement, you can easily substitute coconut milk combined with lemon juice.

1 cup buttermilk = 1 cup full-fat canned coconut milk mixed with 2 teaspoons freshly squeezed lemon juice

¾ cup buttermilk = ¾ cup full-fat canned coconut milk mixed with 1½ teaspoons freshly squeezed lemon juice

⅓ cup buttermilk = ⅓ cup full-fat canned coconut milk mixed with ¾ teaspoon freshly squeezed lemon juice

¼ cup buttermilk = ¼ full-fat canned coconut milk mixed with ½ teaspoon freshly squeezed lemon juice

EGGS. Throughout this book, when I call for eggs, I am referring to grade A large eggs. Each large egg is approximately ¼ cup. You can use organic eggs, or you can use conventional eggs. I am a firm believer in baking with the best ingredients, so if I am going to the trouble of baking something at home, I want it to be really high quality. It is best to use room-temperature eggs in most baked goods. Cold ingredients slow down the baking time and affect the end result. Not to worry, though: if you forget to take the eggs out of the refrigerator, just place them in a bowl and cover them with hot tap water at the beginning of your baking. By the time you need them, the eggs will have warmed up.

Baking gluten-free *and* egg-free is certainly a challenge. Nothing can really replace the egg. You never get the same rise without eggs. However, it has been my goal to provide vegan options alongside recipes that include eggs in every chapter. For instance, most all of my cookie recipes can be made vegan. If you want to bake egg-free, just follow the substitutions in the recipe. All of the

guesswork is taken care of for you. There are recipes in this book that are very reliant on eggs, such as many of my cakes and, of course, brioche. Don't try to sub out the eggs in those recipes.

GETTING MORE NUTRITION AND FLAVOR INTO YOUR FOOD

When I first started to develop my own recipes, I didn't go very far off the beaten path. I used rice flour, potato starch, tapioca starch, and lots of eggs. It didn't take long for me to start to worry about the lack of nutrition in the food I was baking, not to mention the cost of all the gluten-free ingredients. I resolved to find ways of getting more nutritional value into my baked goods.

It was also about this time that I found an old recipe for a cake that used whole poached oranges. I tried that cake and fell in love with it on many levels. The pectin and fiber in the fruit gave the cake structure, moisture, and density, and there was also increased nutritional value in the cake due to the whole-fruit puree it contained. Most of all, the flavor was greatly enhanced by the fruit. It was a win-win situation. I adopted this as my new philosophy and ran with it. It was really fun. Along the way I explored using vegetable purees in all of my breads and made an entire cake with the fiber and sugar contained in dates. All of these recipes are included in this cookbook.

I don't always have time to make my own puree, and I do use the canned vegetable purees from the market. See Resources on page 264 for my favorite brands.

My other secret ingredient is high-quality baby food. The small jars have just enough puree for one loaf of bread. You can also easily broaden your exploration because so many more fruits and vegetables are represented—carrot, parsnip, and squash are all good choices. Just make sure that the baby food is not too watery and use it by weight in each of the individual recipes that call for vegetable or fruit puree. If you are using a puree from the freezer, take it out early enough so that it thaws at room temperature. The best way to do this is to set the leak-proof container of puree in a hot-water bath. It will take 30 to 45 minutes to thaw. You will find that sometimes the water in the fruit/vegetable will separate from the pulp, so just mix the puree together well before using it.

Here are the instructions for making all the purees that are called for in this book. All purees can be frozen and used later. I generally do a bunch of them all on the same day, portion them out in resealable bags, and stack them up in the freezer. Feel free to double the recipes.

SWEET POTATO/RUSSET POTATO PUREE. Peel two medium sweet potatoes or two large russets and cut into 1-inch pieces. Place the pieces in 6 cups of rapidly boiling water and let boil for 15 minutes. The potatoes are done when they yield easily to a poke with a sharp paring knife. Drain off 1 cup of the boiling liquid and set it aside. Transfer the potatoes to a colander to finish draining, letting them cool for about 15 minutes. Place the potatoes into the bowl of a food processor and add $\frac{1}{4}$ cup of the cooking liquid for each potato (i.e., $\frac{1}{2}$ cup for two). Just remember the general rule is to add back cooking liquid at $\frac{1}{4}$ cup per each medium potato. If the potatoes are really small, cut back to 2 tablespoons cooking liquid per potato. Puree until the potato is smooth and creamy. Portion out the puree in resealable bags and store in the freezer; all of my bread recipes require $\frac{1}{2}$ cup (133 grams).

ACORN OR BUTTERNUT SQUASH PUREE. Use one medium whole acorn squash or one medium whole butternut squash. This could not be any easier. Preheat your oven to 350°F. Simply place the whole acorn or butternut squash on a sheet pan lined with foil. No need to peel it or poke it or even wash it. Just place it in the preheated oven and bake until it collapses slightly, about $1\frac{1}{2}$ hours. If you are doing multiple squashes at the same time or if the butternut squash is large, it may take up to 30 minutes longer. It should give a little when you press it with your finger. Remove the pan from the oven and set it aside to cool. Once the squash is cool, cut it in half and scoop out the seeds, then scoop the flesh into a food processor and process until the mixture is smooth and creamy. Portion out the puree in resealable bags and store in the freezer; all of my bread recipes require $\frac{1}{2}$ cup (133 grams).

ORANGE PUREE. Use two or three oranges to make the poached orange puree. Choose thin-skinned organic oranges; I like to use juicing oranges (Valencia). Place the oranges, whole, in a large saucepan and cover with water. I also add a small plate or a lid to cover the whole oranges and keep them submerged (they tend to want to float). Bring the water to a boil, then reduce the heat and simmer for 1 hour. Drain off the water and allow the oranges to cool. Roughly chop the oranges and remove the seeds. In a food processor, blend the coarsely chopped oranges until you have a thick puree. Be sure to include the residual juice from the cutting board. (I like to double or triple the amount of fruit and cook as directed.)

LEMON PUREE. Use three or four small lemons, Meyer or Eureka, to make the poached lemon puree. Choose thin-skinned organic lemons (Meyer lemons are my favorite). Place the lemons in a large saucepan and cover with water. I also add a small plate or a lid to cover the lemons and keep them submerged (they tend to want to float). Bring the water to a boil, then reduce the heat and simmer for 1 hour. Drain off the water and allow the lemons to cool. Roughly chop the lemons and remove the seeds. In a food processor, blend the coarsely chopped lemons until you have a thick puree. Be sure to include the residual juice from the cutting board. (I like to double or triple the amount of fruit and cook as directed.)

APPLE PUREE. Start with 2 pounds of apples (approximately four, any variety), peeled, cored, and cut into eight wedges. Bring 1 cup water to a boil over high heat in a large saucepan with a lid. Add the apples to the boiling water, reduce the heat to low, cover, and let cook undisturbed for 15 minutes. Keep checking to make sure that it doesn't boil dry. Add another ¼ cup of water if it starts to get low. After 15 minutes, check the apples. A knife should easily pierce through an apple wedge. Remove the lid and set aside to cool. Do not drain! Once the apples are cool, place them and the cooking liquid in a food processor and process until smooth.

EQUIPMENT

As you bake your way through this book, you will discover that I often call for smaller pans. I learned early on that surface tension plays a crucial role in creating successful loft and depth of baked goods. Once you remove the gluten, the dough and batters are going to need a little extra help. I would never recommend making a gluten-free sheet cake for this reason (you would be asking too much of the gluten substitutes). Even a 9-inch cake pan is a little on the large side. I prefer to use a 7-inch or 8-inch cake pan for the recipes in this book. In a few instances, I use a 9-inch springform pan.

Build up your tool kit slowly. The most important tool is definitely the scale. As you cook your way through this book, you can buy equipment that the recipes require. For instance, I found the 8½ by 4½-inch loaf pan pictured on page 218 years ago at a flea market.

SCALE. No great baker can get by without a scale. Scales are not expensive. I have had my Escali scale for more than ten years now. OXO makes a good one, too. Refer to page 13 for a tutorial on using a scale. Once you get used to it, you will never go back to measuring cups.

LOAF PAN. Get two 8½ by 4½-inch ones if you don't have them already. You'll need these if you plan to bake from the bread chapter.

CAKE PANS. Have two 8-inch round pans on hand. Select pans that are made of heavy-gauge aluminum or steel. Nonstick is a nice feature but not absolutely necessary because I instruct you to use a nonstick spray and a parchment round for all cakes.

BUNDT PANS. It's good to have one 7-inch (6-cup) nonstick aluminum Bundt pan (such as Nordic Ware) and one 10-inch (12-cup) nonstick Bundt pan. I use these for many of my cake recipes. I like how the pans keep the heat even and that there is very little surface tension due to the center hole. I think it's important to select a Bundt pan with rounded formations and not a lot of edges. I find that the cake is more likely to stick in pans with deep angles and edges. The cake also seems to overcook in those edges. If you are confused about the capacity of your existing Bundt pans, fill them with water and track how many cups they hold. This allows you to use them to the correct capacity of each individual recipe.

TUBE PAN. I like to have one 6-cup tube pan—a circular cake pan with a hollow cone-shaped center. A tube pan differs from a Bundt pan in that it has no edges or shapes. It has a continuous round, smooth form and is used for baking ring-shaped cakes. I find that this is the best piece of equipment for the brioche recipes. You can also use your 6-cup Bundt pan. See picture on page 31.

MUFFIN PAN. A standard 12-cup nonstick muffin pan will work for both muffins and cupcakes. Make sure it is a quality pan, made of a dense metal.

BAKING SHEETS. Choose heavy baking sheets that distribute the heat evenly. Aluminum is a great material but so is stainless steel. The ones they sell at the grocery store are usually not of great quality—they tend to be thin and flimsy. Heavy-gauge metal will disperse the heat more evenly.

FLAT BAKING SHEET (NO SIDES). It is good to have at least one of these for making pies. I like to roll my dough out on parchment. Then I simply pull the parchment and dough onto a baking sheet without sides and place the dough in the refrigerator to chill. A flat sheet is also great for baking galettes. Refer to the pie and galette tutorials on pages 156 and 180, respectively, to see this flat sheet in action. If you don't have a sideless baking sheet, you can use the back of your regular baking sheet.

PIE PLATES. I like the classic 9-inch clear Pyrex pie plates. I love that you can see through the bottom and discern how brown the piecrust is. I also love the edge on these pie plates, which gives you something for the pie dough to hang onto. If the pie plate is without a rim or border, your delicate crust can slump into the bottom in the par bake step. If you are not using Pyrex pie pans, make sure that what you do use is a light-colored metal with an edge to build the crimp of your pie on. I choose light-colored metal because a dark metal can overbrown your pie shell.

SILICONE PASTRY MAT. A silicone mat is crucial for rolling out gluten-free pie dough. I love that there are concentric circles printed on the mat. This makes it so easy to see the diameter of your pie dough. Be careful not to cut out cookies on your silicone mat, because you can cut through to the silicone. I simply slide my parchment off the mat and onto the worktable and then I use my cookie cutters. See Resources on page 265 for my favorite mat.

ROLLING PIN WITH SPACERS. A rolling pin with spacers allows you to get an even thickness on your pie or cookie dough. I discovered this tool when I became a food stylist. The spacers are rubber rings, in sets of two, with different thicknesses. The rolling pin is usually a solid piece of tube-shaped wood. The rubber rings are slid over each end of the pin and allow for only a certain thickness to be obtained. See my version in the pie tutorial on page 156. You will find these pins in high-end kitchen supply shops. See Resources on page 265 for my favorite brands.

INSTANT-READ THERMOMETER. Buy a good-quality thermometer. I encourage you to take the temperature of all of the breads to check for doneness. No need to guess and pray that it is done in the middle. My favorite is made by Thermapen.

MIXING BOWLS. I like plastic mixing bowls with rubber stabilizers on the bottom. The glass and the ceramic ones are pretty, but they are heavy and noisy if you are using a hand mixer. I have a set of four mixing bowls in my kitchen. You don't want to have to keep washing your one mixing bowl while you bake.

MEASURING CUPS FOR LIQUIDS. All liquids should be measured in a liquid measuring cup, ideally one with a spout. Pyrex and OXO are both in my kitchen.

MEASURING CUPS FOR DRY INGREDIENTS. It is important to have a nice set of well-calibrated measuring cups for measuring mix-ins—chocolate chips, nuts, zest, and so on. I tell my students to buy measuring cups from a high-end kitchen store. There are all kinds of cute measuring cups out there. Buy measuring cups that are calibrated well and made for bakers. This is really important.

MEASURING SPOONS. It is important to buy calibrated stainless-steel measuring spoons from a reputable kitchen supply shop. Measuring spoons that are in the shapes of animals or cartoon characters are usually not well calibrated. Those spoons are meant to be decorative. I really have grown attached to my elongated rectangular measuring spoons. They fit into spice jars so much easier than the round spoons. I have three sets of measuring spoons in my kitchen. I don't like to have to keep washing them while baking.

HAND MIXER. Purchase a high-quality mixer with nine speeds. You will usually find that the high-quality one will be a higher price. It is worth the price when you buy a recognizable brand at the top of the line—it is a solid investment. I have had my KitchenAid hand mixer for more than nineteen years. The cheap ones start out too fast and toss around your ingredients. The cheap ones also burn out after several years.

STAND MIXER. For many reasons, a stand mixer makes our lives a lot easier. A stand mixer makes quick work of creaming butter, mixing heavy batters, and kneading doughs, to name just a few of its advantages. KitchenAid is the benchmark of stand mixers, but it is not the only one out there. You can also use your hand mixer with any of the recipes in this book.

FOOD PROCESSOR. I use a food processor a lot in my baking. All of my pie and tart crusts are made in a food processor. The food processor can have a tendency to overstimulate gluten in wheat flour baking. This is a win for those of us who bake gluten-free—there is no gluten to overstimulate. I have a Cuisinart in my kitchen.

PARCHMENT ROUNDS. Parchment rounds are essential for keeping your cakes from sticking to the cake pan. I buy them online precut and ready to go, in both 8- and 9-inch sizes.

PRESS N SEAL. I love this product for covering my mixing bowls whether I am leaving the dough out on the counter or refrigerating it. You get a really nice tight seal.

REYNOLDS WRAP NONSTICK FOIL. I swear that I don't get paid by this company. Not yet anyway. For years, I struggled with how to turn out a cake and not have it stick to the cooling rack. Place a square of this foil slightly larger than the cake on the cooling rack before you turn out the cake. The other nice thing about using this method is that when it comes time to put the cake in the freezer, you simply lift it up by the foil.

GLUTEN-FREE NONSTICK SPRAY. Gluten-free dough and batter are stickier than traditional baking dough and batter. This is mostly due to the powdery starches and the absence of gluten. Spectrum makes a great nonstick high-heat canola spray that ensures your goodies will not stick.

PLASTIC TRAYS. You will notice that there is a lot of freezing and storing of baked goods in this book. I have been dealing with my allergy for so long that I have learned to have most things frozen and ready to go at a moment's notice. Before I put the baked goods in a resealable plastic bag, I usually specify to freeze them on a flat tray first (especially cakes, muffins, piecrusts, portioned cookie dough, quick breads, and yeast breads). I have five or six plastic cafeteria trays that I purchased at a restaurant supply store. They are not expensive, and they are great for freezing all of your baked goods before they go into resealable plastic bags. Once they are frozen solid, you can then feel free to stack and store them in bags without worrying about damaging them. I always store my layer cakes on their sides. I wouldn't be able to do that without my plastic trays. In a pinch you can also freeze things on baking sheets or the flaps cut off cardboard boxes.

BINS OR JARS FOR FLOURS

Baking gluten-free requires particular concentration and focus. It is essential that you adapt your kitchen to this new way of baking. It is so much easier to do that if your pantry is set up in such a way that you are able to access everything in an efficient manner. There is something so rewarding about assembling all of your ingredients before you begin. You can then turn your attention to the careful measurement and precision that gluten-free baking requires.

Instead of dealing with a bunch of open packages of flour that have been taped closed, go out and buy some nice bins with large openings and tight-fitting lids. Buy a container for each of the main ingredients—sorghum flour, tapioca flour, potato starch, almond flour, brown sugar, and granulated sugar. Make sure that the openings are big enough to accept a large spoon for spooning out flour or sugar into your scale. The large opening is also great for filling and refilling your containers. All bins should be clearly labeled on the top of the lid and on the bin itself. It is easy to confuse the bins and the flours. I also have some small containers with lids for my psyllium husk powder and xanthan gum. It is worth noting that your xanthan gum and psyllium husk jars need to be different in shape and color. You don't want to confuse one for the other when you are baking.

The only flour you need to keep in the refrigerator is the almond flour. Almond flour will go bad at room temperature. All of your other flours are safe at cool room temperature. Don't store them near the oven.

Buy some microwave-safe glass quart jars with tight-fitting lids for your clarified butter. Glass jars are easier to put in the microwave. Go ahead and melt the entire amount and use what you need from the jar. A lot of the recipes call for melted and cooled fats.

QUICK BREADS, MUFFINS & SCONES

TIPS FOR SUCCESS

In regular baking, quick breads and muffins are easy—simple and quick to bring together at a moment's notice. Baking gluten-free can also be simple and quick, but there are some guidelines that need to be followed.

The first one is that adding fresh fruit is always risky—sometimes it works and sometimes it doesn't. What it boils down to is moisture. I played with the ratio of berries to batter for a long time to acheive a bread or muffin that is cooked through and free of soggy patches. After all that experimentation, I discovered that by the time I brought the berry ratio down to ensure good results, I lost the berry flavor. As I have mentioned so many times throughout this book, I am often charged with the task of rethinking the process and achieving a desired result in different ways. It is important for me to provide my baking students with success and no nonsense. You will see that for my berry quick breads and muffins, I decided to cook down the fruit and add it as a glaze to achieve that good berry flavor. The fruit glazes do not take long to make, and they bring out the concentrated flavors of the fruit.

The moisture in carrots and zucchini can also hinder the process. You will see that I have you grate your vegetables and squeeze out the moisture in a clean kitchen towel or cheesecloth. Reducing the amount of moisture is absolutely crucial in gluten-free baking. Regular baking is so much more forgiving. The gluten strands that are formed during mixing can hold a great deal of moisture both in terms of oil and liquid. In gluten-free baking you have to be really precise. Don't leave it to chance. How many times have you thrown out something that you baked because it was doughy or raw inside? I have done it more times than I care to admit.

Nonstick cooking spray is crucial but so is properly lining your baking vessel with a parchment overhang. The parchment allows you to remove the bread from the loaf pan soon after it comes out of the oven, without having to touch the hot pan. You never want the baked good to sit in its own steam. This leads to soggy baked goods. Muffins are more forgiving, but I still recommend that you remove them from the muffin pan ten minutes after taking them out of the oven.

I usually use heavy-gauge aluminum or steel loaf and muffin pans. I do not recommend silicone pans for gluten-free baking, and I only recommend glass when baking pies.

Freezing is always a good idea for both the quick breads and muffins. Let them cool to room temperature and then place the loaf or muffins in a resealable plastic bag and freeze them. I thaw the whole loaf or muffins in a 200°F oven for 15 to 20 minutes. You can also slice the breads before freezing and toast them frozen as desired. If you are going to eat them quickly, you can place muffins and quick breads in a container with a tight-fitting lid in the refrigerator for two days. But I freeze most everything and use it directly from the freezer.

1. Cut a length of parchment 8½ inches wide and the entire length of the parchment roll. Place the parchment in the loaf pan so there is an overhang on both long sides of the pan. Spray the pan with nonstick spray and place the batter in the loaf pan on top of the parchment overhang. This will allow you to remove the loaf when it is freshly out of the oven.

banana bread
or muffins

My mother and I both love banana bread. This was the second recipe that I developed for the two of us, right behind the chocolate chip cookie. It is a standard recipe at my house. It tastes exactly like the banana bread that we all know and love. This recipe is great for newcomers to gluten-free baking.

Gluten-free nonstick spray

126 grams (⅔ cup) firmly packed brown sugar

120 grams (1 cup) sorghum flour

72 grams (½ cup) potato starch

52 grams (½ cup) tapioca starch

2 teaspoons ground cinnamon

1 teaspoon double-acting baking powder

1 teaspoon xanthan gum

¾ teaspoon baking soda

½ teaspoon fine salt

⅓ cup melted and slightly cooled clarified butter or coconut oil

¼ cup milk or dairy-free milk, room temperature

2 eggs, room temperature

1 teaspoon vanilla extract

200 grams (1 cup) mashed banana (2 to 3 overripe bananas)

½ cup coarsely chopped pecans, walnuts, sunflower seeds, or pumpkin seeds (optional)

Turbinado sugar, to finish (optional)

1 Preheat the oven to 350°F. Spray an 8½ by 4½-inch loaf pan or 12-cup muffin pan with gluten-free nonstick spray. If using a loaf pan, line the bottom and long sides of the pan with parchment paper so the ends hang over the sides. Lightly coat the parchment paper with the nonstick spray.

2 In the bowl of a stand mixer fitted with the paddle attachment, blend together the brown sugar, sorghum flour, potato starch, tapioca starch, cinnamon, baking powder, xanthan gum, baking soda, and salt.

3 In a 2-cup liquid measuring cup, whisk together the clarified butter, milk, eggs, and vanilla.

4 Add the liquid ingredients to the mixing bowl and mix on low speed until everything is well incorporated, about 2 minutes. Add the banana and pecans (if using) and mix on very low speed until well incorporated, about 1 minute.

5 Transfer the batter to the prepared loaf pan and spread it evenly. For muffins, use a large spoon or cookie scoop to spoon the batter into the pan, filling each cup about three-quarters full. Sprinkle the turbinado sugar over the top, if desired. Bake the loaf for 45 to 50 minutes and the muffins for 20 to 25 minutes, until a toothpick inserted into the middle comes out clean.

6 Remove the pan from the oven. Let the loaf cool in the pan for 10 minutes, then remove it using the parchment paper overhang, and set it on a wire cooling rack. Cool to room temperature, about 1 hour, then slice and serve. Let the muffins cool in the pan until cool enough to handle. Use an offset spatula to remove the muffins and set them on a cooling rack to cool completely.

Note: Store leftovers in a resealable bag in the refrigerator for 2 days. To freeze, let the bread cool to room temperature, then slice. Store slices or muffins in a resealable bag in the freezer for 3 weeks.

carrot bread with currants and pecans
or muffins

MAKES ONE 8½ BY 4½-INCH
LOAF OR 12 MUFFINS

I like to start my day with a muffin, and a carrot muffin is my favorite. After baking, freeze the bread or muffins and defrost them as needed. You can also take this into the realm of a casual dessert by using the Cream Cheese Glaze on page 246.

Gluten-free nonstick spray

120 grams (1 cup) sorghum flour

117 grams (⅔ cup) granulated sugar

52 grams (½ cup) tapioca starch

72 grams (½ cup) potato starch

1 Tablespoon double-acting baking powder

2 teaspoons ground cinnamon, plus more to finish

1 teaspoon baking soda

1 teaspoon xanthan gum

¾ teaspoon fine salt

½ teaspoon ground cardamom

½ cup milk or dairy-free milk, room temperature

½ cup melted and slightly cooled clarified butter or coconut oil

2 eggs, room temperature, or 133 grams (½ cup) unsweetened applesauce

1 teaspoon vanilla extract

90 grams (1 cup) peeled and finely shredded carrots, excess water squeezed out

½ cup finely chopped pecans, finely chopped walnuts, sunflower seeds, or pumpkin seeds

½ cup currants

1 Tablespoon turbinado sugar, to finish

1 Preheat the oven to 350°F. Spray an 8½ by 4½-inch loaf pan or 12-cup muffin pan with gluten-free nonstick spray. If using a loaf pan, line the bottom and long sides of the pan with parchment paper so the ends hang over the sides. Lightly coat the parchment paper with the nonstick spray.

2 In the bowl of a stand mixer fitted with the paddle attachment, blend together the sorghum flour, granulated sugar, tapioca starch, potato starch, baking powder, cinnamon, baking soda, xanthan gum, salt, and cardamom.

3 In a 2-cup liquid measuring cup, whisk together the milk, clarified butter, eggs, and vanilla.

4 Add the milk mixture to the mixing bowl and mix on low speed until everything is well incorporated, about 2 minutes. Add the carrots, pecans, and currants and mix on very low speed until well incorporated, about 1 minute.

5 Transfer the batter to the prepared loaf pan and spread it evenly. For muffins, use a large spoon or cookie scoop to spoon the batter into the pan, filling each cup about three-quarters full. Combine the turbinado sugar and about ½ teaspoon cinnamon, and sprinkle over the top of the loaf or muffins. Bake the loaf for 35 to 40 minutes and the muffins for 20 to 25 minutes, until a toothpick inserted into the middle comes out clean.

6 Remove the pan from the oven. Let the loaf cool in the pan for 10 minutes, then remove it using the parchment paper overhang, and set it on a wire cooling rack. Cool to room temperature, about 1 hour, then slice and serve. Let the muffins cool in the pan until cool enough to handle. Use an offset spatula to remove the muffins and set them on a cooling rack to cool completely.

continued

carrot bread with currants and pecans, continued

Note: Store leftovers in a resealable bag in the refrigerator for 2 days. To freeze, let the bread cool to room temperature, then slice. Store slices or muffins in a resealable bag in the freezer for 3 weeks.

Variation

Zucchini Bread or Muffins: Substitute the carrots with 1 cup shredded zucchini, and substitute the cinnamon and cardamom with 2 teaspoons sweet smoked paprika, 1 teaspoon cumin seed, and 1 Tablespoon Sriracha. Substitute the pecans with ½ cup sunflower seeds. Leave out the currants as well as the cinnamon-and-sugar topping.

Note: Zucchini retains more water than carrots, so it is important to wring the excess water out of the zucchini after shredding. Place the zucchini in a thin layer on top of several layers of paper towels with several more layers of paper towels on top, and press down with your hands to release the moisture. You can also place the shredded zucchini in a kitchen towel and wring it out. Remeasure the zucchini after removing the excess water.

raspberry lemon loaf
or muffins

MAKES ONE 8½ BY 4½-INCH LOAF
OR 12 MUFFINS

For a long time, I struggled with adding fruit to gluten-free baked goods. If I put too much fruit in, I risked having raw batter around the fruit. Too little fruit meant no fruit flavor. I started to have success when I started creating fruit glazes. You get the punch of fruit flavor and no underdone loaf cake. If you don't feel like making the fruit glaze, you can use any of the other glazes starting on page 244.

RASPBERRY GLAZE

6 ounces (1 cup) fresh or frozen raspberries

2 Tablespoons freshly squeezed lemon juice (from 1 lemon)

1 Tablespoon granulated sugar

½ Tablespoon grated lemon zest (from 1 lemon)

23 grams (¼ cup) confectioners' sugar, sifted

LOAF

Gluten-free nonstick spray

96 grams (⅔ cup) potato starch

69 grams (⅔ cup) tapioca starch

60 grams (½ cup) sorghum flour

45 grams (½ cup) gluten-free oat flour

1½ teaspoons double-acting baking powder

1 teaspoon xanthan gum

½ teaspoon baking soda

½ teaspoon fine salt

176 grams (1 cup) granulated sugar

⅓ cup melted and slightly cooled clarified butter or coconut oil

1 Tablespoon finely grated lemon zest (from 1 lemon)

2 eggs, room temperature

¼ cup milk or dairy-free milk, room temperature

1 To make the raspberry glaze: Combine the raspberries, lemon juice, granulated sugar, and lemon zest in a medium saucepan and cook over medium heat, about 5 minutes, mashing the fruit every so often with the back of a heat-safe spatula. Remove the pan from the heat and strain the mixture through a fine-mesh sieve to remove any seeds, skin, or fibrous bits.

2 Return the strained juice to the saucepan and bring to a simmer over medium heat. Simmer until the juice is reduced by half, 2 to 5 minutes. Transfer the juice to a medium bowl and whisk in the confectioners' sugar. Place the bowl in the refrigerator until the glaze sets up. Use immediately or store in an airtight container for up to 2 days, covered with plastic wrap directly touching the top of the glaze to prevent a skin from forming.

3 To make the loaf: Preheat the oven to 350°F. Spray an 8½ by 4½-inch loaf pan or 12-cup muffin pan with gluten-free nonstick spray. If using a loaf pan, line the bottom and long sides of the pan with parchment paper so the ends hang over the sides. Lightly coat the parchment paper with the nonstick spray.

4 In a mixing bowl, whisk together the potato starch, tapioca starch, sorghum flour, oat flour, baking powder, xanthan gum, baking soda, and salt.

continued

5 In the bowl of a stand mixer fitted with the paddle attachment, combine the granulated sugar, clarified butter, and lemon zest, and beat on medium speed until well incorporated, 1 to 2 minutes. Add the eggs and mix until fluffy and light in color, 1 to 2 minutes; it will look like lemon curd. On low speed, add the flour mixture and the milk, and mix until just blended.

6 Transfer the batter to the prepared loaf pan and spread it evenly. For muffins, use a large spoon or cookie scoop to spoon the batter into the pan, filling each cup about three-quarters full. Bake the loaf for 40 to 45 minutes and the muffins for 27 to 30 minutes, until a toothpick inserted into the middle comes out clean.

7 Remove the pan from the oven. Let the loaf cool in the pan for 10 minutes, then remove it using the parchment paper overhang, and set it on a wire cooling rack. Cool to room temperature, about 1 hour. Let the muffins cool in the pan until cool enough to handle. Use an offset spatula to remove the muffins and set them on a cooling rack to cool completely. Just before serving, cut the loaf into slices and drizzle each slice with some of the glaze. Drizzle the glaze over the tops of the muffins and let it set before serving, about 10 minutes.

Note: Store leftovers in a resealable bag in the refrigerator for 2 days. To freeze, let the bread cool to room temperature, then slice. Store slices or muffins in a resealable bag in the freezer for 3 weeks. The glaze will last a week in the refrigerator. You can also just freeze it in a small airtight container and store it along with the bread or the muffins.

Variations

Blueberry Lemon Loaf or Muffins: In the glaze, substitute the raspberries with 6 ounces (1 cup) fresh or frozen organic blueberries. In the loaf, increase to 1 Tablespoon lemon zest (from 1 lemon).

Strawberry Rhubarb Loaf or Muffins: In the glaze, substitute the raspberries with 5 ounces (¾ cup) fresh or frozen strawberries, halved, and 1 ounce (¼ cup) fresh or frozen rhubarb, sliced ¼ inch thick. In the loaf, substitute the lemon zest with 2 Tablespoons orange zest (from 2 navel oranges).

lemon loaf with lemon drizzle
or muffins

MAKES ONE 8½ BY 4½-INCH LOAF
OR 12 MUFFINS

This is a testament to my love of over-the-top lemony goodness. Nice long curls of zest make for a great presentation. Be sure to firmly pack the ¼ cup measure with zest. Sometimes I peel the lemons and then cut the peels into a long julienne (like we did for the photo). Using limoncello (lemon liqueur) really takes the lemony flavor up a notch.

LOAF
Gluten-free nonstick spray

97 grams (⅔ cup) potato starch

69 grams (⅔ cup) tapioca starch

60 grams (½ cup) sorghum flour

45 grams (½ cup) gluten-free oat flour

1½ teaspoons double-acting baking powder

1 teaspoon xanthan gum

½ teaspoon baking soda

½ teaspoon fine salt

176 grams (1 cup) granulated sugar

⅓ cup melted and slightly cooled clarified butter or coconut oil

2 Tablespoons lemon zest (from 2 lemons)

1 teaspoon lemon extract

2 eggs, room temperature

¼ cup milk or dairy-free milk, room temperature

¼ cup poppy seeds (optional)

Turbinado sugar, to finish

LEMON DRIZZLE
¼ cup grated lemon zest, packed (from 4 lemons)

2 Tablespoons granulated sugar

2 Tablespoons freshly squeezed lemon juice (from 1 lemon) or limoncello

1 Tablespoon water

1 To make the loaf: Preheat the oven to 350°F. Spray an 8½ by 4½-inch loaf pan or 12-cup muffin pan with gluten-free nonstick spray. If using a loaf pan, line the bottom and long sides of the pan with parchment paper so the ends hang over the sides. Lightly coat the parchment paper with the nonstick spray.

2 In a bowl, whisk together the potato starch, tapioca starch, sorghum flour, oat flour, baking powder, xanthan gum, baking soda, and salt.

3 In the bowl of a stand mixer fitted with the paddle attachment, beat together the granulated sugar, clarified butter, lemon zest, and lemon extract. Beat in the eggs one at a time until the mixture is light and fluffy; it will look like lemon curd. Add the flour mixture, milk, and poppy seeds (if using), and mix on low speed until just blended.

4 Transfer the batter to the prepared loaf pan and spread it evenly. For muffins, use a large spoon or cookie scoop to spoon the batter into the pan, filling each cup about three-quarters full. Sprinkle the turbinado sugar over the top. Bake the loaf for 44 to 55 minutes and the muffins for 27 to 30 minutes, until a toothpick inserted into the middle comes out clean.

5 While the loaf is in the oven, make the lemon drizzle: In a small skillet or saucepan, mix the lemon zest, granulated sugar, lemon juice, and water. Simmer over very low heat until the lemon zest softens and the sugar dissolves, 5 to 8 minutes. Set aside.

continued

lemon loaf with lemon drizzle, continued

6 Remove the loaf pan from the oven. Immediately pour the lemon drizzle over the hot loaf. Let the loaf cool in the pan for 10 minutes, then remove it using the parchment paper overhang, and set it on a wire cooling rack. Cool to room temperature, about 1 hour, then slice and serve. Let the muffins cool in the pan until cool enough to handle. Use an offset spatula to remove the muffins and set them on a cooling rack to cool completely. Drizzle the glaze over the tops of the muffins and let it set before serving, about 10 minutes.

Note: Store leftovers in a resealable bag in the refrigerator for 2 days. If you plan to freeze, don't drizzle the glaze on the warm bread or muffins; instead, warm and add the drizzle when serving. Let the bread and muffins cool to room temperature, then slice the bread. Store slices or muffins in a resealable bag in the freezer for 3 weeks. The drizzle will last a week in the refrigerator. You can also just freeze it in a small airtight container and store along with the bread or the muffins.

1. After adding the liquid ingredients, add your berries. **2.** Dump the entire contents of the bowl out onto to a length of parchment that is held in place with a silicone mat. **3.** Gently shape and push the dough together with your hands until it forms a tight circle that is ¾ inch in height and approximately 8 inches in diameter. **4.** Carefully slide the parchment, with the dough on top, to a cutting board (so that you're not cutting on the silicone mat). Cut the individual triangles. **5.** Bake immediately or freeze flat on a tray for baking later.

scones four ways

MAKES 8 SCONES

I did not grow up eating scones, even though my mother's side of the family had English heritage. I just don't think anyone wanted to bother making them in the morning, including me. That is why I devised this recipe to make ahead and freeze. Scones are always best when they are hot from the oven. This is true regardless of whether they contain gluten or are gluten-free. They simply don't keep that well. Keep your freezer full of precut raw scones and just bake the number you need. They bake in the same amount of time whether they are frozen or fresh.

GLAZE

94 grams (1 cup) confectioners' sugar

1 Tablespoon lemon or orange juice, plus more as needed

SCONES

150 grams (1¼ cups) sorghum flour, plus more for dusting

97 grams (⅔ cup) potato starch

34 grams (⅓ cup) tapioca starch

2 Tablespoons firmly packed brown sugar

2 teaspoons double-acting baking powder

1 teaspoon xanthan gum

½ teaspoon baking soda

½ teaspoon fine salt

1 Tablespoon loosely packed grated orange or lemon zest (from 1 navel orange or 1 lemon)

½ cup (1 stick) cold unsalted butter, cut into small pieces

1 egg, room temperature

125 grams (½ cup) full-fat sour cream

1 teaspoon vanilla extract

1 egg, lightly beaten with 1 Tablespoon water, heavy cream, or maple syrup, to finish

Turbinado sugar, to finish

1 To make the glaze: Sift the confectioners' sugar through a fine-mesh sieve into a small bowl. Add the juice and blend well. If the glaze is too stiff, add ½ teaspoon additional juice until you reach your desired consistency. Set aside.

2 To make the scones: Preheat the oven to 375°F. Line a baking sheet with parchment paper.

3 In a bowl, whisk together the sorghum flour, potato starch, tapioca starch, brown sugar, baking powder, xanthan gum, baking soda, salt, and zest. With a pastry cutter or fork, cut the butter into the flour mixture until the mixture is crumbly and resembles coarse meal.

4 In a 2-cup liquid measuring cup, whisk the egg until it's very light and foamy. Add the sour cream and vanilla. Add the liquid ingredients to the dry ingredients in the bowl and mix with a wooden spoon until everything comes together. The dough will be soft and somewhat sticky.

5 Transfer the mixture to a countertop dusted with 1 Tablespoon sorghum flour. Dust the top of the dough with more sorghum flour. Using your hands, lightly push the dough together until all of the flour is well incorporated. (Don't play with the dough too much, as the warmth of your hands will melt the butter.) Shape the dough into a ¾-inch-thick circle, 7 to 8 inches in diameter. With a knife, cut the round into 8 even triangles. Place the triangles on the prepared baking sheet. Brush the dough with the egg-water mixture, and sprinkle with the turbinado sugar.

continued

6 Bake for 20 to 25 minutes, until the scones are slightly golden brown and cooked through. Transfer the scones to a wire cooling rack and let them cool to room temperature, about 30 minutes. Drizzle with the glaze and let the glaze set for 15 minutes before serving.

Note: I think this recipe works best if you make the scones just up to the point of baking. Place the shaped (triangular) unbaked scones on a tray and freeze them until solid, at least 4 hours. Once they are frozen, place them in a resealable bag or airtight container and store for up to 1 month. When you're ready, place the triangles on the prepared baking sheet. Brush the dough with the egg-water mixture, and sprinkle with the turbinado sugar. The baking time will be the same.

Variations

Currant and Orange Scones: Add ½ cup currants or raisins in step 4 after the mixture has come together and proceed as directed.

Berry Scones: Add 4 ounces (1 cup) frozen raspberries, blueberries, or blackberries in step 4 after the mixture has come together. Mix until the berries are evenly distributed, then proceed as directed. (It is fine to use fresh berries instead of frozen, but the berries will get crushed and fall apart when you mix and cut the scones.)

Vegan Scones: Replace the butter with an equal amount of Earth Balance Vegan Buttery Sticks. Replace the egg and sour cream with ¼ cup of your favorite alternative milk plus ½ cup unsweetened applesauce. And because I think that the best vegan scones have some berries, use 4 ounces (1 cup) frozen raspberries, blueberries, or blackberries in step 4, mix until they are evenly distributed, then proceed as directed.

cinnamon and praline pecan scones

MAKES 8 SCONES

These are my favorite scones. My colleague and friend Karen Shinto taught me that maple syrup is an excellent browning agent for scones. Buy a good-quality maple syrup and brush it on full-strength. Use it on your frozen scones before popping them in the oven. The maple syrup makes the outside edge crisp and sweet, and it blends so nicely with the cinnamon and praline pecans. Try these scones with the maple glaze on page 246.

PRALINE PECANS

2 Tablespoons unsalted butter

90 grams (¾ cup) coarsely chopped pecans

3 teaspoons ground cinnamon

¼ teaspoon fine salt

3 Tablespoons firmly packed brown sugar

SCONES

150 grams (1¼ cups) sorghum flour, plus more for dusting

97 grams (⅔ cup) potato starch

35 grams (⅓ cup) tapioca starch

2 Tablespoons firmly packed brown sugar

2 teaspoons double-acting baking powder

1 teaspoon xanthan gum

½ teaspoon baking soda

½ teaspoon fine salt

1 Tablespoon loosely packed grated orange or lemon zest (from 1 navel orange or 1 lemon)

½ cup (1 stick) cold unsalted butter, cut into small pieces

1 egg, room temperature

125 grams (½ cup) full-fat sour cream

1 teaspoon vanilla extract

1 teaspoon maple extract

Maple syrup, to finish

1 To make the praline pecans: Melt the butter in a nonstick skillet over low heat. Stir in the pecans, cinnamon, and salt. Toast the nuts, stirring often, for 3 minutes. Add the brown sugar and cook until the color of the nuts deepens slightly and the sugar is dissolved, about 2 minutes. Remove the pan from the heat and spread the pecans on a plate to cool completely.

2 To make the scones: Preheat the oven to 375°F. Line a baking sheet with parchment paper. In a bowl, whisk together the sorghum flour, potato starch, tapioca starch, brown sugar, baking powder, xanthan gum, baking soda, salt, and zest. With a pastry cutter or fork, cut the butter into the flour mixture until the mixture is crumbly and resembles coarse meal. Add in the cooled praline pecans.

3 In a 2-cup liquid measuring cup, whisk the egg until it's very light and foamy. Add the sour cream, vanilla, and maple extract. Add the liquid ingredients to the dry ingredients in the bowl and mix with a wooden spoon until everything comes together. The dough will be soft and somewhat sticky.

4 Transfer the mixture to a countertop dusted with 1 Tablespoon sorghum flour. Dust the top of the dough with more sorghum flour. Using your hands, lightly push the dough together until all of the flour is well incorporated. (Don't play with the dough too much, as the warmth of your hands will melt the butter.) Shape the dough into a ¾-inch-thick circle, 7 to 8 inches in diameter. With a knife, cut the round into 8 even triangles. Place the triangles on the prepared baking sheet. Brush the dough with the maple syrup, and sprinkle with the turbinado sugar and cinnamon.

continued

cinnamon and praline pecan scones, continued

2 Tablespoons turbinado sugar, to finish

2 teaspoons ground cinnamon, to finish

Maple Glaze (page 246)

5 Bake for 20 to 25 minutes, until the scones are slightly golden brown and cooked through. Transfer the scones to a wire cooling rack and let them cool to room temperature, about 30 minutes. Drizzle with the glaze and let the glaze set for 15 minutes before serving.

Note: See the note about freezing scones on page 56.

1. After mixing in the liquid ingredients, dump the entire contents of the mixing bowl out onto parchment that is held in place by a silicone mat. **2.** Gently shape and push the dough together with your hands until you form a square 8 inches by 8 inches. (You can also make round biscuits, as per the recipe instructions.) **3.** Cut the dough into 9 even pieces. **4.** Brush the biscuits with melted butter or heavy cream and bake.

buttermilk biscuits

MAKES 8 BISCUITS

These buttermilk biscuits are so good baked from frozen that I never get up early to make them anymore. After cutting them, place them on a sheet pan or a tray in the freezer until they are frozen, usually overnight. Place the frozen biscuits in a resealable bag and use them straight from the freezer. They bake in the same amount of time. The biscuits are so light, flaky, and buttery. There is no gluten to overwork, so you can keep reshaping every bit of your dough. Biscuits don't keep very well, so only bake the number you need.

90 grams (¾ cup) sorghum flour, plus more for dusting

69 grams (½ cup) sweet rice flour

36 grams (¼ cup) potato starch

26 grams (¼ cup) tapioca starch

1 Tablespoon granulated sugar

1 Tablespoon double-acting baking powder

½ teaspoon baking soda

½ teaspoon xanthan gum

2 Tablespoons buttermilk powder or 1 Tablespoon sweet rice flour

½ teaspoon fine salt

½ cup (1 stick) unsalted butter or Earth Balance Vegan Buttery Sticks, cut into 8 pieces

2 egg whites (¼ cup)

2 fluid ounces (¼ cup) water

1 teaspoon rice vinegar, white vinegar, cider vinegar, or lemon juice

2 Tablespoons heavy cream, melted unsalted butter, or Earth Balance Vegan Buttery Sticks

1 Preheat the oven to 400°F. Line a baking sheet with parchment paper.

2 In a bowl, whisk together the sorghum flour, sweet rice flour, potato starch, tapioca starch, granulated sugar, baking powder, baking soda, xanthan gum, buttermilk powder, and salt. With a pastry cutter or your hands, cut the butter into the flour mixture until the mixture is crumbly and resembles coarse meal. (You can do the recipe up to this point and refrigerate covered overnight. Add the liquid ingredients in the morning and proceed as directed.)

3 In a large bowl, beat the egg whites until very foamy. Add the water, vinegar, and flour mixture to the egg whites all at once. Mix with a rubber spatula or spoon until the dough starts to come together.

4 Transfer the contents of the bowl to a work surface that has been lightly dusted with sorghum flour. Pat the dough into a square about 1 inch thick and 6 by 6 inches in size. (If the dough is really crumbly, add another teaspoon water. If the dough is too sticky, add 1 to 2 Tablespoons sorghum flour.)

continued

5 Using a 2-inch biscuit cutter or a large knife dusted with sorghum flour, cut out as many biscuits as possible. (Make sure your cutter is sharp; using things like juice glasses or tin cans compresses the edges and the biscuits don't rise as well.) Push all the scraps together and continue cutting until you have 8 biscuits. Place the biscuits about 1 inch apart on the baking sheet and brush lightly with the cream or melted butter. You should be able to fit all the biscuits on one baking sheet; they don't expand a lot as they bake.

6 Bake for 15 to 18 minutes. Let the biscuits cool slightly on the baking sheet for a few minutes and then serve immediately.

Note: I like to make the biscuits ahead. After cutting the biscuits out in step 5, transfer them to a resealable bag, arranging them in a single layer. Freeze the biscuits for up to 1 month. Bake directly from the freezer as directed; the biscuits will bake in the same amount of time.

individual microwave muffins

I developed these recipes for my young adult private clients. I felt that it was really important to empower young people who have food allergies. Set aside some time to mix the dry ingredients in individual resealable bags. Later, when it is time for a quick breakfast or a snack, you can just add the wet ingredients. This recipe really doesn't require any baking skill, and it puts the emphasis on taking care of your allergies. The small jars of baby food really come in handy with these recipes.

easy pumpkin muffin

Gluten-free nonstick spray

1 to 2 teaspoons granulated sugar (optional)

DRY INGREDIENTS

23 grams (¼ cup) flaxseed meal or gluten-free oat flour

7 grams (1 Tablespoon) almond meal

1 Tablespoon firmly packed brown sugar

1½ teaspoons pumpkin pie spice, or 1 teaspoon ground cinnamon plus ½ teaspoon ground ginger

1 teaspoon double-acting baking powder

Pinch of fine salt

1 Tablespoon chopped pecans, walnuts, almonds, or sunflower seeds (optional)

WET INGREDIENTS

1 egg, room temperature

20 grams (just over 1 Tablespoon) pumpkin puree

1 Tablespoon clarified butter or coconut oil

1 teaspoon vanilla extract

easy banana or applesauce muffin

Gluten-free nonstick spray

1 to 2 teaspoons granulated sugar (optional)

DRY INGREDIENTS

23 grams (¼ cup) flaxseed meal or gluten-free oat flour

7 grams (1 Tablespoon) almond meal

1 Tablespoon firmly packed brown sugar

1½ teaspoons ground cinnamon

1 teaspoon double-acting baking powder

Pinch of fine salt

1 Tablespoon chopped pecans, walnuts, almonds, or sunflower seeds (optional)

1 Tablespoon chopped dried apple or raisins (optional)

WET INGREDIENTS

1 egg, room temperature

20 grams (just over 1 Tablespoon) banana puree or unsweetened applesauce

1 Tablespoon clarified butter or coconut oil

1 teaspoon vanilla extract

1 Spray a coffee mug with gluten-free nonstick spray (this is very important for unmolding the muffin). You can also sprinkle 1 to 2 teaspoons granulated sugar into the bottom of the mug and tap it around until the sugar covers the bottom.

2 Weigh and measure out all the dry ingredients into a small bowl. (This step can be done ahead and placed in a small container for later. Be sure to label the container.)

3 In another small bowl, combine all the wet ingredients and blend together well with a fork. You don't want chunks of egg in your muffin.

4 Add the wet ingredients to the dry ingredients and mix until well incorporated. With a rubber spatula, scrape the batter into the prepared coffee mug.

5 Place the mug in the microwave and cook on high for 1 minute. Remove the mug from the microwave (if the top looks wet, cook for another 10 seconds). Let the cooked muffin sit in the mug for another 1 to 2 minutes. Unmold the muffin by turning the mug over onto a small plate.

Note: Variations are endless with this recipe. You can add diced dried fruit, chocolate chips, or cocoa nibs. Never add more than 1 Tablespoon of additional ingredients. The number-one rule is to not add more wet ingredients; adding more wet ingredients will lead to a soggy muffin.

skillet maple cornbread
or muffins

MAKES ONE 9-INCH SKILLET, ONE
9-INCH CAKE PAN, OR 9 TO 12 MUFFINS

I love this cornbread! It has a crispy outer edge and a cakey interior. Be sure to use finely ground cornmeal, like Bob's Red Mill, otherwise the cornbread can be gritty. This bread comes together easily and quickly in three easy steps. I bring it to the table in the skillet hot from the oven. Serve it with chili on a cold day or add it to the table at an outdoor barbecue.

Gluten-free nonstick spray

276 grams (2 cups) fine-ground cornmeal

95 grams (½ cup) firmly packed brown sugar

72 grams (½ cup) potato starch

44 grams (¼ cup) granulated sugar

1 Tablespoon double-acting baking powder

1 teaspoon xanthan gum

½ teaspoon fine salt

½ cup canola oil or clarified butter, melted and slightly cooled

1 cup buttermilk (see note, page 26), room temperature

2 eggs, well beaten

1 teaspoon maple extract

1 Preheat the oven to 400°F. Spray a 9-inch oven-safe skillet, such as cast iron, a 9-inch cake pan, or a 12-cup muffin pan with gluten-free nonstick spray.

2 In a large bowl, whisk together the cornmeal, brown sugar, potato starch, granulated sugar, baking powder, xanthan gum, and salt. In a small bowl, whisk together the oil, buttermilk, eggs, and maple extract.

3 Add the milk mixture to the dry ingredients and stir well to combine. Pour the batter into the prepared pan.

4 If baking in the skillet or cake pan, bake for 35 minutes, or until lightly browned around the edges. The center of the cornbread should spring back when gently poked. Bake muffins for 20 to 23 minutes, or until the muffins spring back when gently poked.

5 Remove the pan from the oven. Let cool for 10 minutes, then cut into wedges and serve warm.

Note: Store leftovers in a resealable bag in the refrigerator for up to 24 hours. To freeze, let the cornbread cool to room temperature, then cut. Store wedges or muffins in a resealable bag in the freezer for 3 weeks. The wedges or muffins can be warmed in a 200°F oven for 10 to 15 minutes or thawed in the microwave for 1 minute at 50 percent power. Both are also good toasted directly from the freezer in the toaster oven for 5 to 8 minutes.

CAKES

TIPS FOR SUCCESS

As I have stipulated elsewhere in the book, I think it is important that gluten-free cakes be baked in smaller pans than gluten-based cakes. In my kitchen, I have two 8-inch round pans, one 8-inch square pan, a 9-inch springform pan, and various 6- and 12-cup (10-inch) Bundt pans. I love serving a Bundt cake to company. It is so concise and pretty. Since I am not a fan of big gobs of frosting and am lactose-intolerant, I like to sauté seasonal fruit and serve that with my Bundt cakes.

I have included an extensive array of recipes for frostings, glazes, drips or drizzles, and garnishes for my cakes. My hope is that you will use them freely and according to your palate and the palate of your guests. If a recipe indicates that it is for a Bundt cake, the amount of frosting or glaze is going to be less than what is needed for a layer cake. The headnote for each cake recipe will usually indicate what my favorite frosting and garnish is.

Cake strips are a great baking tool for layer cakes, and it is my feeling that they should always be used when baking layers (refer to the cake tutorial on page 75); they are not needed for Bundt cakes. When a cake goes into the oven without the strips, the outside edge of the pan heats up first and the edge of the cake cooks first. The middle part is slower to cook because the heat takes longer to find its way through the batter. That is why we end up with domed cakes that have to be evened out later. The idea of cake strips is simple: Soak the cake strips and gently squeeze out the water with your thumb and forefinger. They should still be wet but not too drippy. Place the strips evenly around the outside circumference of the cake pan and then fill the pans evenly with batter (weigh the batter for best results). The cake strips keep the outside edge cooled longer. By the time the cake strips dry out in the heat of the oven, the heat is dispersed evenly through the batter. No more domed cakes! This is especially rewarding when it comes to my cakes that are meant to be served as one layer, like the Roasted Banana Cake (page 77) and the Italian Almond Cake (page 100). The presentation is so much better.

It is hard to make a great cake without butter or eggs. However, I have discovered that cakes that use a vegetable or fruit puree (see my vegan cakes on pages 79 and 80) have the best texture and flavor. Butter is so crucial to making a good cake, but you will discover that I tend to use a lot of clarified butter. Clarified butter is lactose-free and still has the rich butter flavor. I feel that making your own clarified butter is the best way to go (see my tutorial on page 25). There are many brands of clarified butter on the market, but my favorite is made by Organic Valley. If you have a butter intolerance or don't like the taste, simply substitute coconut oil.

Not everybody can handle sour cream, and several of my cakes include sour cream. The good news is that you can sub in a vegan sour cream. My recipes were tested with Tofutti brand vegan sour cream (see Resources on page 262).

There are several recipes that call for buttermilk. If you want a lactose-free alternative, you can substitute for each cup of buttermilk, 1 cup full-fat canned coconut milk mixed with 2 teaspoons freshly squeezed lemon juice. Be sure to blend the coconut cream and coconut milk first by gently heating (see page 25), then add the lemon juice and let it cool until it comes time to add it to the cake batter.

For all layer cakes, I like to start with a parchment round in the bottom of each pan. You can find these precut and online, at kitchen supply shops, or in bakery supply shops. You can always trace around the bottom of your baking pans in pencil on a length of parchment and then cut inside the pencil line by ⅛ inch.

All pans should be coated with a releasing agent. My favorite is a high heat canola oil cooking spray made by Spectrum. A light spray used together with nonstick pans and parchment rounds is all you need to ensure beautiful cakes.

Here are a few more tips for ensuring a perfectly even cake: When the cake comes out of the oven, gently run an offset spatula around the perimeter of the cake. The cake expands in the oven. Once it is out of the oven, the cake will immediately start to shrink. If it is stuck anywhere along the edge, uneven shrinking can distort the cake. Another good tip is to turn the cake out onto a piece of Reynolds nonstick foil slightly bigger than the cake layer that has been placed on a wire cooling rack. This way your cake won't stick to the cooling rack and pick up waffle-weave impressions. The foil also allows you to transport the cake from the cooling rack to the refrigerator or the freezer.

I cool and freeze all my cakes before I frost them. I generally keep a layer cake in the freezer so that it is ready to go at a moment's notice. Once a cake has cooled to room temperature, place it flat on a baking sheet or a tray inside your freezer (no need to wrap yet). I generally lift the cake layers onto the tray using the foil that they have been turned out onto. Let the cake freeze solid, and then wrap the length of foil up around the edges of the cake (this prevents flavors from your freezer from getting in and moisture getting out), place in a resealable plastic bag, and freeze. The layers will keep in your freezer for several months. Unwrap and frost the cake while it is frozen. It will take a frozen cake 4 to 5 hours to thaw, so plan accordingly.

I think a frosted cake is a thing of beauty. I also believe birthdays and holidays should include that special touch of frosting and a garnish of candied nuts or carrot curls. In the interest of calorie counting, however, I sometimes like to serve cake with a simple sauté of fruit. This allows me to pull a cake from the freezer and pick up a fruit from the market that is beautiful and in season. For instance, I love a ginger cake with sautéed peaches or cherries.

Here are some simple guidelines for sautéing fruit: Melt 2 Tablespoons butter or coconut oil in a large skillet over low heat. Add 2 Tablespoons granulated sugar or firmly packed brown sugar and ¼ teaspoon cinnamon and stir until the sugar melts. Add 2 cups fruit (stone fruit, berries, cherries, pineapple, mango, figs, or even grapes) and cook until softened and the juices are released, stirring occasionally, 3 to 5 minutes. Remove from the heat and serve over slices of cake. If you like, you can also toast the cake slices in a toaster oven or under the broiler, watching carefully to avoid burning. This works especially well for cake slices that may have dried out.

1. Using a digital scale, divide the batter evenly between two cake pans that have been outfitted with parchment rounds and sprayed with nonstick spray. If it is just one pan, make sure the batter is level. Wipe spilled cake batter off of the edges so that it doesn't burn. **2.** Wring out the pre-soaked cake strips ever so slightly (see page 70). **3.** Attach the dampened cake strips around the sides of each pan. Bake as directed. **4.** Turn the cakes out onto Reynolds nonstick foil that has been lightly sprayed with nonstick spray.

roasted banana cake

This cake can be dressed up or dressed down. For a special-occasion treatment, I like to decorate the cake with what I call banana dust. Place 1 ounce of banana chips in the bowl of a food processor or a coffee grinder and pulse until they turn to a fine meal. Frost the cake with the Cream Cheese Vanilla Bean Frosting for the Bundt cake (page 253) or the Coconut Caramel Sauce, shown in the photo, (page 218) heated until it is spreadable, and then sprinkle the top of the cake with banana dust and some roasted nuts.

ROASTED BANANAS
About 3 bananas

CAKE
Gluten-free nonstick spray

120 grams (1 cup) sorghum flour

108 grams (¾ cup) potato starch

52 grams (½ cup) tapioca starch

1½ teaspoons baking soda

1 teaspoon xanthan gum

½ teaspoon fine salt

126 grams (⅔ cup) firmly packed brown sugar

⅓ cup unsalted butter, room temperature

2 eggs, room temperature

1 teaspoon vanilla extract

½ cup milk or dairy-free milk, room temperature

½ cup chopped walnuts, pecans, sunflower seeds, or pumpkin seeds

1 To make the roasted bananas: Preheat the oven to 400°F. Cut each banana into 4 equal pieces. Place the pieces on a baking sheet lined with parchment paper or nonstick aluminum foil. Roast for 10 to 12 minutes, turning each banana piece halfway through. The bananas will brown slightly and soften. Remove from the oven and let cool. Mash the cooled bananas in a bowl until smooth. Be sure to weigh the roasted bananas so that they equal 176 grams (¾ cup).

2 To make the cake: Lower the oven temperature to 350°F. Place an 8-inch parchment round in an 8-inch cake pan and spray with gluten free nonstick spray. Also outfit the pan with a dampened cake strip; it is easier to do this when the pan is empty.

3 In a bowl, whisk together the sorghum flour, potato starch, tapioca starch, baking soda, xanthan gum, and salt.

4 In the bowl of a stand mixer fitted with the paddle attachment, beat the brown sugar and butter on medium speed until well blended, 1 minute. Add the eggs, one at a time, beating well after each addition. Add the vanilla and roasted bananas. Continue to mix until the color evens out.

5 Reduce the speed to low and add the flour mixture and milk alternately in batches, beginning and ending with the flour mixture (one-third flour, one-half milk, one-third flour, one-half milk, one-third flour). Scrape down the sides of the bowl as needed and mix until the batter is smooth, frothy, and even in color. Fold the walnuts into the batter with a rubber spatula.

continued

roasted banana cake, continued

6 Pour the batter into the prepared pan, smoothing the top. Bake 35 to 40 minutes, until the center springs back when you touch it and a toothpick inserted into the middle comes out clean.

7 Remove the pan from the oven and run a knife or offset spatula around the edge of the cake. Cool the cake in the pan on a wire cooling rack for 10 minutes, then invert the cake onto a piece of foil that has been sprayed with a gluten-free nonstick spray and placed on a wire cooling rack.

8 Once the cake is completely cooled, you can frost with the frosting of your choice.

Note: Store leftovers wrapped in plastic wrap or in an airtight container in the refrigerator for 3 days. If you are not serving the cake immediately, let the cake cool to room temperature, place the cake on a flat tray, and place in the freezer. Once the cake is solid, about 4 hours, place it in a resealable plastic bag and store the cake in the freezer. When you are ready to serve the cake, take it out of the freezer, frost it while it is frozen, and leave it at room temperature until thawed, about 4 hours.

vegan applesauce cake
or muffins

MAKES 10 TO 12 SERVINGS
OR 10 MUFFINS

Serve this cake with a sauté of fresh fruit or the Coconut Caramel Sauce (page 248) and some toasted nuts. You can also just make this recipe as muffins and store them in the freezer for a quick morning treat. You can easily convert this recipe to a vegan banana cake by substituting the same amount of banana puree for the applesauce. That is a great way to use up overripe bananas.

Gluten-free nonstick spray

79 grams (¾ cup) unsalted chopped pecans, walnuts, or sunflower seeds (optional)

142 grams (¾ cup) firmly packed brown sugar

80 grams (⅔ cup) sorghum flour

45 grams (½ cup) gluten-free oat flour

36 grams (¼ cup) potato starch

26 grams (¼ cup) tapioca starch

1 teaspoon xanthan gum

1 teaspoon ground cinnamon

1 teaspoon double-acting baking powder

¾ teaspoon fine salt

½ teaspoon baking soda

½ teaspoon ground nutmeg

¼ teaspoon ground cloves

176 grams (¾ cup) high-quality applesauce

⅓ cup water

¼ cup melted and slightly cooled coconut oil

Sauté of fresh fruit (see page 74) or vegan Coconut Caramel Sauce (page 248)

1 Preheat the oven to 350°F. Spray a 7-inch (6-cup) Bundt pan or 12-cup muffin pan with gluten-free nonstick spray. If using, sprinkle the pecans over the bottom of the Bundt pan or 10 muffin cups.

2 In the bowl of a stand mixer fitted with the paddle attachment, blend together the brown sugar, sorghum flour, oat flour, potato starch, tapioca starch, xanthan gum, cinnamon, baking powder, salt, baking soda, nutmeg, and cloves.

3 In a 2-cup liquid measuring cup, whisk together the applesauce, water, and coconut oil. Add the applesauce mixture to the dry ingredients and mix on low speed until everything is well incorporated, about 1 minute.

4 Transfer the batter to the prepared Bundt pan and spread evenly. For muffins, use a large spoon or cookie scoop and spoon the batter into the pan, filling each cup about three-quarters full. Bake the Bundt cake for 35 to 40 minutes and the muffins for 20 to 25 minutes, until a toothpick inserted into the middle comes out clean.

5 Remove the pan from the oven. Let the cake cool in the pan for 10 minutes, then turn it out onto a cake plate or cake stand. Cool to room temperature, about 20 minutes, then slice and serve. Let the muffins cool in the pan until they are cool enough to handle. Use an offset spatula to remove the muffins and set them on a wire cooling rack to cool completely.

6 Serve the cake or muffins with the sautéed fruit on the side or drizzle with the Coconut Caramel Sauce.

Note: Store leftovers wrapped in plastic wrap or in an airtight container in the refrigerator for 3 days. If you are not serving the cake immediately, let the cake cool to room temperature, then tightly wrap it in plastic wrap and store it in the freezer.

vegan pumpkin cake
or cupcakes

MAKES 10 TO 12 SERVINGS
OR 10 TO 12 CUPCAKES

I developed this recipe for my vegan friends. It is so moist and light that it really doesn't need any adornment. If you want to elevate this cake for a dinner party, serve it with my vegan Coconut Caramel Sauce (page 248). You can also serve the cake with a sauté of fresh fruit and some toasted nuts. This is a holiday-time favorite. The vegans will be so appreciative and your other guests won't complain.

Gluten-free nonstick spray

142 grams (¾ cup) firmly packed brown sugar

80 grams (⅔ cup) sorghum flour

45 grams (½ cup) gluten-free oat flour

36 grams (¼ cup) potato starch

26 grams (¼ cup) tapioca starch

1 Tablespoon ground ginger

1 teaspoon double-acting baking powder

1 teaspoon xanthan gum

1 teaspoon ground cinnamon

¾ teaspoon fine salt

½ teaspoon baking soda

½ teaspoon ground nutmeg

¼ teaspoon ground cloves

176 grams (¾ cup) pumpkin puree

⅓ cup water

¼ cup melted and slightly cooled coconut oil

Sauté of fresh fruit (see page 74) or vegan Coconut Caramel Sauce (page 248)

1 Preheat the oven to 350°F. Spray a 7-inch (6-cup) Bundt pan or 12-cup muffin pan with gluten-free nonstick spray.

2 In the bowl of a stand mixer fitted with the paddle attachment, blend together the brown sugar, sorghum flour, oat flour, potato starch, tapioca starch, ginger, baking powder, xanthan gum, cinnamon, salt, baking soda, nutmeg, and cloves.

3 In a 2-cup liquid measuring cup, whisk together the pumpkin puree, water, and coconut oil.

4 Add the liquid ingredients to the mixing bowl and mix on low speed until everything is well incorporated, about 1 minute.

5 Transfer the batter to the prepared Bundt pan and spread it evenly. For cupcakes, use a large spoon or cookie scoop to spoon the batter into the cupcake pan, filling each cup about three-quarters full. Bake the Bundt cake for 35 to 40 minutes and the cupcakes for 20 to 25 minutes, until a toothpick inserted into the middle comes out clean.

6 Remove the pan from the oven. Let the cake cool in the pan for 10 minutes, then turn it out onto a cake plate or cake stand. Cool to room temperature, about 20 minutes, then slice and serve. Let the cupcakes cool in the pan until cool enough to handle. Use an offset spatula to remove the cupcakes and set them on a wire cooling rack to cool completely.

7 Serve the cake or cupcakes with the sautéed fruit on the side or drizzle with the Coconut Caramel Sauce.

Note: Store leftovers wrapped in plastic wrap or in an airtight container in the refrigerator for 3 days. If you are not serving the cake immediately, let the cake cool to room temperature, then tightly wrap it in plastic wrap and store it in the freezer.

new york–style coffee cake

MAKES 10 TO 12 SERVINGS

This cake is great solo, but I also love it with a sprinkling of powdered sugar. It is also good with the Maple Glaze (page 246) or topped with sautéed fresh, pitted cherries. See my guidelines for sautéing fresh fruit on page 74. This cake is a favorite at any breakfast or brunch, but you can also serve it as an after-dinner dessert.

CRUMB TOPPING

126 grams (⅔ cup) firmly packed brown sugar

60 grams (½ cup) sorghum flour

36 grams (¼ cup) potato starch

26 grams (¼ cup) tapioca starch

4 teaspoons ground cinnamon

1 teaspoon xanthan gum

¼ cup plus 1 Tablespoon melted and slightly cooled clarified butter or coconut oil

Gluten-free nonstick spray

CAKE

96 grams (⅔ cup) potato starch

69 grams (⅔ cup) tapioca starch

60 grams (½ cup) sorghum flour

45 grams (½ cup) gluten-free oat flour

2 teaspoons ground cinnamon

1½ teaspoons double-acting baking powder

1 teaspoon xanthan gum

½ teaspoon ground nutmeg

½ teaspoon baking soda

½ teaspoon fine salt

2 eggs, room temperature

220 grams (1¼ cups) granulated sugar

2 teaspoons vanilla extract

1 cup full-fat sour cream, room temperature

Confectioners' sugar, to finish

1 To make the crumb topping: In a small bowl, whisk together the brown sugar, sorghum flour, potato starch, tapioca starch, cinnamon, and xanthan gum. Pour in the butter and stir until all dry ingredients are moistened.

2 Preheat the oven to 350°F. Spray a 9-inch springform pan with gluten-free nonstick spray and line the bottom of the pan with parchment.

3 To make the cake: In a bowl, whisk together the potato starch, tapioca starch, sorghum flour, oat flour, cinnamon, baking powder, xanthan gum, nutmeg, baking soda, and salt.

4 In the bowl of a stand mixer fitted with the paddle attachment, beat the eggs and granulated sugar on medium speed until well blended, 1 minute. Add the vanilla, sour cream, and flour mixture and beat at medium-low speed for 30 seconds. Do not overbeat.

5 Pour the batter into the prepared pan and sprinkle the crumb topping over the batter; do not press down on the crumb topping.

6 Bake for 40 to 45 minutes, until a toothpick inserted into the middle comes out clean.

7 Remove the pan from the oven and run a knife or offset spatula around the edge of the cake. Let the cake cool in the pan for 20 minutes. Loosen the outer ring of the pan sides and cool completely on a wire cooling rack. To remove the cake from the pan bottom, use two pancake turners to lift the cake onto a cake plate (it is easier to move if the cake is cold). Once the cake has cooled completely, dust it with confectioners' sugar.

continued

Note: Store leftovers wrapped in plastic wrap or in an airtight container in the refrigerator for 3 days. If you are not serving the cake immediately, let the cake cool to room temperature, then tightly wrap it in plastic wrap and store it in the freezer.

Variation

New York–Style Coffee Cake with Apples: In a small bowl, mix together ¼ cup chopped walnuts or pecans, 29 grams (2 Tablespoons) granulated sugar, 2 teaspoons ground cinnamon, and 2 teaspoons potato starch. Peel and core 1 Granny Smith apple and cut it in half (reserve the other half for another purpose). Cut the half apple into four wedges, then cut each wedge into 8 little rectangular chunks. Mix the apples with the nut mixture and set aside.

Follow the directions for the New York–Style Coffee Cake (page 83). After the batter is made (step 4), pour half the batter in the springform pan, then add the apple mixture and disperse evenly over the top of the batter. Add the other half of the batter, followed by the crumb topping. The baking time will not change.

classic chocolate layer cake

MAKES 8 TO 10 SERVINGS

My beloved sister, Janine, loves chocolate cake with lots of chocolate frosting. My brother, Kevin, also loves chocolate. I dedicate this recipe to Janine and Kevin. Try this cake filled with the Chocolate Ganache (page 254) and frosted with the Simple Chocolate Frosting (page 250). It is my go-to recipe for a birthday cake. If you prefer, you can use a purchased jam or marmalade between the two layers.

Gluten-free nonstick spray

120 grams (1 cup) sorghum flour

108 grams (¾ cup) potato starch

61 grams (¾ cup) unsweetened cocoa powder

26 grams (¼ cup) tapioca starch

1 teaspoon xanthan gum

1 teaspoon double-acting baking powder

1 teaspoon baking soda

½ teaspoon fine salt

½ teaspoon espresso powder or instant coffee (optional)

176 grams (1 cup) granulated sugar

¾ cup (1½ sticks) unsalted butter, room temperature

95 grams (½ cup) firmly packed brown sugar

4 eggs, room temperature

1 teaspoon vanilla extract

½ cup milk or dairy-free milk, room temperature

Chocolate Ganache (page 254)

Simple Chocolate Frosting (page 250)

1 Preheat the oven to 350°F. Place two 8-inch parchment rounds in two 8-inch cake pans and spray with gluten-free nonstick spray. Also outfit each pan with a dampened cake strip; this is easier to do when the pans are empty.

2 In a bowl, whisk together the sorghum flour, potato starch, cocoa powder, tapioca starch, xanthan gum, baking powder, baking soda, salt, and espresso powder (if using).

3 In the bowl of a stand mixer fitted with the paddle attachment, beat the granulated sugar, butter, and brown sugar on medium speed until well blended, 1 minute. Add the eggs, one at a time, and the vanilla, scraping down the bowl and beating well after each addition.

4 Reduce the speed to low and add the flour mixture and milk alternately in batches, beginning and ending with the flour mixture (one-third flour, one-half milk, one-third flour, one-half milk, one-third flour). Turn the mixer up to medium speed once the flour or milk is mostly incorporated. Scrape down the sides of the bowl as needed, and mix until the batter is smooth, frothy, and even in color.

5 Divide the batter between the two prepared pans, smoothing the top of each. Bake 32 to 35 minutes, until a toothpick inserted into the middle comes out clean and the center springs back when you touch it.

6 Remove the pans from the oven and run a knife or offset spatula around the edge of each cake. Cool the cakes in the pans on a wire cooling rack for 10 minutes. Line the cooling rack with a piece of aluminum foil and spray the foil with gluten-free nonstick spray. Invert the cake pans onto the prepared cooling rack.

continued

classic chocolate layer cake, continued

7 Once the cakes have cooled completely, freeze them for about 4 hours or overnight before frosting. When the cakes are frozen, spread the Chocolate Ganache on one of the cakes, stack the other cake on top, and then spread the Simple Chocolate Frosting over the top and sides. The cake will take 4 to 5 hours to defrost for serving.

Note: Store leftovers wrapped in plastic wrap or in an airtight container in the refrigerator for 3 days. If you are not serving the cake immediately, let the cake cool to room temperature, then tightly wrap it in plastic wrap and store it in the freezer.

ginger cake

MAKES 10 TO 12 SERVINGS

I call this my three-ginger cake because it has ginger powder, fresh ginger, and candied ginger. The secret is out—I like ginger. This cake can be really casual and served at any time of day. During the holidays, this is my showstopper! I serve it with Maple Glaze (see page 246). You can chop 1 or 2 ounces of candied ginger into a fine julienne to add to the batter or save and use as a garnish.

Gluten-free nonstick spray

120 grams (1 cup) sorghum flour

72 grams (½ cup) potato starch

67 grams (¾ cup) almond meal or sorghum flour

35 grams (⅓ cup) tapioca starch

1 Tablespoon ground ginger

2 teaspoons double-acting baking powder

1½ teaspoons xanthan gum

1 teaspoon ground cinnamon

¾ teaspoon baking soda

¾ teaspoon fine salt

½ teaspoon ground cardamom

190 grams (1 cup) firmly packed brown sugar

½ cup melted and slightly cooled clarified butter or coconut oil

½ cup molasses

1 Tablespoon freshly grated ginger

2 teaspoons vanilla extract

2 eggs, plus 1 egg yolk, room temperature

¾ cup buttermilk (see note, page 26), room temperature

Maple Glaze (page 246)

¼ cup (1–2 ounces) julienne of candied ginger, to finish

1 Preheat the oven to 350°F. Spray a 10-inch Bundt pan with gluten-free nonstick spray.

2 In a bowl, whisk together the sorghum flour, potato starch, almond meal, tapioca starch, ginger, baking powder, xanthan gum, cinnamon, baking soda, salt, and cardamom.

3 In the bowl of a stand mixer fitted with the paddle attachment, combine the brown sugar, clarified butter, molasses, and fresh ginger and beat on medium speed until well blended, 1 minute. Add the vanilla, then add the eggs and egg yolk, one at a time, mixing on low speed after each addition. Add the buttermilk and mix until well combined, about 1 minute.

4 Add the dry ingredients to the mixing bowl in two batches, mixing on low speed after each addition, until all of the ingredients are well incorporated, about 2 minutes. The batter will seem fairly thin for a cake batter, but not to worry.

5 Using a rubber spatula, transfer the batter to the prepared pan and smooth the top. Bake for 40 to 45 minutes, until a toothpick inserted into the middle comes out clean.

6 Remove the pan from the oven. Let the cake cool in the pan for 10 minutes, then turn it out onto a cake plate or cake stand. Once the cake has cooled to room temperature, drizzle it with the Maple Glaze and garnish with the candied ginger. Let the glazed cake set in the refrigerator for 10 minutes before serving.

Note: Store leftovers wrapped in plastic wrap or in an airtight container in the refrigerator for 3 days. If you are not serving the cake immediately, let the cake cool to room temperature then tightly wrap it in plastic wrap and store it in the freezer.

olive oil and cherry bundt cake

MAKES 10 TO 12 SERVINGS

This cake is very moist, and it doesn't really need any adornment. If cherries are in season, I use them as an accompaniment. I sauté 2 cups of pitted and halved cherries in a Tablespoon of butter and a Tablespoon of granulated sugar until they are tender. Then I remove them from the heat and add a Tablespoon of cherry liqueur, Grand Marnier, or brandy. Serve each slice with the warm cherries. You can use frozen cherries for the cherry mixture. Just be sure to thaw them and remove excess moisture before adding them to your batter. The cake is also good with any of the glazes starting on page 244.

Gluten-free nonstick spray

CHERRY MIXTURE

6 ounces cherries, washed, pitted, and cut in half

1 Tablespoon potato starch

CAKE

135 grams (1½ cups) almond meal

120 grams (1 cup) sorghum flour

96 grams (⅔ cup) potato starch

52 grams (½ cup) tapioca starch

1 teaspoon xanthan gum

1 teaspoon double-acting baking powder

½ teaspoon baking soda

½ teaspoon fine salt

1 Tablespoon lemon zest (from 1 lemon)

4 fluid ounces (½ cup) olive oil

264 grams (1½ cups) granulated sugar

1 Tablespoon cherry liqueur (optional)

1 teaspoon vanilla extract

4 eggs, room temperature

1 cup milk or dairy-free milk, room temperature

1 Preheat the oven to 350°F. Spray a 10-inch Bundt pan with gluten-free nonstick spray.

2 To make the cherry mixture: In a small bowl, combine the cherries and potato starch and blend well. Set aside.

3 To make the cake: In a bowl, whisk together the almond meal, sorghum flour, potato starch, tapioca starch, xanthan gum, baking powder, baking soda, and salt.

4 In the bowl of a stand mixer fitted with the paddle attachment, combine the lemon zest, olive oil, and granulated sugar and beat on medium speed until well blended, 1 minute. Add the cherry liqueur (if using) and the vanilla. Add the eggs, one at a time, mixing on low speed after each addition, and mix until the batter is lighter in color and fully incorporated.

5 On low speed, add the flour mixture and the milk alternately in batches, beginning and ending with the flour mixture (one-third flour, one-half milk, one-third flour, one-half milk, one-third flour). Scrape down the sides of the bowl between additions and mix until the batter is smooth and even in color. The batter will seem fairly thin for a cake batter, but not to worry.

6 Working quickly, place the cherry mixture in the prepared Bundt pan and disperse it evenly over the bottom of the pan; the cherries will be somewhat visible on the finished cake. Using a rubber spatula, transfer the batter to the prepared pan and smooth the top. Bake for 42 to 45 minutes, until the top is golden brown and a toothpick inserted in the middle comes out clean.

Citrus Glaze (page 245)

Fresh cherries, washed, pitted, and cut in half (optional)

7 Remove the pan from the oven and let the cake cool in the pan on a wire cooling rack for 15 minutes. Place a serving plate on top of the pan and carefully turn over the plate and the pan so that the cake ends right side up on the plate. Once the cake has cooled completely, drizzle with the Citrus Glaze, and garnish with fresh cherries, if desired.

Note: Store leftovers wrapped in plastic wrap or in an airtight container in the refrigerator for 3 days. If you are not serving the cake immediately, let the cake cool to room temperature, then tightly wrap it in plastic wrap and store it in the freezer.

lemon layer cake

This cake is best served with a lemon frosting. Use the Vanilla Buttercream Frosting (page 255) and substitute the vanilla with 2 Tablespoons of lemon zest. Frost between the two layers and on the top. For color and presentation, I add the Raspberry Glaze from page 47 (Raspberry Lemon Loaf) and fresh raspberries. For a more casual occasion, I use the Citrus Glaze (page 245) on each of the two layers, stack them together, and top with fresh raspberries.

Gluten-free nonstick spray

135 grams (1½ cups) almond meal

120 grams (1 cup) sorghum flour

96 grams (⅔ cup) potato starch

52 grams (½ cup) tapioca starch

1 teaspoon xanthan gum

1 teaspoon double-acting baking powder

½ teaspoon baking soda

½ teaspoon fine salt

1 Tablespoon lemon zest (from 1 lemon)

¾ cup (1½ sticks) unsalted butter, room temperature

264 grams (1½ cups) granulated sugar

2 teaspoons lemon extract

4 eggs, at room temperature

1 cup milk or dairy-free milk, room temperature

Vanilla Buttercream Frosting with lemon zest (page 255; see headnote)

1 Preheat the oven to 350°F. Place two 8-inch parchment rounds in two 8-inch cake pans and spray with gluten-free nonstick spray. Also outfit each pan with a dampened cake strip; this is easier to do when the pans are empty.

2 In a bowl, whisk together the almond meal, sorghum flour, potato starch, tapioca starch, xanthan gum, baking powder, baking soda, and salt.

3 In the bowl of a stand mixer fitted with the paddle attachment, combine the lemon zest, butter, and granulated sugar and beat on medium speed. Add the lemon extract and the eggs, one at a time, mixing on low speed after each addition, until the batter is lighter in color and well incorporated.

4 On low speed, add the flour mixture and the milk, alternately in batches, beginning and ending with the flour mixture (one-third flour, one-half milk, one-third flour, one-half milk, one-third flour). Scrape down the sides of the bowl between additions and mix until the batter is smooth, frothy, and even in color.

5 Using a rubber spatula, transfer the batter to the prepared pans, dividing evenly, and smooth the tops. Bake for 40 to 45 minutes, until the top is golden brown and a toothpick inserted in the middle comes out clean.

6 Remove the pans from the oven and run a knife or offset spatula around the edge of each cake. Let the cakes cool in the pans on a wire cooling rack for 15 minutes. Line the cooling rack with a piece of aluminum foil and spray the foil with gluten-free nonstick spray. Invert the cake pans onto the prepared cooling rack.

continued

lemon layer cake, continued

7 Once the cakes have cooled completely, freeze them for about 4 hours or overnight before frosting. When the cakes are frozen, spread one cake with the lemony Vanilla Buttercream Frosting, stack the other cake on top, and spread the frosting over the top and sides. The cake will take 4 to 5 hours to defrost for serving.

Note: Store leftovers wrapped in plastic wrap or in an airtight container in the refrigerator for 3 days. If you are not serving the cake immediately, let the cake cool to room temperature, then tightly wrap it in plastic wrap and store it in the freezer.

orange and almond butter layer cake

MAKES 8 TO 10 SERVINGS

This is my friend and fellow food stylist Karen Shinto's recipe. Her original recipe called for only a small amount of wheat flour. It was easy to adapt because it already had so much almond flour in the base. I serve it in the summer with the Cream Cheese Vanilla Bean Frosting (page 253) on the top and in the middle and lots of segmented blood oranges swimming on top. That is how we photographed this cake. Not everyone likes almond, so feel free to replace the almond extract with 1 teaspoon of vanilla extract.

Gluten-free nonstick spray

135 grams (1½ cups) almond meal

120 grams (1 cup) sorghum flour

96 grams (⅔ cup) potato starch

52 grams (½ cup) tapioca starch

1 teaspoon xanthan gum

1 teaspoon double-acting baking powder

½ teaspoon baking soda

½ teaspoon fine salt

264 grams (1½ cups) granulated sugar

¾ cup (1½ sticks) unsalted butter, room temperature

1 Tablespoon orange zest (from 1 navel orange)

½ teaspoon almond extract

4 eggs, room temperature

1 cup milk or dairy-free milk, room temperature

Cream Cheese Vanilla Bean Frosting (page 253)

Seasonal fresh fruit, to finish

1 Preheat the oven to 350°F. Place two 8-inch parchment rounds in two 8-inch cake pans and spray with gluten-free nonstick spray. Also outfit each pan with a dampened cake strip; this is easier to do when the pans are empty.

2 In a bowl, whisk together the almond meal, sorghum flour, potato starch, tapioca starch, xanthan gum, baking powder, baking soda, and salt.

3 In the bowl of a stand mixer fitted with the paddle attachment, combine the granulated sugar, butter, and orange zest and beat on medium speed until well blended, 1 minute. Add the almond extract and the eggs, one at a time, mixing on low speed after each addition, until the batter is fluffy and lighter in color.

4 On low speed, add the flour mixture and the milk alternately in batches, beginning and ending with the flour mixture (one-third flour, one-half milk, one-third flour, one-half milk, one-third flour). Scrape down the sides of the bowl between additions and mix until the batter is smooth, frothy, and even in color.

5 Using a rubber spatula, transfer the batter to the prepared pans, dividing evenly, and smooth the tops. Bake for 40 to 45 minutes, until the top is golden brown and a toothpick inserted in the middle comes out clean.

6 Remove the pans from the oven and run a knife or offset spatula around the edge of each cake. Let the cakes cool in the pans on a wire cooling rack for 15 minutes. Line the cooling rack with a piece of aluminum foil and spray the foil with gluten-free nonstick spray. Invert the cake pans onto the prepared cooling rack.

continued

orange and almond butter layer cake, continued

7 Once the cakes have cooled completely, freeze them for about 4 hours or overnight before frosting. When the cakes are frozen, spread one cake with the Cream Cheese Vanilla Bean Frosting, stack the other cake on top, and spread the frosting over the top and sides. The cake will take 4 to 5 hours to defrost for serving. Garnish with seasonal fruit.

Note. Store leftovers wrapped in plastic wrap or in an airtight container in the refrigerator for 3 days. If you are not serving the cake immediately, let the cake cool to room temperature, then tightly wrap it in plastic wrap and store it in the freezer.

chocolate hazelnut tart

MAKES 10 TO 12 SERVINGS

I liked my brownie recipe so much that I wanted it to appear again in a more splendid way. So I dressed it up with hazelnuts and a Chocolate Glaze (page 253). Now the humble brownie is ready for a dinner party. For the photo, I used my 4 by 13½-inch tart pan. Don't attempt to fill more than ¼ inch from the top of the pan. Place the excess batter in a ramekin and bake it alongside the tart.

Gluten-free nonstick spray

48 grams (⅓ cup) potato starch

40 grams (⅓ cup) sorghum flour

½ teaspoon xanthan gum

½ teaspoon double-acting baking powder

½ teaspoon fine salt

½ teaspoon espresso powder or instant coffee (optional)

4 ounces semisweet chocolate

2 ounces unsweetened chocolate

½ cup melted and slightly cooled clarified butter or coconut oil

132 grams (¾ cup) granulated sugar

95 grams (½ cup) firmly packed brown sugar

2 teaspoons vanilla extract

3 eggs, room temperature

2 Tablespoons hazelnut liqueur (Frangelico)(optional)

½ cup coarsely chopped toasted hazelnuts (optional)

Chocolate Glaze (page 253)

1 Preheat the oven to 350°F. Spray a 4 by 13-inch rectangular tart pan or a 9-inch round tart pan with a removable bottom with gluten-free nonstick spray. Place the tart pan on a baking sheet.

2 In a bowl, whisk together the potato starch, sorghum flour, xanthan gum, baking powder, salt, and espresso powder (if using).

3 In a heavy medium-size saucepan over low heat, melt the semisweet chocolate, unsweetened chocolate, and clarified butter. Remove from the heat and whisk in the granulated sugar, brown sugar, and vanilla. Whisk in the eggs, one at a time, and continue to whisk until the mixture is completely smooth and glossy. Add the dry ingredients and mix just until incorporated. Stir in the hazelnut liqueur and hazelnuts (if using).

4 Pour the batter into the prepared pan. Bake for 45 minutes or until a toothpick inserted into the center comes out with wet crumbs.

5 Remove the pan from the oven. Let the tart cool in the pan for 5 minutes. Lift off the outer ring of the pan and let the tart continue to cool. I always find that the tart cuts better if it is refrigerated for a time. Drizzle with Chocolate Glaze before serving.

Note: Store leftovers wrapped in plastic wrap or in an airtight container in the refrigerator for 3 days. If you are not serving the tart immediately, let it cool to room temperature, then tightly wrap it in plastic wrap and store it in the freezer.

italian almond cake

MAKES 8 TO 10 SERVINGS

This cake is best served with only a light sprinkle of powdered sugar. For a dinner party, I serve it with a seasonal fruit compote or lightly sautéed fresh cherries. I developed this recipe for my friends Jaime and Kirk. They are such appreciative eaters. It is always a joy to cook for them.

Gluten-free nonstick spray

²/₃ cup sliced almonds (optional)

2 Tablespoons turbinado or coconut sugar (optional)

113 grams (1 cup + 2 Tablespoons) almond flour or almond meal

45 grams (½ cup) gluten-free oat flour

1 teaspoon xanthan gum

½ teaspoon double-acting baking powder

¼ teaspoon fine salt

176 grams (1 cup) granulated sugar

½ cup melted and slightly cooled clarified butter or coconut oil

1 Tablespoon orange or lemon zest (from 1 navel orange or 1 lemon)

2 teaspoons almond extract

1 Tablespoon amaretto or cherry liqueur (optional)

3 eggs, room temperature

Confectioners' sugar, to finish

1 Preheat the oven to 350°F and place an oven rack in the lower third of the oven. Spray an 8-inch round cake pan with gluten-free nonstick spray. Spread the almonds and turbinado sugar (if using) evenly over the bottom of the pan. If not using the almonds and sugar, place a 8-inch parchment round in the cake pan and spray with gluten-free nonstick spray. Also outfit the pan with a dampened cake strip; this is easier to do when the pan is empty.

2 In a small bowl, whisk together the almond flour, oat flour, xanthan gum, baking powder, and salt.

3 In the bowl of a stand mixer fitted with the paddle attachment, combine the granulated sugar, clarified butter, and citrus zest and beat on medium speed until well blended, 1 minute. Add the almond extract and the amaretto (if using). Add the eggs, one at a time, and mix on low speed after each addition, until the batter is lighter in color. Add the dry ingredients in two batches, mixing on low speed after each addition, until all of the ingredients are well incorporated, about 1 minute.

4 Using a rubber spatula, transfer the batter to the prepared pan and smooth the top. Bake for 35 to 40 minutes, until the top is golden brown and a toothpick inserted into the middle comes out clean.

5 Remove the pan from the oven and run a knife or offset spatula around the edge of the cake. Let the cake cool in the pan on a wire cooling rack for 10 minutes, then turn it out onto a cake plate or cake stand. Dust with confectioners' sugar and serve.

Note: Store leftovers wrapped in plastic wrap or in an airtight container in the refrigerator for 3 days. If you are not serving the cake immediately, let the cake cool to room temperature, then tightly wrap it in plastic wrap and store it in the freezer.

holiday fruitcake

MAKES 8 TO 10 SERVINGS

During the holidays, my mother made a steamed fruitcake, which was an all-day affair. I developed this recipe as a nod to my mother's fruitcake. It is just as moist and delicious as hers but does not require all of the steaming and the waiting of my mother's recipe. I usually cut the cake and serve each slice with a dollop of rum sauce. A little sprinkle of freshly grated nutmeg provides a festive finishing touch for a holiday presentation.

CAKE

Gluten-free nonstick spray

½ cup pistachios, roasted and coarsely chopped

1 cup dried cranberries, coarsely chopped

96 grams (⅔ cup) potato starch

69 grams (⅔ cup) tapioca starch

60 grams (½ cup) sorghum flour

45 grams (½ cup) gluten-free oat flour

1½ teaspoons double-acting baking powder

1 teaspoon xanthan gum

1 teaspoon ground cardamom

½ teaspoon baking soda

½ teaspoon fine salt

220 grams (1¼ cups) granulated sugar

2 Tablespoons canola oil

2 eggs, room temperature

1 cup full-fat sour cream, room temperature

2 teaspoons vanilla extract

1 To make the cake: Preheat the oven to 350°F. Line an 8-inch springform pan with parchment paper and spray the sides and the bottom with gluten-free nonstick spray. Spread the pistachios evenly over the bottom of the pan.

2 Soak the cranberries in enough hot water to cover for 15 minutes, until they plump up slightly. Drain and set aside on an absorbent towel.

3 In a bowl, whisk together the potato starch, tapioca starch, sorghum flour, oat flour, baking powder, xanthan gum, cardamom, baking soda, and salt.

4 In the bowl of a stand mixer fitted with the paddle attachment, beat the granulated sugar and oil until well blended, 1 minute. Add the eggs, one at a time, mixing well after each addition, and beat until cream-colored and light. Add the sour cream, vanilla, and flour mixture and beat at a medium-low speed for 30 seconds. Do not overbeat. With a rubber spatula, fold in the cranberries.

5 With a rubber spatula, spread the batter into the prepared pan. Bake for 75 to 80 minutes, until a toothpick inserted in the center comes out clean.

6 Meanwhile, to make the rum custard sauce: Combine the milk, cream, brown sugar, and cornstarch in a saucepan and whisk together well. Cook on low heat, stirring constantly, until the sauce thickens. Remove from the heat and stir in the rum. Cool slightly before serving. You can also cool the sauce and keep it in the refrigerator for up to 1 week. Warm gently before serving. This makes 1 cup of sauce.

RUM CUSTARD SAUCE

½ cup milk or dairy-free milk

½ cup heavy cream or canned coconut milk

95 grams (½ cup) firmly packed brown sugar

2 teaspoons cornstarch

2 Tablespoons rum

7 Remove the pan from the oven and run a knife or offset spatula around the edge of the cake. Cool the cake in the pan on a wire cooling rack for 20 minutes. Loosen the outer ring of the sides and cool completely on the wire cooling rack. To remove the cake from the pan bottom, turn it out onto a cake plate or cake stand. Gently remove the pan bottom and peel off the parchment. Slice and serve with 1 Tablespoon of sauce on each slice.

Note: Store leftovers wrapped in plastic wrap or in an airtight container in the refrigerator for 3 days. If you are not serving the cake immediately, let the cake cool to room temperature, then tightly wrap it in plastic wrap and store it in the freezer.

carrot layer cake

MAKES 8 TO 10 SERVINGS

I love carrot cake and so does my mother. For this recipe, it really helps to press out the grated carrots. Excessive moisture is never a friend to gluten-free bakers. Don't skimp on the cream cheese frosting—put it on the top, the middle, and all around the sides! I like to decorate the cake with Candied Carrot Curls (page 255), as shown in the photo.

Gluten-free nonstick spray

180 grams (2 cups) grated carrots (2 to 3 carrots)

96 grams (⅔ cup) potato starch

69 grams (⅔ cup) tapioca starch

60 grams (½ cup) sorghum flour

45 grams (½ cup) gluten-free oat flour

2 teaspoons ground cinnamon

1½ teaspoons double-acting baking powder

1¼ teaspoons xanthan gum

1 teaspoon ground cardamom

½ teaspoon baking soda

½ teaspoon fine salt

¼ teaspoon ground nutmeg

220 grams (1¼ cups) granulated sugar

2 Tablespoons canola oil

2 eggs, room temperature

1 cup full-fat sour cream, room temperature

2 teaspoons vanilla extract

¾ cup chopped walnuts (optional)

Cream Cheese Vanilla Bean Frosting (page 253)

Candied Carrot Curls (page 255)

1 Preheat the oven to 350°F. Place two 8-inch parchment rounds in two 8-inch cake pans and spray with gluten-free nonstick spray. Also outfit each pan with a dampened cake strip; this is easier to do when the pans are empty.

2 Press liquid out of the carrots by squeezing them in a clean kitchen towel or in a stack of paper towels.

3 In a bowl, whisk together the potato starch, tapioca starch, sorghum flour, oat flour, cinnamon, baking powder, xanthan gum, cardamom, baking soda, salt, and nutmeg.

4 In the bowl of a stand mixer fitted with the paddle attachment, combine the granulated sugar and oil and beat on medium speed until the oil is distributed, about 1 minute. Add the eggs, one at a time, beating well after each addition. Add the sour cream and vanilla and mix until even in color.

5 Reduce the speed to low and add the flour mixture to the mixing bowl. Mix until smooth, frothy, and even in color, about 1 minute. On very low speed add the carrots and the walnuts (if using) and mix until well incorporated.

6 Divide the batter between the two prepared pans, smoothing the top of each. Bake 40 to 43 minutes, until a toothpick inserted into the middle comes out clean.

7 Remove the pans from the oven and run a knife or offset spatula around the edge of each cake. Cool the cakes in the pans on a wire cooling rack for 10 minutes. Line the cooling rack with a piece of aluminum foil and spray the foil with gluten-free nonstick spray. Invert the cake pans onto the prepared cooling rack.

continued

carrot layer cake, continued

8 Once the cakes have cooled completely, freeze them for about 4 hours or overnight before frosting. After the cakes are frozen, spread the Cream Cheese Vanilla Bean Frosting on one of the cakes, stack the other cake on top, and then spread the frosting around the sides and top. Top with the Candied Carrot Curls. The cake will take 4 to 5 hours to defrost for serving.

Note: Store leftovers wrapped in plastic wrap or in an airtight container in the refrigerator for 3 days. If you are not serving the cake immediately, let the cake cool to room temperature, then tightly wrap it in plastic wrap and store it in the freezer.

poached orange cake with pecans

MAKES 10 TO 12 SERVINGS

It was a revelation when I discovered an old recipe that used whole poached fruit in a cake. Adapting this to gluten-free was a win-win. All the pectin within the fruit gives the cake structure, moisture, and flavor. This cake is best served with a dollop of lightly sweetened whipped cream (page 256). You can also serve it with a fresh fruit compote or a simple glaze (see Glazes, starting on page 244) plus some orange zest, as I did for the photo.

Gluten-free nonstick spray

⅓ cup coarsely chopped pecans (optional)

96 grams (⅔ cup) potato starch

90 grams (1 cup) almond meal

69 grams (⅔ cup) tapioca starch

60 grams (½ cup) sorghum flour

45 grams (½ cup) gluten-free oat flour

1½ teaspoons baking soda

1 teaspoon ground cardamom

¾ teaspoon xanthan gum

¼ teaspoon fine salt

340 grams (1½ cups) orange puree (see page 29)

1 teaspoon orange extract

¾ cup (1½ sticks) unsalted butter, room temperature

132 grams (¾ cup) granulated sugar

1 Tablespoon grated orange zest (from 1 navel orange)

4 eggs, room temperature

1 Preheat the oven to 325°F. Spray a 10-inch Bundt pan with gluten-free nonstick spray. If using, sprinkle the pecans evenly over the bottom of the pan.

2 In a bowl, whisk together the potato starch, almond meal, tapioca starch, sorghum flour, oat flour, baking soda, cardamom, xanthan gum, and salt. In a small bowl, whisk together the orange puree and orange extract.

3 In the bowl of a stand mixer fitted with the paddle attachment, beat the butter, granulated sugar, and orange zest on medium speed until well blended, 1 minute. Add the eggs, one at a time, mixing after each addition, until light in color, 1 to 2 minutes, then beat in the orange puree mixture. Add the dry ingredients to the mixing bowl and mix on very low speed until well incorporated.

4 With a rubber spatula, spread the batter into the prepared pan. Bake 45 to 50 minutes, until the top is golden brown and a toothpick inserted into the middle comes out clean.

5 Remove the pan from the oven. Let the cake cool in the pan on a wire cooling rack for 10 minutes, then turn it out onto a cake plate or cake stand. Be sure to turn out the cake before it cools too much because the pecans can stick to the bottom of the pan.

Note: Store leftovers wrapped in plastic wrap or in an airtight container in the refrigerator for 3 days. If you are not serving the cake immediately, let the cake cool to room temperature, then tightly wrap it in plastic wrap and store it in the freezer.

poached lemon cake

I like to serve this poached fruit cake with a simple Citrus Glaze (page 245), using the lemon variation. For a birthday or other special occasion, I dice or julienne some purchased candied lemon peel and place it on the top. Fresh raspberries are also great as a simple decoration.

Gluten-free nonstick spray

96 grams (⅔ cup) potato starch

90 grams (1 cup) almond meal

69 grams (⅔ cup) tapioca starch

60 grams (½ cup) sorghum flour

45 grams (½ cup) gluten-free oat flour

1½ teaspoons baking soda

1 teaspoon ground cardamom

¾ teaspoon xanthan gum

¼ teaspoon fine salt

340 grams (1½ cups) poached lemon puree (see page 29)

1 teaspoon lemon extract, or 1 Tablespoon limoncello

¾ cup (1½ sticks) unsalted butter, room temperature

132 grams (¾ cup) granulated sugar

1 Tablespoon lemon zest (from 1 lemon)

4 eggs, room temperature

Citrus Glaze (page 245)

1 Preheat the oven to 325°F. Spray a 10-inch Bundt pan with gluten-free nonstick spray.

2 In a bowl, whisk together the potato starch, almond meal, tapioca starch, sorghum flour, oat flour, baking soda, cardamom, xanthan gum, and salt. In a small bowl, whisk together the lemon puree and lemon extract.

3 In the bowl of a stand mixer fitted with the paddle attachment, beat the butter, granulated sugar, and lemon zest on medium speed until well blended, 1 minute. Add the eggs, one at a time, mixing after each addition, until light in color, 1 to 2 minutes, then beat in the lemon puree mixture. Add the dry ingredients to the mixing bowl and mix on very low speed until well incorporated.

4 With a rubber spatula, spread the batter into the prepared cake pan. Bake 45 to 50 minutes, until the top is golden brown and a toothpick inserted into the middle comes out clean.

5 Remove the pan from the oven. Let the cake cool in the pan on a wire cooling rack for 10 minutes, then turn it out onto a cake plate or cake stand. If you decide to glaze the cake, wait until it cools to room temperature.

Note: Store leftovers wrapped in plastic wrap or in an airtight container in the refrigerator for 3 days. If you are not serving the cake immediately, let the cake cool to room temperature, then tightly wrap it in plastic wrap and store it in the freezer.

date cake with pecans

When I discovered that whole poached fruit made for a great cake, I started looking around for my next pectin- and fiber-rich ingredient—dates! Try this cake with the Coffee Glaze (page 245), sautéed fruit (see page 74), or Candied Pecans (page 256). It is so moist that it can also be served plain.

Gluten-free nonstick spray

⅓ cup coarsely chopped pecans

¾ cup water

12 ounces (about 3 cups) pitted small Medjool dates

2 Tablespoons dark rum, or 2 teaspoons rum extract

2 Tablespoons brewed espresso, or 2 teaspoons instant espresso powder mixed with 2 Tablespoons hot water

96 grams (⅔ cup) potato starch

69 grams (⅔ cup) tapioca starch

60 grams (½ cup) sorghum flour

45 grams (½ cup) gluten-free oat flour

1 Tablespoon double-acting baking powder

1½ teaspoons baking soda

1 teaspoon ground cinnamon

¾ teaspoon xanthan gum

¼ teaspoon ground nutmeg

¼ teaspoon fine salt

⅛ teaspoon ground cloves

¾ cup (1½ sticks) unsalted butter, room temperature

142 grams (¾ cup) firmly packed brown sugar

4 eggs, room temperature

Coffee Glaze (page 245)

1 Preheat the oven to 325°F. Spray a 10-inch Bundt pan with gluten-free nonstick spray. Spread the pecans evenly over the bottom of the pan.

2 In a medium microwave-safe bowl, combine the water, dates, rum, and espresso. Microwave at high power for 2 minutes. You can also combine the ingredients in a small saucepan and heat until the liquids are hot. Transfer the date mixture to a food processor and let it stand until the dates are softened. Puree until smooth.

3 In a bowl, whisk together the potato starch, tapioca starch, sorghum flour, oat flour, baking powder, baking soda, cinnamon, xanthan gum, nutmeg, salt, and cloves.

4 In the bowl of a stand mixer fitted with the paddle attachment, beat the butter and brown sugar on medium speed until well blended, 1 minute. Add the eggs, one at a time, and the date puree, mixing on low speed after each addition until well incorporated. Add the dry ingredients and mix on low speed until well incorporated.

5 With a rubber spatula, spread the batter into the prepared pan. Bake 55 to 60 minutes, until the top is golden brown and a toothpick inserted into the middle comes out clean.

6 Remove the pan from the oven. Let the cake cool in the pan on a wire cooling rack for 10 minutes, then turn it out onto a cake plate or cake stand. Be sure to turn out the cake before it cools too much because the pecans can stick to the bottom of the pan. If you decide to glaze the cake, wait until it cools to room temperature.

Note: Store leftovers wrapped in plastic wrap or in an airtight container in the refrigerator for 3 days. If you are not serving the cake immediately, let the cake cool to room temperature, then tightly wrap it in plastic wrap and store it in the freezer.

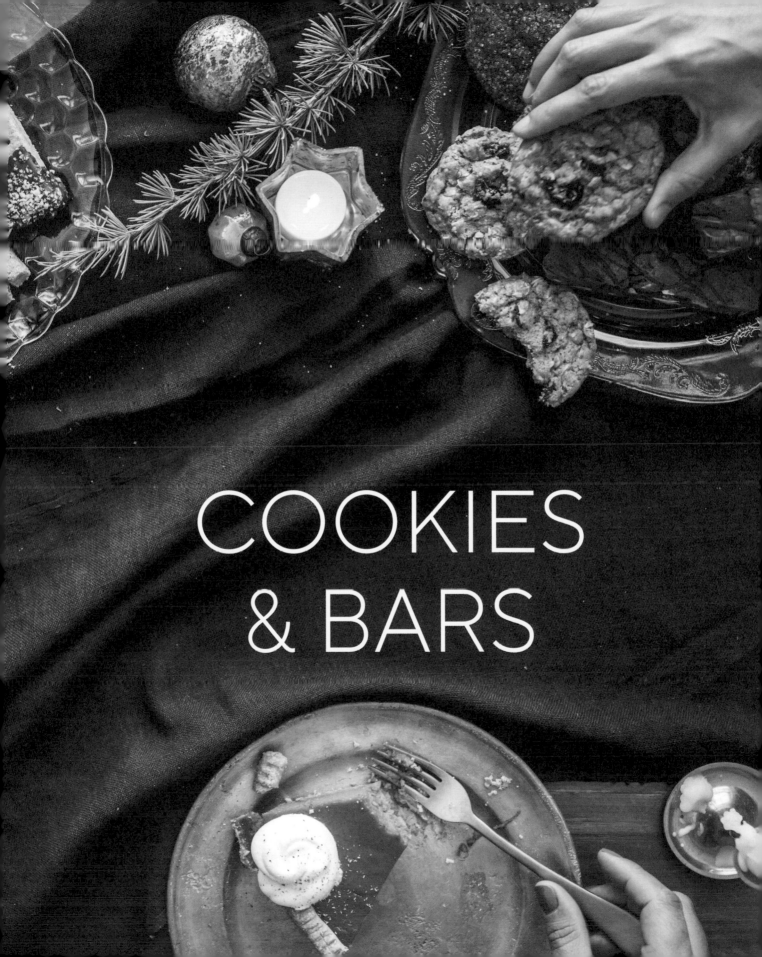

COOKIES
& BARS

TIPS FOR SUCCESS

I love having cookie dough in the freezer at all times. There is something immensely comforting about knowing that I can have a really good gluten-free treat at a moment's notice. Sometimes I just bake off two at a time as a form of portion control. The other nice thing is that when I am tempted by grocery-store gluten-free cookies, I know that I can come home and have something that is so much better.

Always mix together the butter and sugar first and then add the eggs one at a time, mixing after each addition. (Refer to cookie tutorial on the opposite page.) This method is generally used for cakes, but it also gives great structure to gluten-free cookies. This method dissolves the sugar into the fat, ensuring a crisp exterior. Mixing the eggs in one at a time adds aeration and a tender interior. The final step is to carefully measure out the dry ingredients in a separate bowl and mix really well. The creaming method ensures that all ingredients are well combined and suspended in the fat and sugar. It also guarantees that you will have nice tight cookies that will be less likely to spread out over the cookie sheet when baking.

Cookie dough should always be set aside to chill in the refrigerator before it is baked. This allows the fat to solidify, which also keeps the cookies from spreading as they bake. Setting the cookies aside in the refrigerator or freezer also allows for full hydration. The dry ingredients and the liquid ingredients meld together more completely, and you will avoid a gritty, flat cookie. The interior will be light and cakey. If you want to take it one step further, portion out the cookies and freeze the balls of dough on a flat tray. Once the cookies are frozen, you can place them all in a freezer-safe resealable plastic bag. Write the name of the cookies and the baking time on the bag and bake them as needed. The baking time does not change for frozen cookies. I think the best cookies come from a frozen state. That is my preferred method.

Some of my cookie recipes can be made as bars. I grew up on bar cookies. My mother liked how quick and easy they were to make.

If bar cookies can be made from the recipe, it will be noted at the bottom of the directions. Make these adjustments: Reduce the fat by ¼ cup. Bake in an 8 by 13-inch or 9 by 12-inch pan outfitted with parchment paper with an overhang on two sides. Refrigerate the entire pan and allow the dough to solidify before baking. Bake at 325°F for 35 to 40 minutes, until the cookie dough puffs up and browns at the edges. The center will appear soft. Let the bars cool completely in the pan. Once the bars are cool, refrigerate the entire pan until solid and then cut into bars. You can also freeze the entire pan of raw dough and bake at your convenience. The baking time does not change for frozen cookies. Be sure to wrap the pan really well in plastic wrap before freezing.

1. Cream together the fat and sugar, and then add the eggs one at a time, mixing between each addition. The batter should be light and fluffy at the end of mixing. Refrigerate the dough and allow the fat to solidify.

2. Scoop cookies with a cookie scoop.

3. Here is a simple food-styling trick that gives your cookies a better presentation: Hold back some of your mix-ins—nuts, chocolate chips, etc. Scoop out the dough and add additional mix-ins onto the top of each cookie.

chocolate chip cookies

MAKES 30 TO 40 COOKIES, USING
A 1-OUNCE COOKIE SCOOP

This is the first baked goodie that I converted to gluten-free. As I learned more and became more accomplished as a gluten-free baker, I always went back to my chocolate chip cookie and revised it. Over the years, it has been adapted fourteen times! I feel really confident that this is my best version ever. To make bar cookies, see page 114.

108 grams (¾ cup) potato starch

90 grams (1 cup) gluten-free oat flour

90 grams (¾ cup) sorghum flour

45 grams (½ cup) almond meal, pecan meal, sunflower meal, or hazelnut meal (see note)

1½ teaspoons baking soda

1 teaspoon xanthan gum

1 teaspoon fine salt

285 grams (1½ cups) firmly packed brown sugar

¾ cup melted and slightly cooled clarified butter or coconut oil

2 eggs, room temperature, or 133 grams (½ cup) unsweetened applesauce

1 Tablespoon vanilla extract

10 to 12 ounces (2 to 2¼ cups) chocolate chips

½ cup chopped unsalted pecans, walnuts, or sunflower seeds (optional)

Gluten-free nonstick spray

Note: If you have an allergy to almond meal, replace it with another 45 grams (½ cup) gluten-free oat flour.

1 In a mixing bowl, whisk together the potato starch, oat flour, sorghum flour, almond meal, baking soda, xanthan gum, and salt.

2 In the bowl of a stand mixer fitted with the paddle attachment, mix together the brown sugar and clarified butter on medium speed. Add the eggs and vanilla, and mix until fluffy and light in color, 1 to 2 minutes.

3 Add the dry ingredients to the mixing bowl and mix on low speed until well incorporated. On very low speed, mix in the chocolate chips and the pecans (if using).

4 Cover the bowl and refrigerate the dough for at least 3 hours or up to 5 days. This step is important, so the dry ingredients have a chance to absorb all the moisture, which keeps the cookies from spreading too much when baked.

5 When you're ready to bake the cookies, preheat the oven to 350°F. Lightly spray a baking sheet with gluten-free nonstick spray or line it with parchment paper.

6 With a 1-ounce cookie scoop or a tablespoon measure, portion out the dough and roll it into 1-inch balls. Arrange the balls on the prepared baking sheet 2 inches apart, and slightly flatten each ball with the palm of your hand.

7 Bake for 12 to 14 minutes, until the cookies are light golden brown. Remove the pan from the oven and let the cookies cool on the baking sheet for 10 minutes, then transfer them with a metal spatula to a wire cooling rack to cool completely.

Note: Store the cookies in an airtight container for 5 days at room temperature. The dough can also be portioned and frozen for baking at a moment's notice. The baking time does not change for baking from frozen cookie dough.

double chocolate chip cookies

MAKES 30 TO 40 COOKIES,
USING A 1-OUNCE COOKIE SCOOP

There are so many chocolate lovers in my family and within my circle of friends that I had to have this recipe in my arsenal for family gatherings and parties.

108 grams (¾ cup) potato starch

90 grams (1 cup) gluten-free oat flour

90 grams (¾ cup) sorghum flour

45 grams (½ cup) almond meal or pecan, sunflower, or hazelnut meal (see note)

40 grams (½ cup) cocoa powder

1½ teaspoons baking soda

1 teaspoon xanthan gum

1 teaspoon fine salt

285 grams (1½ cups) firmly packed brown sugar

¾ cup melted and slightly cooled clarified butter or coconut oil

2 eggs, room temperature, or 133 grams (½ cup) unsweetened applesauce

1 Tablespoon vanilla extract

10 to 12 ounces (2 to 2¼ cups) chocolate chips

½ cup unsalted chopped pecans, walnuts, or sunflower seeds (optional)

Gluten-free nonstick spray

Note: If you have an allergy to almond meal, substitute with another 45 grams (½ cup) gluten-free oat flour.

1 In a bowl, combine the potato starch, oat flour, sorghum flour, almond meal, cocoa powder, baking soda, xanthan gum, and salt.

2 In the bowl of a stand mixer fitted with the paddle attachment, combine the brown sugar and clarified butter and mix at medium speed until well incorporated, about 1 minute. Add the eggs and vanilla and beat until fluffy and light in color, 1 to 2 minutes. On low speed, add the dry ingredients to the mixing bowl and mix until all of the ingredients are well blended. On very low speed, mix in the chocolate chips and the pecans (if using).

3 Cover the bowl and refrigerate the dough for at least 3 hours or up to 5 days. Don't skip the refrigeration. The cookies won't spread as much if the dry ingredients have a chance to absorb all the moisture.

4 When you're ready to bake the cookies, preheat the oven to 350°F. Lightly spray a baking sheet with gluten-free nonstick spray or line it with parchment paper.

5 With a 1-ounce cookie scoop or a tablespoon measure, portion out the dough and roll into 1-inch balls. Place the balls on the prepared baking sheet 2 inches apart, and slightly flatten each cookie with your thumb. Bake for 12 to 15 minutes, until light golden brown.

6 Remove the pan from the oven and let the cookies cool on the baking sheet for 10 minutes, then transfer them with a metal spatula to a wire cooling rack to cool completely.

Note: Store the cookies in an airtight container for 5 days at room temperature. The dough can also be portioned and frozen for baking at a moment's notice. The baking time does not change for baking from frozen cookie dough.

To make bar cookies, see page 114.

almond butter cookies

MAKES 30 TO 40 COOKIES, USING
A 1-OUNCE COOKIE SCOOP

For a long time, this was my peanut butter cookie. Over time I learned that I could substitute just about any nut butter, including sunflower butter (made from seeds, not nuts). In my teaching and recipe development, I needed to be adaptable to all allergens. I think that it works best to measure the nut butter by weight. It is so messy in a measuring cup. To make bar cookies, see page 114.

108 grams (¾ cup) potato starch

90 grams (1 cup) gluten-free oat flour

90 grams (¾ cup) sorghum flour

45 grams (½ cup) almond meal, pecan meal, sunflower meal, or hazelnut meal (see note)

1½ teaspoons baking soda

1 teaspoon xanthan gum

1 teaspoon fine salt

285 grams (1½ cups) firmly packed brown sugar

134 grams (½ cup) almond butter, peanut butter, or sunflower seed butter

¼ cup melted and slightly cooled clarified butter or coconut oil

2 eggs, room temperature, or 133 grams (½ cup) unsweetened applesauce

2 teaspoons almond extract

10 to 12 ounces (2 to 2¼ cups) chocolate chips (optional)

½ cup coarsely chopped almonds, peanuts or sunflower seeds (optional)

Gluten-free nonstick spray

Note: If you have an allergy to almond meal, replace it with another 45 grams (½ cup) gluten-free oat flour.

1 In a bowl, combine the potato starch, oat flour, sorghum flour, almond meal, baking soda, xanthan gum, and salt.

2 In the bowl of a stand mixer fitted with the paddle attachment, combine the brown sugar, almond butter, and clarified butter on medium speed. Add the eggs and almond extract, and mix until fluffy and light in color, 1 to 2 minutes.

3 Add the dry ingredients to the mixing bowl and mix on low speed until well incorporated. On very low speed, mix in the chocolate chips and the almonds (if using).

4 Cover the bowl and refrigerate the dough for at least 3 hours or up to 5 days. This step is important, so the dry ingredients have a chance to absorb all the moisture, which keeps the cookies from spreading too much when baked.

5 When you're ready to bake the cookies, preheat the oven to 350°F. Lightly spray a baking sheet with gluten-free nonstick spray or line it with parchment paper.

6 With a 1-ounce cookie scoop or a tablespoon measure, portion out the dough and roll it into 1-inch balls. Arrange the balls on the prepared baking sheet 2 inches apart, and slightly flatten each ball with your thumb.

7 Bake for 12 to 14 minutes, until the cookies are light golden brown. Remove the pan from the oven and let the cookies cool on the baking sheet for 10 minutes, then transfer them with a metal spatula to a wire cooling rack to cool completely.

Note: Store the cookies in an airtight container for 5 days at room temperature. The dough can also be portioned and frozen for baking at a moment's notice. The baking time does not change for baking from frozen cookie dough.

gingersnap cutout cookies

MAKES 37 THREE-INCH COOKIES

During the holidays it is essential for me to have a gingerbread recipe. I use the cutouts for decorations on the tree as well as for dessert. You can also use this recipe for building a gingerbread house. I bake the pieces for the house according to the timings in this cookie recipe. You will need to keep your eye on them, as larger pieces will take longer to bake. My secret is to bake all the shapes again at 200°F for an additional 10 to 15 minutes. You want to crisp them until they are really firm and then build your gingerbread house.

150 grams (1¼ cups) sorghum flour, plus more as needed

95 grams (½ cup) firmly packed brown sugar

72 grams (½ cup) potato starch

52 grams (½ cup) tapioca starch

2 teaspoons ground ginger

1 teaspoon xanthan gum

1 teaspoon baking soda

1 teaspoon ground cinnamon

½ teaspoon ground cardamom

½ teaspoon ground cloves

¼ teaspoon fine salt

¼ cup molasses

1 egg plus 1 egg yolk, room temperature

1 Tablespoon melted and slightly cooled clarified butter or coconut oil, plus more as needed

Teff or sorghum flour, for dusting and rolling (it will disappear as the cookies bake)

1 In a medium mixing bowl, whisk together the sorghum flour, brown sugar, potato starch, tapioca starch, ginger, xanthan gum, baking soda, cinnamon, cardamom, cloves, and salt.

2 In a liquid measuring cup, combine the molasses, egg, egg yolk, and clarified butter.

3 Add the molasses mixture to the dry ingredients and stir with a rubber spatula. You will have a crumbly dough at first, but it will come together. Keep stirring until the dough begins to form a ball. If it seems dry, add 1 teaspoon melted clarified butter. If the dough is too wet, add 1 Tablespoon sorghum flour. Add one or the other of these ingredients incrementally until you achieve the desired consistency. The dough should be the consistency of Play-Doh. Knead the dough until it is smooth, pliable, and even in color.

4 Divide the dough into 3 even portions, shape into disks, wrap each disk separately with plastic wrap, and place all three disks in a resealable bag. Refrigerate for 1 hour.

5 Preheat the oven to 350°F. Line a baking sheet with parchment paper.

6 Remove the dough from the refrigerator and let it sit for 5 to 10 minutes. Place a piece of parchment paper on top of a silicone baking mat (this keeps the parchment from moving around when you are rolling the dough out). Lightly flour the parchment paper with teff flour and place one of the portions of dough on the parchment paper. Keeping both sides of the dough floured, roll the dough to a ¼-inch thickness.

continued

gingersnap cutout cookies, continued

7 Cut the dough with your favorite 3-inch cookie cutters. With a small offset spatula, gently peel up each cookie and place on the prepared baking sheet. If you are going to use the cookies as ornaments, use a small drinking straw to cut a small hole in the top of each cookie. I also like to freeze the full baking sheet of cookies for about 10 minutes before baking.

8 Bake the cookies, one sheet at a time, for 8 to 10 minutes. If the cookies are larger than 3 inches, bake for 10 to 12 minutes. Remove the pan from the oven and let the cookies cool on the baking sheet for 10 to 15 minutes, then transfer them with a metal spatula to a wire cooling rack to cool completely. Once the cookies are cool, you can decorate them with royal icing (see Resources on page 262) and sprinkle with decorative sugars or candy.

Note: If you like crunchier gingerbread cookies, place them side by side on a baking sheet in a 200°F oven and bake for an additional 10 minutes to dry them out.

Variation

This dough lends itself well to making gingerbread houses. You can also use a clean rubber stamp to decorate the dough. Press the stamp lightly into the top of the dough. If you place the tray of cookies in the freezer for about 10 minutes before baking, the impressions will remain through baking.

almond thumbprint cookies

I like to use apricot or raspberry jam or orange marmalade for these cookies. There is something so elegant about all of those jewel tones on the same plate, especially during the holidays. The key is making the cookies abundant with jam. My trick is to add more jam immediately after they come out of the oven. Another trick is to form all of the cookies with the thumb indent. Fill them with jam and freeze them. Bake them from their frozen state, and you will find that they stay more compact and hold the jam better.

135 grams (1½ cups) almond meal, pecan meal, sunflower meal, or hazelnut meal (see note)

108 grams (¾ cup) potato starch

90 grams (1 cup) gluten-free oat flour

90 grams (¾ cup) sorghum flour

1½ teaspoons baking soda

1 teaspoon xanthan gum

1 teaspoon fine salt

285 grams (1½ cups) firmly packed brown sugar

¾ cup melted and slightly cooled clarified butter or coconut oil

2 eggs, room temperature, or 133 grams (½ cup) unsweetened applesauce

1 Tablespoon almond extract

1 cup coarsely chopped sliced almonds

Gluten-free nonstick spray

1 cup orange marmalade or raspberry or apricot jam (make sure it is a dense jam rather than a runny jam), or a combination

Note: If you have an allergy to almond meal, replace it with another 45 grams (½ cup) gluten-free oat flour.

1 In a medium mixing bowl, whisk together the almond meal, potato starch, oat flour, sorghum flour, baking soda, xanthan gum, and salt.

2 In the bowl of a stand mixer fitted with the paddle attachment, combine the brown sugar and clarified butter on medium speed. Add the eggs and almond extract and mix until fluffy and light in color, 1 to 2 minutes.

3 Add the dry ingredients to the mixing bowl and mix on low speed until well incorporated. On very low speed, mix in the almonds.

4 Cover the bowl and refrigerate the dough for at least 3 hours or up to 5 days. This step is important, so the dry ingredients have a chance to absorb all the moisture, which keeps the cookies from spreading too much when baked.

5 When you're ready to bake the cookies, preheat the oven to 350°F. Lightly spray a cookie sheet with gluten-free nonstick spray or line it with parchment paper.

6 With a 1-ounce cookie scoop or a tablespoon measure, portion out the dough and roll it into 1-inch balls. Arrange the balls on the prepared baking sheet 2 inches apart. With your thumb, slightly flatten each ball and make a small well in the center of each cookie. Place a scant teaspoon of jam in the middle of each cookie.

continued

7 Bake for 15 to 18 minutes, until the cookies are light golden brown. (I like to add another ¼ to ½ teaspoon jam to each cookie after the cookies come out of the oven.) Remove the pan from the oven and let the cookies cool on the baking sheet for 10 minutes, then transfer them with a metal spatula to a wire cooling rack to cool completely.

Note: Store the cookies in an airtight container for 5 days at room temperature. The dough can also be portioned and frozen for baking at a moment's notice. The baking time does not change for baking from frozen cookie dough.

For instructions on making bar cookies, see page 114 and follow the directions until baking. Bake at 325°F for 35 minutes. Remove the pan from the oven and with an offset spatula, spread an even layer of jam on top of the cookies. Bake for an additional 5 to 8 minutes. Let the cookies cool completely in the pan, and then refrigerate before cutting and serving.

snickerdoodle cookies

MAKES 30 TO 40 COOKIES, USING
A 1-OUNCE COOKIE SCOOP

There is something really unique about a snickerdoodle cookie. When I started researching it, I discovered that there is a slight sour flavor underneath all of that cinnamon and sugar. The sour comes from the cream of tartar. For a soft crunch, roll the cookies in granulated sugar and cinnamon as directed. For a denser crunchy cookie, use turbinado sugar and cinnamon on the outside. For instructions on making bar cookies, see page 114.

120 grams (1½ cups) gluten-free oat flour

108 grams (¾ cup) potato starch

90 grams (1 cup) almond meal, pecan meal, sunflower meal, or hazelnut meal (see note)

90 grams (¾ cup) sorghum flour

2 teaspoons cream of tartar

1½ teaspoons baking soda

1 teaspoon xanthan gum

1 teaspoon fine salt

285 grams (1½ cups) firmly packed brown sugar

¾ cup melted and slightly cooled clarified butter or coconut oil

2 eggs, room temperature, or 133 grams (½ cup) unsweetened applesauce

1 Tablespoon vanilla extract

Gluten-free nonstick spray

3 Tablespoons granulated sugar, to finish

1 Tablespoon ground cinnamon, to finish

Note: If you have an allergy to almond meal, replace it with another 45 grams (½ cup) gluten-free oat flour.

1 In a bowl, combine the oat flour, potato starch, almond meal, sorghum flour, cream of tartar, baking soda, xanthan gum, and salt.

2 In the bowl of a stand mixer fitted with the paddle attachment, combine the brown sugar and clarified butter on medium speed. Add the eggs and vanilla, and mix until fluffy and light in color, 1 to 2 minutes.

3 Add the dry ingredients to the mixing bowl and mix on low speed until well incorporated.

4 Cover the bowl and refrigerate the dough for at least 3 hours or up to 5 days. This step is important, so the dry ingredients have a chance to absorb all the moisture, which keeps the cookies from spreading too much when baked.

5 When you're ready to bake the cookies, preheat the oven to 350°F. Lightly spray a baking sheet with gluten-free nonstick spray or line it with parchment paper. In a small bowl, combine the granulated sugar and cinnamon.

6 With a 1-ounce cookie scoop or a tablespoon measure, portion out the dough and roll it into 1-inch balls. Roll each ball in the cinnamon-sugar mixture. Arrange the balls on the prepared baking sheet 2 inches apart and slightly flatten each ball with your thumb.

7 Bake for 12 to 14 minutes, until the cookies are light golden brown. Remove the pan from the oven and let the cookies cool on the baking sheet for 10 minutes, then transfer them with a metal spatula to a wire cooling rack to cool completely.

Note: Store the cookies in an airtight container for 5 days at room temperature. The dough can also be portioned and frozen for baking at a moment's notice. The baking time does not change for baking from frozen cookie dough.

oatmeal and dried cherry cookies

MAKES 30 TO 40 COOKIES, USING
A 1-OUNCE COOKIE SCOOP

Sour cherries are another favorite of mine. I like how they add color and tartness. You can also substitute ½ cup of dried currants or your favorite raisin. Try baking all of the cookies and then making them into sandwich cookies (see photo) using the Vanilla Buttercream Frosting (page 255). These will be a big hit at a child's birthday party. For instructions on making bar cookies, see page 114.

108 grams (¾ cup) potato starch

90 grams (1 cup) gluten-free oat flour

90 grams (¾ cup) sorghum flour

45 grams (½ cup) almond meal, pecan meal, sunflower meal, or hazelnut meal (see note)

1½ teaspoons baking soda

1 teaspoon xanthan gum

1 teaspoon ground cinnamon

1 teaspoon fine salt

½ teaspoon ground ginger

½ teaspoon ground nutmeg

285 grams (1½ cups) firmly packed brown sugar

¾ cup melted and slightly cooled clarified butter or coconut oil

2 eggs, room temperature, or 133 grams (½ cup) unsweetened applesauce

1 Tablespoon vanilla extract

202 grams (2 cups) rolled oats (not quick cooking)

½ cup coarsely chopped dried cherries

Note: If you have an allergy to almond meal, replace it with another 45 grams (½ cup) gluten-free oat flour.

1 In a bowl, whisk together the potato starch, oat flour, sorghum flour, almond meal, baking soda, xanthan gum, cinnamon, salt, ginger, and nutmeg.

2 In the bowl of a stand mixer fitted with the paddle attachment, combine the brown sugar and clarified butter on medium speed. Add the eggs and vanilla and mix until fluffy and light in color, 1 to 2 minutes.

3 Add the dry ingredients to the mixing bowl and mix on low speed until well incorporated. On very low speed, mix in the rolled oats and dried cherries.

4 Cover the bowl and refrigerate the dough for at least 3 hours or up to 5 days. This step is important, so the dry ingredients have a chance to absorb all the moisture, which keeps the cookies from spreading too much when baked.

5 When you're ready to bake the cookies, preheat the oven to 350°F. Lightly spray a baking sheet with gluten-free nonstick spray or line it with parchment paper.

6 With a 1-ounce cookie scoop or a tablespoon measure, portion out the dough and roll it into 1-inch balls. Arrange the balls on the prepared baking sheet 2 inches apart, and slightly flatten each ball with your thumb.

7 Bake for 12 to 14 minutes, until the cookies are light golden brown. Remove the pan from the oven and let the cookies cool on the baking sheet for 10 minutes, then transfer them with a metal spatula to a wire cooling rack to cool completely.

Note: Store the cookies in an airtight container for 5 days at room temperature. The dough can also be portioned and frozen for baking at a moment's notice. The baking time does not change for baking from frozen cookie dough.

ginger cookies

MAKES 30 TO 40 COOKIES, USING A 1-OUNCE COOKIE SCOOP

I love a good ginger cookie. I love the crisp cookies that are called gingersnaps (see my Gingersnap Cutout Cookies on page 121 for that one). These cookies are cakey on the inside and crisp on the outside. I love to roll them in turbinado sugar before baking. Sometimes I also add a little piece of candied ginger to the center of each cookie. There is no such thing as too much ginger!

120 grams (1 cup) sorghum flour

108 grams (¾ cup) potato starch

60 grams (¾ cup) gluten-free oat flour

45 grams (½ cup) almond meal (see note)

2 teaspoons ground ginger

1 teaspoon xanthan gum

1 teaspoon baking soda

1 teaspoon ground cinnamon

¾ teaspoon fine salt

½ teaspoon ground cardamom

¼ teaspoon ground cloves

190 grams (1 cup) firmly packed brown sugar

¾ cup melted and slightly cooled clarified butter or coconut oil

1 egg, room temperature, or ¼ cup canned pumpkin puree or unsweetened applesauce

¼ cup molasses

2 teaspoons freshly grated ginger

Gluten-free nonstick spray

¼ cup turbinado or coconut sugar, to finish

Note: If you have an allergy to almond meal, substitute with another 45 grams (½ cup) gluten-free oat flour.

1 In a bowl, whisk together the sorghum flour, potato starch, oat flour, almond meal, ginger, xanthan gum, baking soda, cinnamon, salt, cardamom, and cloves.

2 In the bowl of a stand mixer fitted with the paddle attachment, combine the brown sugar and clarified butter and beat at medium speed until well incorporated, about 1 minute. Add the egg, molasses, and fresh ginger and beat until fluffy and light in color, 1 to 2 minutes. On low speed, add the dry ingredients to the mixing bowl and mix just until all of the ingredients are blended.

3 Cover the bowl and refrigerate the dough for at least 3 hours or up to 5 days. This step is important so the dry ingredients have a chance to absorb all the moisture, which keeps the cookies from spreading too much when baked.

4 Preheat the oven to 350°F. Lightly spray a baking sheet with gluten-free nonstick spray or line it with parchment paper.

5 With a 1-ounce cookie scoop or a tablespoon measure, portion the dough and roll into 1-inch balls. Dip the top half of each ball into the turbinado sugar. Place the balls, sugar-side up, on the prepared cookie sheet 2½ inches apart. (Any sugar on the bottom of the cookie will burn.) Slightly flatten each cookie with your thumb.

6 Bake for 12 to 14 minutes, until light golden brown. Remove the pan from the oven and let the cookies cool on the baking sheet for 10 minutes, then transfer them with a metal spatula to a wire cooling rack to cool completely.

Note: Store the cookies in an airtight container for 5 days at room temperature. The dough can also be portioned and frozen for baking at a moment's notice. Bake the cookies directly from the freezer; the baking time does not change for frozen cookie dough.

banana cookies

MAKES 32 COOKIES, USING A 1-OUNCE COOKIE SCOOP

These cookies remind me of the best part of a muffin—the top. Unlike a lot of my other cookie recipes, these should be baked immediately. The ratio of liquid is higher, and the leavening will dissipate if the batter is set aside for too long.

Gluten-free nonstick spray

90 grams (⅔ cup) sorghum flour

75 grams (⅔ cup) buckwheat flour

72 grams (½ cup) potato starch

45 grams (½ cup) almond meal (see note)

2 teaspoons ground cinnamon

1½ teaspoons double-acting baking powder

1 teaspoon xanthan gum

1 teaspoon baking soda

½ teaspoon ground cardamom

½ teaspoon fine salt

285 grams (1½ cups) firmly packed brown sugar

½ cup melted and slightly cooled clarified butter or coconut oil

2 eggs, room temperature

2 teaspoons vanilla extract

200 grams (1 cup) mashed banana (2 to 3 ripe bananas)

½ cup coarsely chopped pecans (optional)

Note: If you have an allergy to almond meal, substitute with another 45 grams (½ cup) gluten-free oat flour.

1 Preheat the oven to 350°F. Lightly spray a baking sheet with gluten-free nonstick spray or line it with parchment paper.

2 In a bowl, whisk together the sorghum flour, buckwheat flour, potato starch, almond meal, cinnamon, baking powder, xanthan gum, baking soda, cardamom, and salt.

3 In the bowl of a stand mixer fitted with the paddle attachment, combine the brown sugar and clarified butter on medium speed. Add the eggs and vanilla, and mix until fluffy and light in color, 1 to 2 minutes. On low speed, mix in the banana. Add the dry ingredients to the mixing bowl and mix on low speed until well incorporated. On very low speed, mix in the pecans (if using).

4 With a 1-ounce cookie scoop or a tablespoon measure, portion out the dough and arrange the scoops of dough on the prepared baking sheet 2 inches apart.

5 Bake for 15 to 18 minutes, until the cookies are firm and light golden brown. Remove the pan from the oven and transfer the cookies with a metal spatula to a wire cooling rack to cool completely.

Note: Store the cookies in an airtight container for 1 week at room temperature. You can also freeze them in a resealable plastic bag for up to a month.

brownies

MAKES 12 BROWNIES

I never developed a brownie recipe until I was asked to do this book. It seemed like a no-brainer. As it turns out, I was wrong—getting the right mix of fudgy and cakey was no easy task. I am very proud of this recipe and it turns out to be so easy! I always find that the brownies cut better if they are refrigerated for several hours after cooling to room temperature.

Gluten-free nonstick spray

48 grams (⅓ cup) potato starch

40 grams (⅓ cup) sorghum flour

½ teaspoon xanthan gum

½ teaspoon double-acting baking powder

½ teaspoon fine salt

½ teaspoon espresso powder or instant coffee (optional)

½ cup clarified butter or coconut oil

4 ounces (about ¾ cup) semisweet chocolate, as chips or coarsely chopped

2 ounces (about ⅓ cup) unsweetened chocolate, coarsely chopped

132 grams (¾ cup) granulated sugar

95 grams (½ cup) firmly packed brown sugar

2 teaspoons vanilla extract

3 eggs, room temperature

½ cup toasted, coarsely chopped nuts, such as walnuts or pistachios (optional)

1 Preheat the oven to 350°F. Spray an 8-inch square baking pan with gluten-free nonstick spray. Line the bottom and long sides of the pan with parchment paper so the ends hang over the sides. Lightly spray the pan again.

2 In a bowl, whisk together the potato starch, sorghum flour, xanthan gum, baking powder, salt, and espresso powder (if using).

3 Melt the clarified butter and chocolates together in a heavy medium-size saucepan over low heat. Remove from the heat and whisk in the sugars and vanilla. Whisk in the eggs, one at a time, and continue to whisk until the mixture is completely smooth and glossy. Add in the dry ingredients and whisk until just incorporated. With a rubber spatula, fold in the nuts (if using).

4 Transfer the batter to the prepared pan and spread evenly. Bake the brownies for 45 minutes, until a toothpick inserted into the center comes out with wet crumbs.

5 Remove the pan from the oven. Let the brownies cool in the pan for 5 minutes, then remove them using the parchment paper overhang and place on a wire cooling rack. Cool to room temperature, about 20 minutes, then slice and serve. Nice clean cuts will happen more readily if you refrigerate the brownies for several hours before cutting. But nobody at my house ever wants to wait that long.

Note: Store the brownies in an airtight container for 5 days at room temperature. Or freeze the brownies and thaw for several hours before eating them.

pumpkin cookies
(for shahla joon)

MAKES 32 COOKIES, USING A
1-OUNCE COOKIE SCOOP

I developed this recipe for my best girlfriend, Shahla. She is Iranian, and Joon is a term of endearment in Farsi. Similarly to the Banana Cookies (page 131), these cookies should be baked right away. I love frosting them with the Cream Cheese Glaze on page 246.

Gluten-free nonstick spray

90 grams (⅔ cup) sorghum flour

60 grams (⅔ cup) gluten-free oat flour

72 grams (½ cup) potato starch

45 grams (½ cup) almond meal (see note)

1 Tablespoon ground ginger

1½ teaspoons double-acting baking powder

1 teaspoon ground cinnamon

1 teaspoon xanthan gum

1 teaspoon baking soda

½ teaspoon ground nutmeg

½ teaspoon fine salt

285 grams (1½ cups) firmly packed brown sugar

¾ cup melted and slightly cooled clarified butter or coconut oil

2 eggs, room temperature

2 teaspoons vanilla extract

234 grams (1 cup) pumpkin puree

½ cup coarsely chopped pecans (optional)

½ cup mini chocolate chips (optional)

Note: If you have an allergy to almond meal, substitute with another 45 grams (½ cup) gluten-free oat flour.

1 Preheat the oven to 350°F. Lightly spray a baking sheet with gluten-free nonstick spray or line it with parchment paper.

2 In a bowl, combine the sorghum flour, oat flour, potato starch, almond meal, ginger, baking powder, cinnamon, xanthan gum, baking soda, nutmeg, and salt.

3 In the bowl of a stand mixer fitted with the paddle attachment, combine the brown sugar and clarified butter on medium speed. Add the eggs and vanilla, and mix until fluffy and light in color, 1 to 2 minutes. Mix in the pumpkin puree on low speed.

4 Add the dry ingredients to the mixing bowl and mix on low speed until well incorporated. On very low speed, mix in the pecans and chocolate chips (if using).

5 With a 1-ounce cookie scoop or a tablespoon measure, portion out the batter. Arrange the scoops on the prepared baking sheet 2 inches apart.

6 Bake for 15 to 18 minutes, until the cookies are firm and light golden brown. Remove the pan from the oven and transfer the cookies with a metal spatula to a wire cooling rack to cool completely. The cookies will solidify as they cool.

Note: Store the cookies in an airtight container for 1 week at room temperature. You can also freeze them in a resealable plastic bag for up to a month.

fat daddy cookies

MAKES 30 TO 40 COOKIES, USING A 1-OUNCE COOKIE SCOOP

Some people just aren't happy with one kind of cookie. They want all the goodies in one cookie. This cookie is for all the hedonists out there. You can simplify the amount of mix-ins that you use. However, the rolled oats are crucial to the structure of the cookies. To make bar cookies, see page 114.

120 grams (1 cup) sorghum flour

106 grams (¾ cup) potato starch

90 grams (1 cup) gluten-free oat flour

45 grams (½ cup) almond meal, pecan meal, sunflower meal, or hazelnut meal (see note)

40 grams (½ cup) unsweetened cocoa powder

1½ teaspoons baking soda

1 teaspoon xanthan gum

1 teaspoon fine salt

285 grams (1½ cups) firmly packed brown sugar

¾ cup melted and slightly cooled clarified butter or coconut oil

2 eggs, room temperature, or 133 grams (½ cup) unsweetened applesauce

2 teaspoons vanilla extract

151 grams (1½ cups) gluten-free rolled oats

10 ounces (about 2 cups) semisweet chocolate chips

¼ cup dried fruit (dried apricots are my favorite), chopped into ¼-inch pieces

½ cup roasted, unsalted pecans, walnuts, or sunflower seeds

Gluten-free nonstick spray

Note: If you have an allergy to almond meal, substitute with another 45 grams (½ cup) gluten-free oat flour.

1 In a bowl, whisk together the sorghum flour, potato starch, oat flour, almond meal, cocoa powder, baking soda, xanthan gum, and salt.

2 In the bowl of a stand mixer fitted with the paddle attachment, combine the brown sugar and clarified butter on medium speed. Add the eggs and vanilla, and mix until fluffy and light in color, 1 to 2 minutes.

3 Add the dry ingredients to the mixing bowl and mix on low speed until well incorporated. On very low speed, mix in the rolled oats, chocolate chips, dried fruit, and pecans.

4 Cover the bowl and refrigerate the dough for at least 3 hours or up to 5 days. This step is important, so the dry ingredients have a chance to absorb all the moisture, which keeps the cookies from spreading too much when baked.

5 When you're ready to bake the cookies, preheat the oven to 350°F. Lightly spray a baking sheet with gluten-free nonstick spray or line it with parchment paper.

6 With a 1-ounce cookie scoop or a tablespoon measure, portion out the dough and roll it into 1-inch balls. Arrange the balls on the prepared baking sheet 2 inches apart, and slightly flatten each ball with your thumb.

7 Bake for 12 to 14 minutes, until the cookies are light golden brown. Remove the pan from the oven and let the cookies cool on the baking sheet for 10 minutes, then transfer them with a metal spatula to a wire cooling rack to cool completely.

Note: Store the cookies in an airtight container for 5 days at room temperature. The dough can also be portioned and frozen for baking at a moment's notice. The baking time does not change for baking from frozen cookie dough.

grandma blake's butter cookies (shortbread)

MAKES 16 COOKIES

Grandma Blake loved what she called "butter cookies." She was always experimenting with cooking and baking. She rarely made the same thing twice, but this was a staple in the cookie jar. She never dipped them in chocolate—that is my little extra touch.

120 grams (1 cup) sorghum flour

95 grams (½ cup) firmly packed brown sugar

52 grams (½ cup) tapioca starch

48 grams (⅓ cup) potato starch

45 grams (½ cup) gluten-free oat flour

1 teaspoon xanthan gum

½ teaspoon fine salt

¾ cup (1½ sticks) cold unsalted butter or Earth Balance Vegan Buttery Sticks, sliced into ¼-inch pieces

1 teaspoon vanilla extract

Chocolate Glaze (page 253) (optional)

1 Preheat the oven to 350°F. Place a 9-inch nonstick tart pan on a baking sheet.

2 In the bowl of a food processor, combine the sorghum flour, brown sugar, tapioca starch, potato starch, oat flour, xanthan gum, and salt. Pulse until well blended. Add the butter and vanilla, and process until the mixture forms a smooth, soft dough, about 1 minute.

3 With your hands, spread the dough evenly into the prepared tart pan. With the back of a spoon or the bottom of a measuring cup, smooth the top of the dough. Place a 2-inch round biscuit cutter directly into the center of the dough and remove the center circle of dough. Put the cutter back into the center of the dough (this helps with heat distribution when baking).

4 Bake until the top puffs (it will stay fairly blond in color), 20 to 25 minutes. Remove the pan from the oven and turn the oven off. With a chef's knife, score the shortbread into 16 even wedges, cutting halfway through the shortbread. Using a wooden skewer, poke 8 to 10 holes into each wedge.

5 Return the shortbread to the turned-off oven and prop the door open with a wooden spoon, leaving a 1-inch gap. Allow the shortbread to dry out for about 1 hour. Remove the shortbread from the oven and allow it to cool. Cut the shortbread at the scored marks to separate, and serve. If desired, drizzle the shortbread with dark chocolate that has been melted in the microwave.

Note: Refrigerate the cookies in an airtight container for 5 days or freeze for up to a month.

coconut and pecan german chocolate cookies

MAKES 30 TO 40 COOKIES

I think this recipe works best as bar cookies because they are easier. However, the thumbprint version is more elegant. They will be the hit of the bake sale with either presentation. Press a thumb into the center of each portioned cookie, freeze them, and add the coconut-pecan filling just before baking. This will give you a tight cookie that will hold the tasty filling.

FILLING

1 cup evaporated milk or dairy-free milk

95 grams (½ cup) firmly packed brown sugar

2 egg yolks

¼ cup melted and slightly cooled clarified butter

1½ teaspoons vanilla extract

1 cup chopped pecans or sunflower seeds

1½ cups flaked unsweetened coconut

COOKIES

120 grams (1 cup) sorghum flour

106 grams (¾ cup) potato starch

90 grams (1 cup) gluten-free oat flour

90 grams (1 cup) almond meal (see note)

20 grams (¼ cup) unsweetened cocoa powder (do not use Dutch processed)

1½ teaspoons baking soda

1 teaspoon xanthan gum

1 teaspoon fine salt

285 grams (1½ cups) firmly packed brown sugar

¾ cup melted and slightly cooled clarified butter or coconut oil

1 To make the filling: In a medium saucepan, whisk together the evaporated milk, brown sugar, egg yolks, clarified butter, and vanilla. Cook over low heat, stirring constantly, until the mixture is puffy, begins to thicken, and reaches 180°F on an instant-read thermometer, 15 to 20 minutes. Pour the mixture into a bowl and cool to room temperature. Stir in the pecans and coconut and set aside.

2 To make the cookies: In a bowl, whisk together the sorghum flour, potato starch, oat flour, almond meal, cocoa powder, baking soda, xanthan gum, and salt.

3 In the bowl of a stand mixer fitted with the paddle attachment, combine the brown sugar and clarified butter on medium speed. Add the eggs and vanilla, and mix until fluffy and light in color, 1 to 2 minutes.

4 Add the dry ingredients to the mixing bowl and mix on low speed until well incorporated.

5 Cover the bowl and refrigerate the dough for at least 3 hours or up to 5 days. This step is important so the dry ingredients have a chance to absorb all the moisture, which keeps the cookies from spreading too much when baked.

6 When you're ready to bake the cookies, preheat the oven to 350°F. Lightly spray a cookie sheet with gluten-free nonstick spray or line it with parchment paper.

continued

coconut and pecan german chocolate cookies, continued

2 eggs, room temperature, or 133 grams (½ cup) unsweetened applesauce

2 teaspoons vanilla extract

Gluten-free nonstick spray

Note: If you have an allergy to almond meal, substitute with another 90 grams (1 cup) gluten-free oat flour.

7 With a 1-ounce cookie scoop or a tablespoon measure, portion out the dough and roll it into 1-inch balls. Arrange the balls on the prepared baking sheet 2 inches apart. With your thumb, slightly flatten each ball and make a small well in the center of each cookie. Place a teaspoon of the coconut-pecan filling in the middle of each cookie.

8 Bake for 15 to 18 minutes, until the cookies are light golden brown. Remove the pan from the oven and let the cookies cool on the baking sheet for 10 minutes, then transfer them with a metal spatula to a wire cooling rack to cool completely.

Note: Store the cookies in an airtight container for 5 days at room temperature. The dough can also be portioned and frozen for baking at a moment's notice. The baking time does not change for baking from frozen cookie dough.

For instructions on making bar cookies, see page 114 and follow the directions until baking. Bake at 325°F for 30 minutes. Remove the pan from the oven and with an offset spatula, spread an even layer of coconut-pecan filling on top of the cookies. Bake for an additional 10 to 12 minutes. Let the cookies cool completely in the pan, and then refrigerate before cutting and serving.

sugar cookies

MAKES 32 THREE-INCH COOKIES

The key to successful gluten-free rollout cookies is to roll out the dough in small batches. You don't have to worry about ending up with tough cookies from rerolling the scraps. It is overworked gluten that causes tough cookies. Keep the dough well floured so that the rolling pin doesn't stick. Feel free to decorate the cookies as you please. If you are proficient with piping and royal icing, see Resources on page 262 for my recommendations.

132 grams (¾ cup) granulated sugar

80 grams (⅔ cup) sorghum flour, plus more for dusting

72 grams (½ cup) potato starch

69 grams (⅔ cup) tapioca starch

67 grams (¾ cup) gluten-free oat flour, plus more as needed

1 Tablespoon loosely packed grated lemon zest (from 1 lemon)

1 teaspoon xanthan gum

½ teaspoon baking soda

½ teaspoon fine salt

¼ cup melted and slightly cooled clarified butter or coconut oil

1 egg, room temperature, or ¼ cup unsweetened applesauce

2 Tablespoons honey

2 Tablespoons freshly squeezed lemon juice (from 1 lemon)

1 Preheat the oven to 350°F. Line a baking sheet with parchment paper.

2 In a bowl, whisk together the granulated sugar, sorghum flour, potato starch, tapioca starch, oat flour, lemon zest, xanthan gum, baking soda, and salt.

3 In a liquid measuring cup, combine the clarified butter, egg, honey, and lemon juice.

4 Add the butter mixture to the dry ingredients and stir with a rubber spatula. You will have a crumbly dough at first, but it will come together. Stir until the dough begins to form a ball. If it seems dry, add 1 teaspoon melted clarified butter. If the dough is too wet, add 1 Tablespoon oat flour. The dough should be the consistency of Play-Doh. Knead the dough until it is smooth, pliable, and even in color. Divide the dough into 3 even portions.

5 Place a piece of parchment paper on top of a silicone baking mat (this keeps the parchment from moving around when you are rolling out the dough). Lightly flour the parchment paper with sorghum flour and place one of the portions of dough on the parchment paper. Keep both sides of the dough floured and roll the dough to a ¼-inch thickness.

6 Cut the dough with your favorite 3-inch cookie cutters. With a small offset spatula, gently peel up each cookie and place on the prepared baking sheet. If you are going to use the cookies as ornaments, use a small drinking straw to cut a small hole in the top of each cookie. I also like to freeze the full baking sheet of cookies for about 10 minutes before baking.

continued

7 Bake, one sheet at a time, for 9 to 10 minutes. If the cookies are larger than 3 inches, bake for 12 to 15 minutes. Remove the pan from the oven and let the cookies cool on the baking sheet for 10 minutes, then transfer them with a metal spatula to a wire cooling rack to cool completely. Once the cookies are cool, you can decorate them with royal icing (see Resources on page 262) and sprinkle with decorative sugars or candy.

Notes: Store the cookies in an airtight container for 5 days at room temperature. To freeze, place the cookies in a resealable plastic freezer bag. Thaw them at room temperature for several hours or in the microwave for $1\frac{1}{2}$ minutes at 50 percent power.

If you like crunchier cookies, after the first bake, place the cookies side by side on a baking sheet in a 200°F oven and bake for an additional 10 minutes to dry them out.

You can also use a clean rubber stamp to decorate the dough. Press the stamp lightly into the top of the dough. If you place the tray of cookies in the freezer for about 10 minutes before baking, the impressions will remain through baking.

Variations

To roll out the cookies at a later time: Flatten each of the three portions into a disk shape and wrap each disk in plastic wrap. Place in a resealable bag and refrigerate for about an hour. Remove the dough from the refrigerator and let it sit out for 5 to 10 minutes before rolling out.

For slice-and-bake cookies: Roll the dough into a log shape, wrap with parchment paper, and refrigerate. Once the dough has solidified, cut into $\frac{1}{4}$-inch slices and proceed as directed.

s'mores bars

I have so many happy memories of spending time at my grandparents' cabin. It was an actual log cabin that Grandma and Grandpa built from scratch. It had a big fireplace with a stone hearth. My Aunt Lana was always in charge of bringing the makings for s'mores.

108 grams (¾ cup) potato starch

90 grams (1 cup) gluten-free oat flour

90 grams (¾ cup) sorghum flour

45 grams (½ cup) almond meal, pecan meal, sunflower meal, or hazelnut meal (see note)

1½ teaspoons baking soda

1 teaspoon xanthan gum

1 teaspoon fine salt

285 grams (1½ cups) firmly packed brown sugar

½ cup melted and slightly cooled clarified butter or coconut oil

2 eggs, room temperature, or 133 grams (½ cup) unsweetened applesauce

2 teaspoons vanilla extract

6 ounces (about 1¼ cups) semisweet chocolate chips

10 ounces (about 6 cups) mini marshmallows

Note: If you have an allergy to almond meal, substitute with another 45 grams (½ cup) gluten-free oat flour.

1 Line the bottom and long sides of a 9 by 12-inch or 9 by 13-inch cake pan with parchment paper so the ends hang over the long sides.

2 In a mixing bowl, whisk together the potato starch, oat flour, sorghum flour, almond meal, baking soda, xanthan gum, and salt.

3 In the bowl of a stand mixer fitted with the paddle attachment, combine the brown sugar and clarified butter on medium speed. Add the eggs and vanilla, and mix until fluffy and light in color, 1 to 2 minutes. Add the dry ingredients to the mixing bowl and mix on low speed until well incorporated.

4 With your hands, press the dough evenly into the prepared pan. Refrigerate the pan until the dough has solidified, about 30 minutes.

5 Preheat the oven to 325°F. Bake the bars for 35 to 40 minutes, until the top has puffed and the edges are browned. The center will appear soft.

6 Take the pan out of the oven and immediately scatter the chocolate chips and the marshmallows over the hot bars. Set the oven to broil and allow it to heat up for about 5 minutes. Place the pan under the broiler to brown the marshmallows and melt the chocolate. This will take 5 to 8 minutes depending on your broiler; you may need to rotate the pan several times.

7 Let the bars cool completely in the pan, and then refrigerate before cutting and serving. Cut the bars into thirds along the length of the pan and into sixths along the width of the pan.

Notes: Store the bars in an airtight container for 5 days at room temperature. To freeze, place the bars in a resealable plastic freezer bag. Thaw them at room temperature for several hours or in the microwave for 1½ minutes at 50 percent power.

If you are proficient with a kitchen torch, you can torch the bars instead of broiling until the marshmallows are light golden brown and the chocolate is melted.

sticky toffee date bars

MAKES 18 BARS

I have always said that dates are nature's caramel. This recipe proves it! The toffee sauce is by no means traditional. It is my way of getting more dates into the mix and adding a punch of flavor without a bunch more refined sugar. It makes enough for a thin layer of sweetness on top. If you want to live dangerously, double the toffee sauce recipe. The bars are easier to cut if you frost the bars first and then refrigerate for several hours. If you want round cookies, I would bake them first and frost them with the toffee sauce after they have cooled or sandwich the toffee sauce between two cookies. This recipe can be made completely vegan by using coconut oil.

BARS

108 grams (¾ cup) potato starch

90 grams (1 cup) gluten-free oat flour

90 grams (¾ cup) sorghum flour

45 grams (½ cup) almond meal, pecan meal, sunflower meal, or hazelnut meal (see note)

1½ teaspoons baking soda

1 teaspoon xanthan gum

1 teaspoon fine salt

285 grams (1½ cups) firmly packed brown sugar

½ cup melted and slightly cooled clarified butter or coconut oil

2 eggs, room temperature, or 133 grams (½ cup) unsweetened applesauce

1 Tablespoon vanilla extract

6 ounces (about 1½ cups) pitted small Medjool dates, coarsely chopped

TOFFEE SAUCE

72 grams (¼ cup) cashew butter

¼ cup maple syrup

2 Tablespoons melted coconut oil or clarified butter

1 To make the bars: Line the bottom and long sides of a 9 by 12-inch or 9 by 13-inch pan with parchment paper so the ends hang over the long sides.

2 In a mixing bowl, whisk together the potato starch, oat flour, sorghum flour, almond meal, baking soda, xanthan gum, and salt.

3 In the bowl of a stand mixer fitted with the paddle attachment, combine the brown sugar and clarified butter on medium speed. Add the eggs and vanilla, and mix until fluffy and light in color, 1 to 2 minutes. Add the dry ingredients to the mixing bowl and mix on low speed until well incorporated. On very low speed, mix in the chopped dates.

4 With your hands, press the dough evenly into the prepared pan. Refrigerate until the dough has solidified, about 30 minutes.

5 To make the toffee sauce: While the dough is chilling, place the cashew butter, maple syrup, coconut oil, dates, vanilla, and salt in a small blender or food processor and puree until smooth. The sauce should be kept in the refrigerator in an airtight container if you are not baking the bars immediately.

6 Preheat the oven to 325°F. Bake the bars for 35 to 40 minutes, until the top has puffed and the edges are browned. The center will appear soft. Immediately drizzle the toffee sauce over the hot bars.

4 pitted Medjool dates

1 teaspoon vanilla extract

Pinch of fine salt

Note: If you have an allergy to almond meal, substitute with another 45 grams (½ cup) gluten-free oat flour.

7 Let the bars cool completely in the pan, and then refrigerate before cutting and serving. Cut the bars into thirds along the length of the pan and into sixths along the width of the pan.

Notes: The toffee sauce can be stored in the refrigerator for 2 weeks. Microwave the cold sauce for 1 minute at 50 percent power to make it a pourable consistency.

Store the bars in an airtight container for 5 days at room temperature. To freeze, place the bars in a resealable plastic freezer bag. Thaw them at room temperature for several hours or in the microwave for 1½ minutes at 50 percent power.

almond biscotti

MAKES 18 BISCOTTI

I do not have Italian heritage but I do love a biscotti cookie. The dough in this recipe is wet and sticky. It is best to use wet or oiled hands when patting the dough into the log shapes.

Gluten-free nonstick spray

176 grams (1 cup) granulated sugar

60 grams (½ cup) sorghum flour, plus more for dusting

52 grams (½ cup) tapioca starch

45 grams (½ cup) gluten-free oat flour

1¼ teaspoons double-acting baking powder

1 teaspoon xanthan gum

¼ teaspoon fine salt

2 eggs, room temperature

1 Tablespoon Amaretto or another almond liqueur

2 teaspoons almond extract

2 teaspoons vanilla extract

1 Tablespoon melted clarified butter

¾ cup slivered almonds, lightly toasted

1 Preheat the oven to 300°F. Lightly spray a baking sheet with gluten-free nonstick spray and dust with 1 Tablespoon sorghum flour.

2 In the bowl of a stand mixer fitted with the paddle attachment, mix together the granulated sugar, sorghum flour, tapioca starch, oat flour, baking powder, xanthan gum, and salt. Add the eggs, Amaretto, almond extract, vanilla, and clarified butter and beat on medium speed until well combined. On very low speed, mix in the almonds. The dough will be very sticky and wet.

3 Lightly wet your hands. Shape the dough into two slightly flattened logs, 8 inches long, 2 inches wide, and 1 inch high. Place the logs 2½ inches apart on the prepared baking sheet.

4 Bake for 40 to 50 minutes, until light golden brown. The logs will spread and flatten. Transfer the logs with a metal spatula to a cutting board and cool for 8 minutes.

5 Using a serrated knife, slice the logs diagonally into ½-inch-wide biscotti. Place the biscotti back on the baking sheet with the cut surfaces down and return the pan to the oven. Bake 15 to 20 minutes, until golden brown. Turn the biscotti over and bake another 12 to 15 minutes, until golden brown on the other side. Remove from the oven and cool the biscotti completely on a wire cooling rack.

Note: Store the biscotti in an airtight container for 1 week or in the freezer for up to a month.

Variation

Hazelnut Biscotti: To make hazelnut biscotti, substitute the Amaretto with 3 Tablespoons Frangelico or another hazelnut liqueur, the almond extract with 1½ teaspoons anise extract, and the almonds with 1 cup coarsely chopped hazelnuts, lightly toasted and skins removed.

PIES
& TARTS

TIPS FOR SUCCESS

Pies and tarts are always a little bit daunting, even for those of us who bake all the time. The key with gluten-free crusts is to understand that the dough is always going to be a bit fragile and crumbly. The upside of gluten-free pies and tarts is that you really can't toughen the dough. There is no gluten to overwork! Like so much of gluten-free baking, this taught me to stop fighting with the dough and develop new techniques to ensure success.

All of the pie dough recipes in this book are made in a food processor, and that is the first step in making it easier. If you don't have a food processor, you can make the dough in a bowl by cutting in the cubed butter and adding the sour cream with a hand mixer. Always begin by weighing the dry ingredients into a bowl and whisking them together, making sure that they are mixed well. As I have stated elsewhere in the book, always measure the xanthan gum precisely and accurately. Level off the measuring spoon with a straightedge or offset spatula. This is so important! Next, cut your butter into small pieces. I generally slice the butter lengthwise, turn the stick, and slice it again lengthwise. Then I slice across the stick, making little ½-inch squares. (Refer to the piecrust tutorial on page 156). Scatter the butter over the flour mixture in the food processor, replace the lid, and pulse the food processor until the butter is distributed throughout the flour. Take off the lid of the food processor again and add the sour cream. Replace the lid and turn the machine on. You will be able to see how the dough is crumbly at first and then forms a ball and spins on the blade. This usually takes 20 to 30 seconds. Be patient—it will come together and form a ball.

This next part is so important: don't add any more liquid unless the dough needs it. The liquid is dependent on where you live. I live in San Francisco and my flour tends to be damp because it draws moisture from the air even though I store the flour in plastic containers with a tight seal. You may live in a part of the world that is more on the dry side and you will need more moisture for the dough to come together. This is why I wanted to include the how-to photos in my book. Understanding the right level of moisture is crucial to your success. If the dough is too wet, don't struggle with it—just start over and add less liquid. The good news is that once you get the hang of it, it will generally be the same each time. Write the amount of liquid on a sticky note and place it in the book for the next time you make a pie.

I think that it works best to make the pie dough ahead of time and wait at least one day before rolling it out. This allows for full absorption of the liquids, and the dough becomes more pliable and less fragile. This isn't mandatory, but it is helpful.

The next point of concern is getting the pie dough into the pie plate. Follow the instructions and roll the dough out on parchment that has been placed on a silicone pastry mat. Consider buying the rolling pin with the thickness spacers for a nice even thickness (see the pie tutorial on page 156). The silicone mat is essential for keeping the parchment in place, but you can certainly get by without it. There is no need to place another sheet of parchment on the top of the dough, just keep the dough floured really well so that it doesn't stick to the rolling pin. Slide the parchment and rolled dough onto the back of a sheet pan (I like to use a flat baking sheet that does not have sides). Remove the dough from the refrigerator and place the 9-inch pie plate upside down on the rolled dough. Carefully flip the baking sheet, dough, and pie plate all at once. Remove the baking sheet and let the dough sink into the pie plate.

It works best to make the shell and the pie on the same day. If you are short on time, freeze the piecrust to bake later: Place the unbaked piecrust in the freezer for 30 minutes. Remove from the freezer and tightly wrap in plastic wrap or place in a resealable plastic bag. Store in the freezer for up to a month. This way, you can divide the work between two different days. I generally keep several unbaked piecrusts in the freezer, ready to go at a moment's notice. If they are wrapped tightly in plastic and placed in a resealable bag, you will be able to keep them for several months in the freezer.

I have included recipes for various fruit pies, but I think that it is nice to make a pie based on whatever you find in the market that is beautiful and in season. Here are a few simple rules for improvising a pie using my piecrust recipes:

1 A 9-inch pie generally takes 2½ to 3 pounds of stone fruit or apples or 6 cups of berries.

2 If the fruit is particularly juicy, cut the fruit and place it in a bowl with ¼ cup sugar; let it macerate for about 30 minutes. Apples and blueberries don't really release much juice and don't need to macerate. Stone fruit (including cherries), strawberries, blackberries, and rhubarb all require maceration.

3 Pour off the accumulated juices to ensure that you will have a more successful pie that cuts easily and holds its shape. Too much juice will make a soupy, soggy pie.

Save the juice that you pour off and reduce it in a nonstick skillet over medium heat until it is reduced by half (5–7 minutes) and use it as a topping for the pie when you serve it. Remember to use the additional sugar called for in the recipe, as you will have lost some of the sugar in the macerating process.

4 Potato starch is my thickener of choice for the fillings. It is already in the pantry because you are using it elsewhere in your baking. Thirty-six grams (¼ cup) works great for all of the stone fruits and berries. Add potato starch, spices, and other ingredients called for in the individual pie filling recipe (use my Strawberry and Rhubarb Pie and Peach Pie as guides for sugar and spices). Finally, taste for sugar levels and add more if you feel it needs it.

I have noticed something over the course of baking so many pies. Pies are best baked ahead. Hot out of the oven, the crust is not my favorite. The crumb is very expanded from the heat of the oven—the flavor is great, but the texture is gritty. I find that everything settles down after the pie has cooled to room temperature and been refrigerated overnight. This requires some advance planning but is well worth the extra effort. I would never make this recommendation with any other gluten-free baked good. I often recommend that you freeze everything after it has cooled to room temperature. But a pie only gets better with time. It needs to be covered lightly with plastic wrap and placed in the refrigerator. It may have something to do with the butter solidifying and intensifying. Make your pies and refrigerate them! The leftovers are best stored in the refrigerator for 4 to 5 days covered in plastic wrap. Pie does not freeze well; both the crust and the filling lose their texture and become soggy.

A word about vegan pies: Use the vegan piecrust recipe and then follow the instructions for each of the individual pie recipes, always choosing the vegan options as you go. You will need to forgo the almond cobbler topping because it contains eggs. My suggestion would be to switch to the streusel topping and use the coconut oil option. Happy baking!

1. Cut the cold butter into ½-inch dice and add it to the food processor on top of the dry ingredients. 2. Process until the butter is incorporated. Add the sour cream to the bowl and run the food processor until a dough forms and it starts to whirl around on the blade. This can take a while so be patient. 3. Roll out the dough on a piece of parchment that has been placed on a silicone mat. 4. Slide the parchment and dough onto a flat baking sheet or the back of a rimmed baking sheet. 5. Turn your pie plate over onto the rolled dough and carefully flip the baking sheet and pie plate simultaneously. 6. Carefully peel back the parchment and let the dough slide into the pie plate. 7. Peel back the parchment and cut the dough off at the edge of the pie plate.

1. Gather scraps of dough and roll them into a coil. Place the coil on the top edge of your unbaked piecrust.
2. Crimp the top edge of your pie using one of these simple crimping techniques (the edges of a fluted pastry wheel, the inside of a spoon, or your fingers).

CRIMPING TUTORIAL - TART

1. Turn your tart pan over onto the freshly rolled dough. With your fingers, gently press down on the edge of the pan to cut the dough. **2.** Carefully flip the baking sheet and the tart pan simultaneously and allow the dough to slide into the bottom of the tart pan. Gently lift away the parchment. Gather the scraps of dough and roll them into a coil, filling in the sides of a tart. **3.** Press the coil firmly into the sides of the tart pan.

piecrust

Piecrust takes patience and precision, but the end result is so satisfying. A beautiful pie is a thing to behold. When I was a kid, I didn't want a birthday cake. I requested a cherry pie. I still prefer a pie on my birthday.

60 grams (½ cup) sorghum flour, plus more for dusting

48 grams (⅓ cup) potato starch

34 grams (⅓ cup) tapioca starch

34 grams (¼ cup) sweet rice flour

1 Tablespoon granulated sugar

1½ teaspoons xanthan gum

½ teaspoon fine salt

½ cup (1 stick) cold unsalted butter, cut into ½-inch dice

1 Tablespoon full-fat sour cream

1 teaspoon ice water, plus more as needed

1 Preheat the oven to 375°F and adjust the oven rack to the lower-middle position.

2 In the bowl of a food processor, combine the sorghum flour, potato starch, tapioca starch, sweet rice flour, granulated sugar, xanthan gum, and salt. Pulse several times to blend the dry ingredients. Remove the lid and add the butter; pulse until the butter is cut in. Remove the lid and add the sour cream. Blend it together until the mixture forms a ball, 20 to 30 seconds. Add the water only if the mixture looks dry and crumbly. Add 1 teaspoon at a time until you get the right consistency.

3 Turn the dough out onto a countertop and knead it gently. It should look and act just like regular pie dough. If the dough seems too wet, add 1 Tablespoon sorghum flour and knead until it is evenly distributed. Repeat if necessary.

4 Place a sheet of parchment paper on top of a silicone mat; the silicone mat is to keep the parchment paper stable. Flatten the dough into a disk and roll the dough on the parchment paper until it is 11 to 12 inches in diameter. Keep the top surface of your dough sprinkled with sorghum flour to ensure that your dough rolls out evenly without sticking to the rolling pin.

5 Slide the parchment paper and dough onto the back of a sheet pan. Place the 9-inch pie plate upside down on the dough. Carefully flip the baking sheet, dough, and pie plate all at once. Remove the baking sheet and let the dough sink into the pie plate.

6 Carefully peel away the parchment paper, keeping the dough centered over the pie plate, and ease the dough into the pie plate. This crust can be somewhat delicate; if it cracks, just push it back together. You don't have to fold over the edge and crimp this crust; I simply trim the dough to the edge of the pie plate and create a decorative edge with a spoon or fork. For a more traditional crimped edge, reroll your scraps and make several long coils, ½ inch in diameter. Place the coil along the top edge of your pie plate in a continuous circle. This will allow you to have an edge that can be crimped. Refer to the crimping tutorial (page 157) to establish your favorite way of finishing the pie.

7 At this point, I like to freeze the piecrust for 25 to 30 minutes while I make the filling of my pie (see second note). Remove the piecrust from the freezer and, with a fork, poke holes in the bottom of the piecrust and a little bit up the sides. Carefully place a piece of aluminum foil or parchment paper in the piecrust and fill with rice, lentils, or beans. Partially bake the piecrust according to the requirements of each recipe. It is important not to remove the weights right after baking, as they will have a tendency to stick. After cooling, the weights will come out cleaner and easier.

Notes: If you are not using the dough immediately, wrap it in plastic wrap and refrigerate it for up to a week or freeze it for up to a month. Bring the dough back to room temperature before rolling it out. This helps the pliability if the dough is left to rest.

To freeze a piecrust to bake later, place the unbaked piecrust in the freezer for 30 minutes. Remove from the freezer and tightly wrap in plastic wrap. Store in the freezer for up to a month.

For a double crust, make the recipe twice in two batches in a food processor. Don't blend all the flours and butters; it will overwhelm the food processor.

Variation

If you are making individual pies (3–3½ inches), divide the dough into 6 equal pieces by weight and then follow the directions outlined in step 5. Use the accumulated scraps to fashion the crimped edge of each little pie.

vegan piecrust

MAKES ONE 9-INCH PIECRUST

Try to find vegan sour cream if you can (see Resources, page 262). It makes a big difference in the flavor. Or you can use cold water as directed.

60 grams (½ cup) sorghum flour, plus more for dusting

48 grams (⅓ cup) potato starch

34 grams (⅓ cup) tapioca starch

34 grams (¼ cup) sweet rice flour

1 Tablespoon granulated sugar

1½ teaspoons xanthan gum

½ teaspoon fine salt

½ cup (1 stick) cold Earth Balance Vegan Buttery Sticks, cut into ½-inch dice

1 Tablespoon vegan sour cream or ice water, plus 1 teaspoon ice water, if needed

1 Preheat the oven to 375°F and adjust the oven rack to the lower-middle position.

2 In the bowl of a food processor, combine the sorghum flour, potato starch, tapioca starch, sweet rice flour, granulated sugar, xanthan gum, and salt. Pulse several times to blend the dry ingredients. Remove the lid and add the butter replacement; pulse until cut in. Remove the lid and add the vegan sour cream. Blend together until the mixture forms a ball, 20 to 30 seconds. Add the extra water only if the mixture looks dry and crumbly. Add 1 teaspoon at a time until you get the right consistency.

3 Turn the dough out onto a countertop and knead it gently. It should look and act just like regular pie dough. If the dough seems too wet, add 1 Tablespoon sorghum flour and knead until it is evenly distributed. Repeat if necessary.

4 Place a sheet of parchment paper on top of a silicone mat; the mat is to keep the parchment paper stable. Flatten the dough into a disk and roll the dough on the parchment paper until it is 11 to 12 inches in diameter. Keep the top surface of your dough sprinkled with sorghum flour to ensure that your dough rolls out evenly without sticking to the rolling pin.

5 Slide the parchment paper and dough onto the back of a sheet pan. Place the 9-inch pie plate upside down on the dough. Carefully flip the baking sheet, dough, and pie plate all at once. Remove the baking sheet and let the dough sink into the pie plate.

6 Carefully peel away the parchment paper, keeping the dough centered over the pie plate, and ease the dough into the pie plate. This crust can be somewhat delicate; if it cracks, just push it back together. You don't have to fold over the edge and crimp this crust; I simply trim the dough to the edge of the pie plate and create a decorative edge with a spoon or fork. For a more traditional crimped edge, reroll your scraps and make several long coils, 1/2 inch in diameter. Place the coil along the top edge of your pie plate in a continuous circle. This will allow you to have an edge that can be crimped. Refer to the crimping tutorial (page 157) to establish your favorite way of finishing the pie.

7 At this point, I like to freeze the piecrust for 25 to 30 minutes while I make the filling (see note). Remove the piecrust from the freezer and, with a fork, poke holes in the bottom of the piecrust and a little bit up the sides. Carefully place a piece of aluminum foil or parchment paper in the piecrust and fill with rice, lentils, or beans. Partially bake the piecrust according to the requirements of each recipe. It is important not to remove the weights right after baking, as they will have a tendency to stick. After cooling, the weights will come out cleaner and easier.

Notes: If you are not using the dough immediately, you can wrap it in plastic wrap and refrigerate it for up to a week, or freeze it for up to a month. Bring the dough back to room temperature before rolling it out. This helps the pliability if the dough is left to rest.

To freeze the piecrust to bake later, place the unbaked piecrust in the freezer for 30 minutes. Remove from the freezer and tightly wrap in plastic wrap. Store in the freezer for up to a month.

tart crust

MAKES ONE 9-INCH TART CRUST
OR SIX 3½-INCH INDIVIDUAL
TART CRUSTS

60 grams (½ cup) sorghum flour,
plus more for dusting

48 grams (⅓ cup) potato starch

34 grams (⅓ cup) tapioca starch

34 grams (¼ cup) sweet rice flour

1 Tablespoon granulated sugar

1½ teaspoons xanthan gum

½ teaspoon fine salt

½ cup (1 stick) cold unsalted
butter, cut into ½-inch dice

1 Tablespoon full-fat sour cream

1 teaspoon ice water, plus more
as needed

I have included this as a separate recipe because the technique is different than for making my regular piecrust. See page 157 for a tart crust crimping tutorial.

1 Preheat the oven to 375°F and adjust the oven rack to the lower-middle position.

2 In the bowl of a food processor, combine the sorghum flour, potato starch, tapioca starch, sweet rice flour, granulated sugar, xanthan gum, and salt. Pulse several times to blend the dry ingredients. Remove the lid and add the butter; pulse until the butter is cut in. Remove the lid and add the sour cream. Blend together until the mixture forms a ball, 20 to 30 seconds. Add the water only if the mixture looks dry and crumbly. Add 1 teaspoon at a time until you get the right consistency.

3 Turn the dough out onto a countertop and knead it gently. It should look and act just like regular pie dough. If the dough seems too wet, add 1 Tablespoon sorghum flour and knead until it is evenly distributed. Repeat if necessary.

4 Place a sheet of parchment paper on top of a silicone mat; the mat is to keep the parchment paper stable. Flatten the dough into a disk and roll the dough on the parchment paper until it is 11 to 12 inches in diameter. Keep the top surface of your dough sprinkled with sorghum flour to ensure that your dough rolls out evenly without sticking to the rolling pin.

5 Slide the parchment paper and dough onto the back of a sheet pan. Place a 9-inch tart pan with the removable bottom, bottom side up, in the center of the dough. Press down on the tart pan gently so that the edge of the tart pan cuts the dough. Holding the tart pan in place, pick up the baking sheet and carefully flip it over so that the tart pan is right side up on the counter. Remove the baking sheet and run a rolling pin over the edge of the pan to cut the dough completely. Carefully pull away the parchment paper. Gently ease and press the dough into the pan, reserving the scraps. Roll dough scraps into ½-inch rope, line the edge of the tart pan with rope, and gently press into the fluted sides. Don't try to roll the ropes too long. Keep them short, 4 to 5 inches in length, and fill in the sides as needed. Finally, smooth out all seams in the rope and make sure it is an even thickness.

6 At this point, I like to freeze the tart crust for 25 to 30 minutes while I make the filling of my tart (see note). Remove the tart crust from the freezer and, with a fork, poke holes in the bottom of the crust and a little bit up the sides. Carefully place a piece of aluminum foil or parchment paper in the tart crust and fill with rice, lentils, or beans. Partially bake the crust according to the requirements of each recipe. It is important not to remove the weights right after baking, as they will have a tendency to stick. After cooling, the weights will come out cleaner and easier.

Notes: If you are not using the dough immediately, you can wrap it in plastic wrap and refrigerate it for up to a week or freeze it for up to a month. Bring the dough back to room temperature before rolling it out. This helps the pliability if the dough is left to rest.

To freeze the tart crust to bake later, place the unbaked tart crust in the freezer for 30 minutes. Remove from the freezer and tightly wrap in plastic wrap. Store in the freezer for up to a month.

Variation

If you are making individual tarts (3–3½ inch), divide the dough into 6 equal pieces by weight and then follow the directions outlined in step 5. Use the accumulated scraps to fashion the sides of each tart.

almond cobbler topping for pie

MAKES ENOUGH FOR ONE
9-INCH PIE

Gluten-free toppings on pies are very challenging, and I never feel like they look very good. I invented this as a top crust, and I suppose it makes the pie more of a cobbler/pie hybrid. Try this as a top crust for your favorite berry pie. It sops up the juices and makes for a heavenly pie. Refer to the Peach Pie with Almond Topping (page 189) for specific instructions on how to use it.

90 grams (1 cup) almond flour

80 grams (⅔ cup) sorghum flour

69 grams (¼ cup + 2 Tablespoons) sweet rice flour

36 grams (¼ cup + 1 Tablespoon) potato starch

3 Tablespoons granulated sugar

2 teaspoons double-acting baking powder

1 teaspoon xanthan gum

½ teaspoon baking soda

½ teaspoon fine salt

6 Tablespoons (¾ stick) cold unsalted butter or Earth Balance Vegan Buttery Sticks, cut into 8 slices

¼ cup buttermilk (see note, page 26)

2 eggs

2 teaspoons almond extract

1 Preheat the oven to 375°F and adjust the oven rack to the center of the oven. Line a baking sheet with parchment paper.

2 In the bowl of a food processor, combine the almond flour, sorghum flour, sweet rice flour, potato starch, granulated sugar, baking powder, xanthan gum, baking soda, and salt. Pulse several times to blend the dry ingredients. Remove the lid and add the butter; pulse until the mixture is crumbly and resembles coarse meal. Transfer the mixture to a mixing bowl. (You can do the recipe to this point and refrigerate, covered, overnight. In the morning, proceed with the following steps.)

3 In a separate bowl, combine the buttermilk, eggs, and almond extract and beat well. Add the buttermilk mixture to the dry ingredients and mix with a rubber scraper until the dough starts to come together.

4 This topping works best with a par-baked bottom crust; place the filling of your choice in the piecrust first. Spoon the almond cobbler over the filling in big lumps. With dampened hands, smooth the surface of the cobbler and make sure that it is pressed right up to the crimped edge.

5 Bake the pie according to the instructed time of the individual recipe.

streusel topping for pie

MAKES ENOUGH FOR ONE
9-INCH PIE

I include this recipe in case you feel like adding it to your own improvised pie. Sometimes I add this to the Strawberry and Rhubarb Pie (page 187) instead of using the cutout shapes. Use the recipe for one piecrust, add your filling, and place the raw streusel topping over the strawberry-rhubarb filling before it goes into the oven. I like to make this ahead and store it in an airtight container in the freezer. It is nice to have on hand alongside your unbaked frozen pie shells.

126 grams (⅔ cup) firmly packed brown sugar

60 grams (½ cup) sorghum flour

36 grams (¼ cup) potato starch

26 grams (¼ cup) tapioca starch

2 teaspoons ground cinnamon

¾ teaspoon xanthan gum

1 cup pecans, coarsely chopped (optional)

¼ cup plus 1 Tablespoon melted and slightly cooled clarified butter or coconut oil

1 In a bowl, whisk together the brown sugar, sorghum flour, potato starch, tapioca starch, cinnamon, xanthan gum, and pecans (if using). Pour the clarified butter into the dry ingredients and stir with a fork until all of the dry ingredients are moistened. Continue to process with the fork or your fingers until you achieve a crumbly consistency. Set aside in the refrigerator to cool.

2 Add the topping after you add the filling, and bake for the instructed time of the individual recipe.

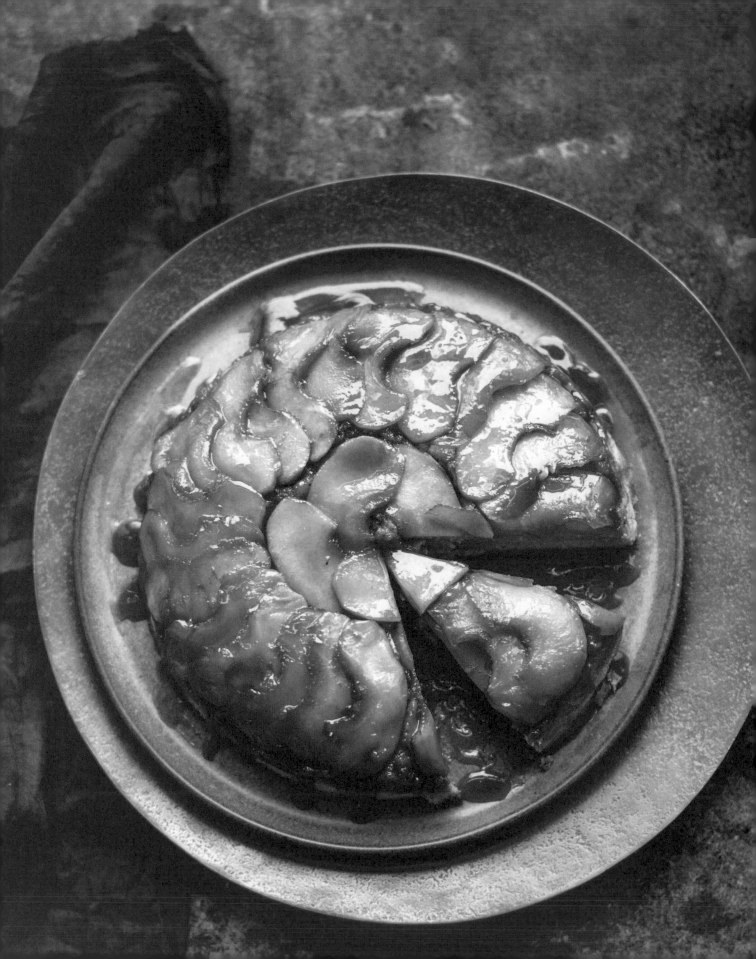

apple tarte tatin

Honestly this is a bit of a cheat but a really good one and so much easier than the French version. This tart has a soft, cakey batter that is spooned over the apples—no need to roll out dough. After baking, you turn it over and the cakey part is on the bottom. The cake sops up all the heavenly caramel sauce. It is best to make this ahead and let it sit at room temperature for several hours, or you can refrigerate it overnight and bring to room temperature before serving. I like to serve it with the Ginger Jam (page 249), but it is also really good with whipped cream and toasted sliced almonds.

3 apples, each peeled, cored, and cut into ½ inch pieces

2 Tablespoons freshly squeezed orange juice (from 1 to 2 oranges)

1 Tablespoon orange zest (from 1 orange)

¼ cup (½ stick), plus 6 Tablespoons (¾ stick), cut into ¼-inch slices, unsalted butter or Earth Balance Vegan Buttery Sticks

142 grams (¾ cup) firmly packed dark brown sugar

1 Tablespoon ground cinnamon

½ teaspoon fine salt (divided)

¼ cup currants

2 teaspoons, plus 1 teaspoon vanilla extract

90 grams (1 cup) almond flour

80 grams (⅔ cup) sorghum flour

69 grams (¼ cup plus 2 Tablespoons) sweet rice flour

36 grams (¼ cup plus 1 Tablespoon) potato starch

3 Tablespoons granulated sugar

2 teaspoons double-acting baking powder

1 teaspoon xanthan gum

1 Preheat the oven to 375°F. Line a baking sheet with parchment paper.

2 Place the apples, orange juice, and zest in a small mixing bowl and stir. Set aside while you make the caramel.

3 Melt the ¼ cup butter in a nonstick skillet over medium-high heat. Stir in the brown sugar, cinnamon, and ¼ teaspoon of the salt. Cook, swirling the skillet occasionally, until the mixture turns a medium amber color, about 3 minutes. Remove the skillet from the heat, add the apple mixture and the 2 teaspoons vanilla extract, and stir to combine. Set aside to cool while you make the topping.

4 In the bowl of a food processor, combine the almond flour, sorghum flour, sweet rice flour, potato starch, granulated sugar, baking powder, xanthan gum, baking soda, and the remaining ¼ teaspoon salt. Pulse several times to blend the dry ingredients. Remove the lid and add the sliced 6 tablespoons butter; pulse until the mixture is crumbly and resembles coarse meal. Transfer the mixture to a mixing bowl.

5 In a separate bowl, combine the remaining 1 teaspoon vanilla, the buttermilk, and eggs and beat well.

6 Add the buttermilk mixture to the dry ingredients and mix with a rubber scraper until the dough starts to come together.

continued

apple tarte tatin, continued

½ teaspoon baking soda

¼ cup buttermilk (see note, page 26)

2 eggs, room temperature

½ cup sliced almonds, to finish

7 When the apple slices are cool enough to handle, arrange the apples in another 8-inch skillet, slightly over-lapping and fanning the apples around the outer edge of the skillet. Save a few apple slices to fill in the center circle. Sprinkle the currants over and between the apples. If you don't feel like fussing you can also just spread the sautéed apples evenly over the skillet and skip the fanning.

8 Carefully spoon the dough over the apples in big lumps. With dampened hands, smooth the surface of the dough and make sure that it is pressed right up to the edge. Place the skillet on the prepared baking sheet and bake for 25 to 30 minutes, until the top is puffed and golden brown.

9 On a separate baking sheet lined with parchment, scatter the sliced almonds. Bake for 5 to 8 minutes in the same oven, on a separate oven rack, underneath the tart. Watch the almonds carefully and remove from the oven when they are golden.

10 Remove the skillet from the oven and place on a wire cooling rack. Let the tart cool for 30 minutes. Place a serving plate over the top of the skillet and, using a kitchen towel, carefully invert the tart onto the plate. Serve with the toasted almonds, Ginger Jam, and ice cream or whipped cream (if using).

Note: Leftovers can be covered with plastic wrap and kept in the refrigerator for 4 days.

banana tarte tatin

MAKES ONE 9-INCH TART,
OR 8 TO 10 SERVINGS

This dessert is always a huge hit with family and friends. It is usually better the next day, so make it ahead and store it in the refrigerator overnight. The bottom soaks up the juices and the flavors intensify. I love this dessert with Caramel Sauce (page 254) or Flavored Whipped Cream (page 256)—or both!

¼ cup (½ stick) unsalted butter or Earth Balance Vegan Buttery Sticks

142 grams (¾ cup) firmly packed dark brown sugar

1 teaspoon ground cinnamon

¼ teaspoon fine salt

6 medium bananas (enough to fill the skillet)

2 Tablespoons dark rum, or 2 teaspoons rum extract

1 teaspoon vanilla extract

90 grams (1 cup) almond flour

80 grams (⅔ cup) sorghum flour

69 grams (¼ cup plus 2 Tablespoons) sweet rice flour

36 grams (¼ cup plus 1 Tablespoon) potato starch

3 Tablespoons granulated sugar

2 teaspoons double-acting baking powder

1 teaspoon xanthan gum

½ teaspoon baking soda

¼ teaspoon fine salt

6 Tablespoons cold unsalted butter (¾ stick) or Earth Balance Vegan Buttery Sticks, cut into ¼-inch slices

¼ cup buttermilk (see note, page 26)

2 eggs, room temperature

1 Preheat the oven to 375°F. Line a baking sheet with parchment paper.

2 Melt the ½ stick of butter in a 9-inch skillet over medium heat. Stir in the brown sugar, cinnamon, and salt. Cook, swirling the skillet occasionally, until the mixture turns a medium amber color, about 3 minutes. Remove the skillet from the heat.

3 Working quickly, cut the bananas into 1-inch-thick slices.

4 Arrange the bananas in the skillet with the ends facing up, working from the center outward. You should have enough to completely fill the pan (enjoy any leftovers as a snack). Drizzle the rum and vanilla over the bananas. Set aside.

5 In the bowl of a food processor, combine the almond flour, sorghum flour, sweet rice flour, potato starch, granulated sugar, baking powder, xanthan gum, baking soda, and salt. Pulse several times to blend the dry ingredients. Remove the lid and add the butter slices; pulse until the mixture is crumbly and resembles coarse meal. Transfer the mixture to a mixing bowl.

6 In a separate bowl, combine the buttermilk, eggs, and rum extract, and beat well.

7 Add the buttermilk mixture to the dry ingredients and mix with a rubber scraper until the dough starts to come together.

8 Carefully spoon the dough over the bananas in big lumps. With dampened hands, smooth the surface of the dough, being careful of the hot skillet, and make sure that it is pressed right up to the edge. Place the skillet on the prepared baking sheet and bake for 25 to 30 minutes, until the top is puffed and golden.

continued

banana tarte tatin, continued

1 teaspoon rum extract

½ cup shredded unsweetened coconut (optional)

Caramel Sauce (page 254) or Flavored Whipped Cream (page 256)

9 On a separate baking sheet lined with parchment, scatter the shredded coconut. Bake for 5 to 8 minutes in the same oven, on a separate oven rack, underneath the tart. Watch the shredded coconut carefully and remove it from the oven when it is golden.

10 Remove the skillet from the oven and place on a wire cooling rack. Let the tart cool for 30 minutes. Place a serving plate over the top of the skillet and, using a kitchen towel, carefully invert the tart onto the plate. Sprinkle the shredded coconut over the top, if using. Serve with Caramel Sauce or Flavored Whipped Creamg.

Note: Leftovers can be covered with plastic wrap and kept in the refrigerator for 4 days.

dutch apple pie

MAKES ONE 9-INCH PIE,
OR 8 TO 10 SERVINGS

My grandmother and grandfather had apple trees in their backyard. As a kid, I was always in charge of climbing the tree and collecting the apples. Grandma, in return, made an apple pie with them. If you are a cinnamon lover like I am, feel free to double the cinnamon in the streusel topping.

1 piecrust, partially baked at 375°F for 25 to 30 minutes, or until golden, and cooled to room temperature (see page 158)

FILLING

4 Tablespoons butter or coconut oil

2½ pounds Granny Smith apples (about 4–5 apples), peeled, cored, and sliced crosswise into ½-inch slices

44 grams (¼ cup) granulated sugar

¼ cup freshly squeezed orange juice, 1 Tablespoon reserved

1 Tablespoon orange zest (from 1 orange)

1 Tablespoon potato starch

2 teaspoons ground cinnamon

¼ teaspoon fine salt

TOPPING

126 grams (⅔ cup) firmly packed brown sugar

60 grams (½ cup) sorghum flour

36 grams (¼ cup) potato starch

26 grams (¼ cup) tapioca starch

2 teaspoons ground cinnamon

¾ teaspoon xanthan gum

1 cup pecans, coarsely chopped (optional)

¼ cup plus 1 Tablespoon melted and slightly cooled clarified butter or coconut oil

Ice cream or Cardamom Custard (see page 203)

1 To make the filling: In a large mixing bowl, stir together the apples, granulated sugar, orange juice, orange zest, cinnamon, and salt. Set aside.

2 Melt butter in a large non-stick skillet over medium heat until frothy. Add apple slices and sauté apples until just tender, 6 to 7 minutes. Let apples cool while you make the streusel topping.

3 To make the topping: In a bowl, whisk together the brown sugar, sorghum flour, potato starch, tapioca starch, cinnamon, and xanthan gum. Mix in the pecans (if using). Pour the clarified butter into the dry ingredients and stir with a fork until all of the dry ingredients are moistened. Continue to process with the fork or your fingers until you achieve a crumbly consistency. Set aside in the refrigerator to cool.

4 In a small bowl, combine the reserved orange juice (1 Tablespoon) and potato starch. Blend until you have a smooth paste.

5 Combine the orange juice paste with the reserved apples. Blend well.

6 Preheat the oven to 350°F. Line a baking sheet with aluminum foil. Transfer the apple mixture to the piecrust and press into an even layer. Pinch the crumb topping into ¼- to ½-inch pieces and sprinkle over the top of the apples. Place the pie on the prepared baking sheet and bake until the topping is golden and crisp, 30 to 35 minutes, rotating the pie halfway through baking.

7 Remove the pie from the oven and let it cool to room temperature on a wire cooling rack, 2 to 3 hours. I honestly think the pie is best served the next day. Refrigerate after it cools. Serve with ice cream or Cardamom Custard (see page 203).

lemon meringue pie

MAKES SIX 3–3½-INCH PIES, FOUR
4-INCH PIES, OR ONE 9-INCH PIE

I have written this recipe for individual meringue pies but you can also make it in a 9-inch pie pan. Lemon meringue pie was Grandfather Blake's favorite dessert. This one is dedicated to William Blake (Bill).

1 egg white, beaten

Six 3–3½-inch piecrusts baked at 375°F for 20 minutes, or until golden (page 158), or 1 tart crust, partially baked at 375°F for 25 to 30 minutes, or until golden (page 164)

176 grams (1 cup) granulated sugar

⅔ cup freshly squeezed lemon juice (from 3 lemons)

¼ cup lemon zest (from 4 lemons)

Pinch of fine salt

2 eggs, room temperature

7 egg yolks, reserving 3 egg whites for the meringue

4 Tablespoons (½ stick) unsalted butter, cut into 4 pieces, or melted and cooled coconut oil

3 Tablespoons heavy cream or full-fat canned coconut milk

MERINGUE

3 reserved egg whites

¼ teaspoon cream of tartar

58 grams (⅓ cup) granulated sugar

½ teaspoon vanilla extract

1 Preheat the oven to 375°F.

2 Lightly brush the egg white over the 3–3½-inch piecrusts while they are still warm. (The egg white acts as a barrier and keeps the crust crisp when you pour in the filling.)

3 In a medium saucepan, combine the granulated sugar, lemon juice, lemon zest, and salt. Cook over low heat until the mixture starts to bubble at the edges. Remove the pan from the heat.

4 In a small mixing bowl, whisk together the eggs and egg yolks. Whisk ⅓ cup of the hot lemon mixture into the egg mixture; stir well and then add the egg mixture into the saucepan.

5 Add the butter and cook over medium-low heat, stirring constantly, until the mixture thickens and registers 170°F on an instant-read thermometer. Pour the mixture through a fine-mesh sieve into a bowl and stir in the cream.

6 Pour the lemon filling into the piecrusts. Bake the pies on a baking sheet until the filling is shiny and wobbles slightly when shaken, 10 to 12 minutes. (It will be the same amount of time whether you are making the individual pies or the 9-inch pie.)

7 Remove the baking sheet from the oven and let the pies cool to room temperature on a wire cooling rack, about 2 hours.

8 To make the meringue: Preheat the oven to 350°F. In the bowl of a stand mixer fitted with the whip attachment, combine the egg whites and cream of tartar and whip on high speed until soft peaks form. Reduce to medium speed and add the granulated sugar 1 Tablespoon at a time until the egg whites turn glossy and stiff peaks form. Add the vanilla and blend well. Spread the meringue over the pies, making certain it touches the edges of the crusts all around. This will keep the meringue from shrinking as it bakes. Place the pies on a baking sheet

continued

lemon meringue pie, continued

and place in the oven for 12 to 15 minutes, until the meringue is golden brown (see note). Cool to room temperature and chill before serving. Once the meringue is on top, the pies should be served that same day. The pies can be refrigerated prior to placing the meringue for 4 days. After the meringue is on top, the pie really does not keep that well.

Note: If you are proficient with a kitchen torch, you can also torch the meringue until it is light golden brown.

1. Bring the dough to room temperature. Line a silicone mat with a piece of parchment paper. Place the dough on the parchment. **2.** If the edges are cracking, gently warm and shape the dough with your hands. The edges will smooth out with the heat of your hands. **3.** Generously dust the top of the dough with flour. Roll out the dough until you have an even circle that is 12 to 13 inches in diameter. At this point you can slide the parchment off of the silicone mat and onto a flat baking sheet. **4.** Spread the cold frangipane filling evenly onto the dough leaving a 1 to 1½ inch border on all sides of the circle. **5.** Place the fruit onto the frangipane filling, making sure that the fruit is not clumped or too heavy in any one area. Be sure to use the amounts stipulated in the recipe; too much fruit can lead to a soggy filling. **6.** Gently lift the parchment over the edges of the tart and nudge the dough to fold over to create a folded edge all over. This takes a careful and steady hand. If the pastry breaks, just press it together with your fingers. Place the galette into the oven.

frangipane and cherry galette

MAKES ONE 10-INCH GALETTE,
OR 10 TO 12 SERVINGS

I really love the presentation of a rustic tart or galette. There is something so beautiful about a frangipane galette. I have included a couple of fruit variations at the bottom of the recipe. It is important to adhere to the fruit quantities, as too much fruit juice can leave your almond filling soggy.

FRANGIPANE FILLING

90 grams (1 cup) almond flour

88 grams (½ cup) granulated sugar

¼ teaspoon fine salt

1 large egg, plus 1 large egg white

2 teaspoons almond extract

1 teaspoon vanilla extract

6 Tablespoons (¾ stick) unsalted butter, room temperature, cut into 6 pieces

SHELL

60 grams (½ cup) sorghum flour, plus more for dusting

48 grams (⅓ cup) potato starch

34 grams (⅓ cup) tapioca starch

34 grams (¼ cup) sweet rice flour

28 grams (⅓ cup) golden flaxseed meal

2 Tablespoons granulated sugar

1¾ teaspoons xanthan gum

½ teaspoon fine salt

½ cup (1 stick) cold unsalted butter, cut into ½-inch dice

2 Tablespoons full-fat sour cream

1 teaspoon ice water, if needed

20 cherries, pitted and cut in half

1 egg white, beaten

1 Tablespoon turbinado sugar, to finish

1 Adjust the oven rack to the lower-middle position and preheat the oven to 350°F. Line a baking sheet with parchment paper.

2 To make the frangipane filling: Pulse the almond flour, granulated sugar, and salt in a food processor until well blended. Add the egg and egg white, almond extract, and vanilla and process until combined, about 10 seconds.

3 Add the butter and process until no lumps remain, about 10 seconds. Scrape the bottom and sides of the bowl with a rubber spatula and process to combine thoroughly, about 10 seconds longer. Refrigerate the filling while you make the galette shell (see notes).

4 To make the shell: In the bowl of a food processor, combine the sorghum flour, potato starch, tapioca starch, sweet rice flour, flaxseed meal, granulated sugar, xanthan gum, and salt. Pulse several times to blend the dry ingredients. Remove the lid and add the butter; pulse until the butter is cut in. Remove the lid and add the sour cream. Blend together until the mixture forms a ball, 20 to 30 seconds. Add the ice water only if the mixture looks dry and crumbly. Add 1 teaspoon at a time until you get the right consistency.

5 Turn the dough out onto a countertop and knead it gently. It should look and act just like regular pie dough. If the dough seems too wet, add 1 Tablespoon sorghum flour and knead until it is evenly distributed. Repeat if necessary.

continued

6 Place a sheet of parchment paper on top of a silicone mat; the silicone mat is to keep the parchment stable. Flatten the dough into a disk and roll the dough on the parchment paper until it is 15 inches in diameter. Keep the top surface of your dough sprinkled with sorghum flour to ensure that your dough rolls out evenly without sticking to the rolling pin. Slide the parchment paper and dough onto the back of a sheet pan.

7 Remove the frangipane filling from the refrigerator and spread it in a circle in the center of the dough, leaving a 2-inch border at the edge. Smooth the frangipane with an offset spatula or a rubber scraper and place the cherry halves evenly over the frangipane. Using the parchment to help lift the dough at the edges, fold the outer 2 inches of dough up and over the filling, pleating the dough every 2 or 3 inches as needed. Brush the galette with the beaten egg white and sprinkle with turbinado sugar. Slide the parchment onto the back of a baking sheet and refrigerate the galette 15 minutes before baking.

8 Place the baking sheet and galette in the oven. Bake for 40 to 45 minutes, until golden on all edges. Let the galette cool on the baking sheet, about 5 minutes. Slide it onto a wire cooling rack using the parchment. Let cool until the frangipane filling has thickened, about 25 minutes. Serve warm or at room temperature.

Notes: The galette will keep in the refrigerator for up to a week, covered in plastic wrap. It does not freeze well.

If you would like to make the frangipane filling ahead, the filling can be refrigerated in an airtight container for up to 3 days. Before using, let stand at room temperature about 30 minutes to soften, stirring three or four times.

This dough is best if made several days ahead of time, wrapped in plastic, and refrigerated. This allows for greater absorption of the liquid and increases the pliability of the dough. It can be frozen for up to a month. Bring the dough back to room temperature before rolling it out.

Variation

This recipe also works well with fresh figs (8 quartered, any variety) or apricots (10 pitted and halved) instead of the cherries. Just be sure not to overstuff or overlap the fruit. Too much fruit and the filling won't bake properly.

chocolate ganache tart

MAKES ONE 9-INCH ROUND TART,
OR 8 TO 10 SERVINGS

This is such an easy tart to make. It is very rich with chocolate flavor so I dress it up with toasted hazelnuts and whipped cream. It is also terrific with sautéed fruit (see page 74).

1 tart crust, partially baked at 375°F for 25 to 30 minutes or until golden (page 164)

½ cup plus 2 Tablespoons heavy cream or full-fat canned coconut milk

11 ounces (about 2¼ cups) semisweet or bittersweet chocolate, chopped or in chips

Chopped toasted hazelnuts, to finish

Pinch of Maldon salt, to finish

1 In a small saucepan, warm the cream over medium heat until you see little bubbles at the edges. Add the chocolate and turn off the heat. Wait 1 minute and stir until glossy.

2 Pour the chocolate directly on top of the crust. Allow it to set in a cool place for an hour before serving. You can also pop it in the refrigerator for 15 to 30 minutes if you're in a rush. Just before serving, sprinkle with hazelnuts and Maldon salt.

Note: If making ahead and refrigerating for more than 2 hours, the ganache may lose some of its sheen. Remove from the refrigerator and allow to temper for 30 minutes to 2 hours before serving so that the ganache softens. You can also very quickly run a crème brûlée torch over the surface of the tart to get the sheen back.

strawberry and rhubarb pie

MAKES ONE 9-INCH PIE,
OR 8 TO 10 SERVINGS

This is a summertime classic. Rhubarb grows wild in my home state of Montana. All you have to do is drive around and you will find it by the roadside. I had to include this recipe as a nod to my roots and growing up in Montana. This pie is best eaten after some refrigerator time, usually by the next day. The filling becomes jammy and easier to cut.

1¼ pounds (6 cups) rhubarb, sliced ½ inch thick

1 pound (3 cups) strawberries, hulled and halved (if smaller than 1 inch) or quartered (if larger than 1 inch)

132 grams (¾ cup) granulated sugar, plus 44 grams (¼ cup)

1 Tablespoon lemon zest (from 1 lemon)

1 double piecrust (see page 158), room temperature

Sorghum flour, for dusting

36 grams (¼ cup) potato starch

1 Tablespoon fruit pectin, low sugar or no sugar added (I use Pomona's Universal Pectin)

Pinch of fine salt

1 egg white, beaten

1 Tablespoon granulated sugar for cut-out shapes

1 In a large mixing bowl, toss the rhubarb and strawberries together with ¾ cup of the granulated sugar and the lemon zest. Let sit and macerate for at least 30 minutes or up to an hour.

2 Adjust the oven racks to the upper-middle and lower-middle positions and preheat the oven to 400°F. Line a baking sheet with parchment paper.

3 Place a sheet of parchment paper on top of a silicone mat; the silicone mat is to keep the parchment paper stable. Flatten the first half of the piecrust dough into a disk and roll the dough on the parchment paper until it is 11 to 12 inches in diameter. Keep the top surface of your dough sprinkled with sorghum flour to ensure that your dough rolls out evenly without sticking to the rolling pin.

4 Slide the parchment paper and dough onto the back of a sheet pan. Place the 9-inch pie plate upside down on the dough. Carefully flip the baking sheet, dough, and pie plate all at once. Remove the baking sheet and let the dough sink into the pie plate.

5 Carefully peel away the parchment paper, keeping the dough centered over the pie plate, and ease the dough into the pie plate. This crust can be somewhat delicate; if it cracks, just push it back together. You don't have to fold over the edge and crimp this crust; I simply trim the dough to the edge of the pie plate and create a decorative edge with a spoon or fork. Place the piecrust in the refrigerator to chill.

6 Place another sheet of parchment paper on top of the silicone mat. Flatten the other half of the dough into a disk and roll the dough on the parchment paper until it is 11 to 12 inches in diameter.

continued

7 Cut out shapes using your favorite cookie cutters. You will need enough to cover the pie. Place the shapes on the prepared baking sheet about 1/2 inch apart. Cover the pie shapes in plastic wrap and place them in the refrigerator.

8 Line a baking sheet with aluminum foil.

9 Drain off the juices that have accumulated around the strawberry-rhubarb mixture.

10 Combine 1/4 cup of the granulated sugar, the potato starch, pectin, and salt in a small bowl. Stir the sugar mixture into the strawberry-rhubarb mixture and mix well. Immediately pour the filling into the piecrust.

11 Place the filled pie on the prepared baking sheet and bake on the lower rack until the crust is a deep golden brown and the filling is bubbling, about 15 minutes. Remove the baking sheet from the oven and transfer the pie to a wire cooling rack. Let the pie cool at room temperature and refrigerate the pie overnight.

12 Brush the pie shapes with the beaten egg white and sprinkle with the remaining 1 Tablespoon granulated sugar. Bake the pie shapes at 400°F for 15 to 20 minutes. Remove the pan from the oven and let the shapes cool slightly and then shingle them over the top of the pie. The baked pie shapes can be held at room temperature, covered, for up to 6 hours before going stale. After you assemble the pie, store the leftovers in the refrigerator for up to a week, covered in plastic wrap.

Note: For a more traditional crimped edge, reroll your scraps and make several long coils, 1/2 inch in diameter. Place the coils along the top edge of your pie plate in a continuous circle. This will allow you to have an edge that can be crimped. Refer to the crimping tutorial (page 157) to establish your favorite way of finishing the pie.

peach pie with almond topping

MAKES ONE 9-INCH PIE,
OR 8 TO 10 SERVINGS

The almond topping makes this a pie/cobbler hybrid. I invented this to avoid having a top crust. Not only is the topping easier and faster than adding a top crust, the presentation is also fun and whimsical. Feel free to use the Streusel Topping (page 247) as an alternate and more traditional presentation.

1 piecrust, partially baked at 375°F for 25 to 30 minutes, or until golden, and cooled to room temperature (see page 158)

2½ pounds peaches
(5 to 6 medium peaches)

176 grams (1 cup) granulated sugar

90 grams (1 cup) almond flour

80 grams (½ cup) sorghum flour

69 grams (¼ cup plus
2 Tablespoons) sweet rice flour

72 grams (½ cup plus
1 Tablespoon) potato starch

2 teaspoons double-acting baking powder

1 teaspoon xanthan gum

½ teaspoon baking soda

½ teaspoon fine salt

6 Tablespoons (¾ stick) cold unsalted butter or Earth Balance Vegan Buttery Sticks, cut into 8 slices

⅓ cup buttermilk (see note, page 26)

2 eggs, room temperature

1 teaspoon almond extract

2 Tablespoons freshly squeezed lemon juice (from 1 lemon)

Pinch of ground cardamom

Pinch of ground cinnamon

Pinch of ground nutmeg

Pinch of fine salt

1 Fill a large Dutch oven with hot water and bring to a boil over high heat. Cut a small X into the bottom of each peach, cutting only through the outer peel. Carefully lower each peach into the boiling water. Let the peaches cook for 2 minutes. Remove and place them in an ice bath. Let them sit until they are cool. Wrap each peach with a kitchen towel and carefully peel off the skin. Pit and cut each peach into 8 segments.

2 Place the peaches in a small bowl with the granulated sugar. Let the peaches macerate while you make the topping.

3 Preheat the oven to 425°F. Line a baking sheet with parchment paper.

4 In the bowl of a food processor, combine the almond flour, sorghum flour, sweet rice flour, ¼ cup plus 1 Tablespoon of the potato starch, the baking powder, xanthan gum, baking soda, and salt. Pulse until well combined. Remove the lid and add the butter; pulse until the mixture is crumbly and resembles coarse meal. Transfer the mixture to a mixing bowl. (You can do the recipe to this point and refrigerate, covered, overnight. In the morning, proceed with step 5.)

5 In a separate bowl, combine the buttermilk, eggs, and almond extract and beat well. Add the buttermilk mixture to the dry ingredients and mix with a rubber scraper until the dough starts to come together.

6 Pour off about half the juice that has accumulated around the peaches, and add to the peaches the remaining ¼ cup potato starch, the lemon juice, cardamom, cinnamon, nutmeg, and salt. With your hands, gently mix the peaches until all of the ingredients are combined. Pour the peach mixture into the partially baked piecrust.

continued

peach pie with almond topping, continued

2 Tablespoons turbinado sugar, to finish

¼ cup slivered almonds, to finish

7 Carefully spoon the almond topping over the peaches in big lumps. With dampened hands, smooth the surface of the topping and make sure that it is pressed right up to the edge. Sprinkle the turbinado sugar over the entire top of the pie. I like to place the slivered almonds around the outer edge of the pie (see photo). Place the filled pie on the prepared baking sheet and bake for 25 to 30 minutes. Rotate the pie and reduce the oven temperature to 375°F. Continue baking for 20 to 25 minutes, until the almond topping is golden brown and the juices are bubbling at the edge.

8 Remove the baking sheet from the oven, place on a wire cooling rack, and let cool to room temperature. Cover with plastic wrap and refrigerate overnight before serving. I really feel that this pie is better the second day.

Note: The pie will keep in the refrigerator for 1 week, covered in plastic wrap.

pumpkin pie

MAKES ONE 9-INCH PIE,
OR 8 TO 10 SERVINGS

A holiday classic. I like to form the piecrust the day before and place it on a tray in the freezer. I also like to cook the pumpkin with the spices the day before. This allows the filling to cool down completely. The next day you can partially bake the piecrust, finish the filling, and bake the pie in the morning. This pumpkin pie will satisfy both your gluten-free guests and the gluten eaters.

1 piecrust, partially baked at 375°F for 25 to 30 minutes, or until golden, and cooled to room temperature (see page 158)

1 can (15 ounces) pumpkin puree

190 grams (1 cup) firmly packed brown sugar

2 teaspoons ground ginger

2 teaspoons ground cinnamon

1 teaspoon vanilla extract

½ teaspoon fine salt

¼ teaspoon ground cardamom

¼ teaspoon ground nutmeg

1 cup half-and-half

4 eggs, room temperature

1 Preheat the oven to 375°F.

2 In a bowl, whisk together the pumpkin puree, brown sugar, ginger, cinnamon, vanilla, salt, cardamom, and nutmeg. Transfer the mixture to a heavy 2-quart saucepan, setting aside the bowl. Bring the filling to a sputtering simmer over medium heat and cook, stirring constantly, until it is thick and shiny, about 5 minutes (this step is crucial to remove the canned flavor from the pumpkin and to bloom the spices). Pour the filling back into the mixing bowl and let it cool until just warm to the touch.

3 In a separate small bowl, whisk together the half-and-half and eggs. If the filling is still quite warm, add a small amount of it to the egg mixture to temper, then add the rest of the filling and mix together.

4 Pour the filling into the partially baked piecrust so it reaches just below the crimped edge. (You will most likely have some filling left over.) Bake the pie for 20 minutes and then cover it with aluminum foil, taking care not to touch the filling. This keeps the edges from browning too much before the custard is done. Continue baking for 25 to 30 minutes more, until the filling is puffed and dry-looking and the center slightly jiggles. At this point, I turn off the oven and prop open the door with the handle of a wooden spoon. This allows the pie to come down in temperature very slowly, keeping the custard from cracking, about 1 hour.

5 Remove the pie from the oven and continue to cool on a wire cooling rack for at least 2 hours before slicing and serving. I think the pie is best served at room temperature.

Note: If you don't plan to serve the pie right away, let it cool completely to room temperature, then cover it with plastic wrap and store it in the refrigerator for 1 week. Bring the pie to room temperature before serving for the best flavor.

vegan pumpkin pie

MAKES ONE 9-INCH PIE,
OR 8 TO 10 SERVINGS

This vegan pie is so good that you don't need to make an issue about it—just serve it to everyone. Be sure to cook the pumpkin with the spices and flaxseed meal as directed. This activates the flax meal to bind the custard in the absence of the eggs. This pie is best eaten the day after it is baked and refrigerated overnight. Bring it back to room temperature for the best flavor.

1 vegan piecrust, partially baked at 375°F for 25 to 30 minutes, or until golden, and cooled to room temperature (see page 162)

1 can (15 ounces) pumpkin puree

190 grams (1 cup) firmly packed brown sugar

¼ cup flaxseed meal

2 teaspoons ground ginger

2 teaspoons ground cinnamon

1 teaspoon vanilla extract

½ teaspoon fine salt

¼ teaspoon ground cardamom

¼ teaspoon ground nutmeg

1 cup full-fat canned coconut milk

3 Tablespoons cornstarch

1 Preheat the oven to 375°F.

2 In a bowl, whisk together the pumpkin puree, brown sugar, flaxseed meal, ginger, cinnamon, vanilla, salt, cardamom, and nutmeg. Transfer the mixture to a heavy 2-quart saucepan, setting aside the bowl. Bring the filling to a sputtering simmer over medium heat and cook, stirring constantly, until the puree is thick and shiny, about 5 minutes (this step is crucial to remove the canned flavor from the pumpkin and to bloom the spices). Pour the filling back into the mixing bowl and let it cool until just warm to the touch.

3 In a separate small bowl, whisk together the coconut milk and cornstarch until a thick slurry forms. Add the slurry to the warm pumpkin filling mixture and blend well.

4 Pour the filling into the partially baked piecrust so it reaches just below the crimped edge. (You most likely will have some filling left over.) Bake the pie for 20 minutes and then cover it with aluminum foil, taking care not to touch the filling. This keeps the edges from browning too much before the custard is done. Continue baking for 25 to 30 minutes more, until the filling is puffed and dry-looking and the center slightly jiggles. At this point, I turn off the oven and prop open the door with the handle of a wooden spoon. This allows the pie to come down in temperature very slowly, keeping the custard from cracking, about 1 hour.

5 Remove the pie from the oven and continue to cool on a wire cooling rack for at least 2 hours before slicing and serving. I think the pie is best served at room temperature.

Note: If you don't plan to serve the pie right away, let it cool completely to room temperature, then cover it with plastic wrap and store it in the refrigerator for 1 week. Bring the pie to room temperature before serving for the best flavor.

pecan pie

MAKES ONE 9-INCH PIE,
OR 8 TO 10 SERVINGS

Here, the pie filling is cooked over low heat on the stove top. It is then poured into the warm piecrust and cooked slowly for a full hour. This low-and-slow approach will ensure that the filling will cook evenly and not be dried out at the edges. This pecan pie will satisfy both your gluten-free guests and the regular eaters. There is no need to make two versions.

1 piecrust, partially baked at 375°F for 25 to 30 minutes, or until golden, still warm (see page 158)

6 Tablespoons melted clarified butter or coconut oil

190 grams (1 cup) firmly packed dark brown sugar

½ teaspoon fine salt

3 eggs, room temperature

¾ cup light corn syrup

1 Tablespoon vanilla extract

8 ounces (2 cups) pecans, toasted and coarsely chopped

1 After baking the piecrust, turn down the oven temperature to 275°F.

2 Place the clarified butter in a heat-safe bowl over a skillet filled with 2 inches of barely simmering water. Stir in the brown sugar and salt, and blend until the sugar is dissolved. Remove the bowl from the heat and whisk in the eggs, corn syrup, and vanilla, mixing until smooth.

3 Return the bowl to the simmering water and continue to cook and stir until the mixture is shiny and registers 130°F on an instant-read thermometer. Remove the bowl from the heat and stir in the pecans.

4 Pour the pecan mixture into the piecrust and bake until the filling looks set but still jiggles slightly, 50 to 60 minutes.

5 Remove the pie from the oven and let it cool on a wire cooling rack until the filling has set, about 2 hours. Serve slightly warm or at room temperature. If you are not serving the pie immediately, it can be stored in the refrigerator for up to a week, covered with plastic wrap.

coconut cream pie

MAKES ONE 9-INCH PIE, OR 8 TO 10 SERVINGS

I didn't grow up with coconut cream pie. I was introduced to it as an adult. Sometimes I have found that it can be overly sweet and cloying, but not this recipe. It took me a while to get it right, but I am really happy with these results. Consider topping it with whipped cream that has a purchased caramel sauce or one of my caramel recipes swirled in (as we did in the photo). See page 154 for caramel sauce.

1 piecrust, partially baked at 375°F for 25 to 30 minutes, or until golden, and cooled to room temperature (see page 158)

FILLING

1 cup whole milk or dairy-free milk, room temperature

1 can (13.5 fluid ounces) full-fat coconut milk

117 grams (⅔ cup) granulated sugar, divided

28 grams (½ cup) unsweetened shredded coconut

¼ teaspoon fine salt

5 egg yolks

55 grams (¼ cup) cornstarch

2 Tablespoons unsalted butter or Earth Balance Vegan Buttery Sticks, cut into 2 pieces

2 teaspoons vanilla extract

TOPPING

1½ cups heavy cream, chilled

1½ Tablespoons granulated sugar

1½ teaspoons dark rum (optional)

1 teaspoon vanilla extract

1 Tablespoon unsweetened shredded coconut, toasted, to finish

1 To make the filling: In a medium saucepan, bring the milk, coconut milk, ⅓ cup of the granulated sugar, the coconut, and salt to a simmer over medium-high heat, stirring occasionally.

2 As the coconut milk mixture begins to simmer, whisk the egg yolks, cornstarch, and remaining ⅓ cup granulated sugar together in a bowl until smooth. Slowly whisk 1 cup of the simmering coconut milk mixture into the yolk mixture to temper, then slowly whisk the tempered yolk mixture into the saucepan. Reduce the heat to medium and cook, whisking vigorously, until the mixture has thickened and a few bubbles burst on the surface, about 30 seconds. Take the pan off the heat and whisk in the butter and vanilla. Let the mixture cool until just warm, stirring often, about 5 minutes.

3 Pour the coconut filling into the piecrust. Lay a sheet of plastic wrap directly on the surface of the filling to prevent a skin from forming. Refrigerate until the filling is chilled and set, at least 4 hours or up to 24 hours.

4 To make the topping: Before serving, using a stand mixer fitted with a whip attachment, blend the cream, granulated sugar, rum (if using), and vanilla on medium-low speed until foamy, about 1 minute. Increase the speed to high and whip until soft peaks form, 1 to 3 minutes. Spread the whipped cream on the pie, sprinkle with the coconut, and serve.

CRISPS &
COBBLERS

TIPS FOR SUCCESS

Crisps and cobblers are so simple and satisfying and are my go-to dessert for a casual meal with friends. I love going to the farmers' market and finding whatever inspires me. It is always best to weigh your fruit, at home or at the market, and adhere to the amounts stated in each of the individual recipes. The second part is finding a nice partnership, such as peaches and cherries or nectarines and blueberries. It is fun to be experimental. Here is the big secret to making your own combination a success: macerate the fruit! Prepare your fruit—wash, peel, core, chop—and place it in a large mixing bowl with ¼ cup of sugar. Stir well and let sit for 30 minutes. After the time is up, drain the accumulated juices from the bowl and proceed with the recipe. Remember to use the additional sugar called for in the recipe, as you will have lost some of the sugar in the macerating process. That is all there is to it. Use my crisp topping, my cobbler topping, or even my vegan crisp topping, and follow these general guidelines for baking a crisp or cobbler.

1 Use a 6-cup-capacity oven-safe baking dish sprayed with gluten-free nonstick spray (very important).

2 Macerate the fruit for 30 minutes and pour off the accumulated juices. Save the juice that you pour off and reduce it in a nonstick skillet over medium heat for 5 to 7 minutes (until it is reduced by half) and use it as a topping for the crisp or cobbler when you serve it.

3 Add back in sugar to taste.

4 Use potato starch for thickening—36 grams (¼ cup).

5 You can use frozen fruit, but the end result will have more liquid (you will be skipping the macerating step). Place the frozen fruit in the baking dish with an additional 2 Tablespoons of potato starch—18 grams plus 36 grams equals 54 grams total. You may need to increase the baking time by 5 to 10 minutes.

6 Set the oven temperature to 350°F.

7 The cobblers and crisps with apples bake for 45 minutes.

8 The cobblers and crisps with stone fruits and berries bake for 30 to 40 minutes.

You can improvise with the toppings as well. The cobblers generally have added nuts (½ cup), but you can leave out the nuts and add the same amount of chopped dried fruit or shredded unsweetened coconut instead. The crisp topping includes rolled oats or quinoa flakes. I find that extra-thick rolled oats remain a little too chewy for my taste, so just stick to regular rolled oats. You can also add more nuts, chopped dried fruit, or shredded coconut.

Finally, don't plan on serving a crisp or cobbler directly from the oven. It is best when it has had several hours to congeal. You can always rewarm it gently for serving. It is good with ice cream or plain or Flavored Whipped Cream (see page 256). You can store the crisp or cobbler in the refrigerator for up to a week, covered in plastic wrap. It is my feeling that crisps or cobblers do not freeze well, as they tend to get soggy when they thaw.

CRISP AND COBBLER TUTORIAL

1. Chop the fruit according to the recipe instructions and place in a bowl. Add ¼ cup sugar and set the fruit aside to macerate while you make the crisp or cobbler topping. This method is only necessary with stone fruits, strawberries, rhubarb, and cherries. **2.** Pour off accumulated juice and add back half the juice to the recipe. This keeps the crisp or cobbler from being too wet. Remember to use the additional sugar called for in the recipe, as you will have lost some of the sugar in the macerating process.

apple crisp with cardamom custard

MAKES 8 SERVINGS

A fruit crisp is a quick and easy dessert. For me, it is always about the presentation. I have several beautiful casserole dishes that go from the oven to the table. The cardamom custard elevates this dessert to dinner-party status. To make a pear crisp, substitute 2 pounds pears, peeled, cored, and thickly sliced for the apples.

CARDAMOM CUSTARD

5 cardamom pods

10 fluid ounces (1¼ cups) heavy cream or canned full-fat coconut milk

1 teaspoon vanilla extract

2 egg yolks

1½ teaspoons granulated sugar

1 teaspoon cornstarch

Gluten-free nonstick spray

TOPPING

142 grams (¾ cup) firmly packed brown sugar

45 grams (½ cup) gluten-free oat flour

36 grams (¼ cup) potato starch

26 grams (¼ cup) tapioca starch

2 teaspoons ground cinnamon

1¼ teaspoons double-acting baking powder

½ teaspoon xanthan gum

½ teaspoon fine salt

1 egg

101 grams (1 cup) rolled oats or 100 grams (1 cup) quinoa flakes

⅓ cup melted clarified butter or coconut oil

APPLES

2 pounds apples, peeled, cored, and sliced ¼ inch thick

44 grams (¼ cup) granulated sugar

36 grams (¼ cup) potato starch

2 teaspoons ground cinnamon

1 To make the cardamom custard: Grind the cardamom pods to a powder using a mortar and pestle or spice grinder. Place a heavy saucepan over medium heat and add the cardamom, cream, and vanilla. Bring to a boil, then reduce the heat and simmer for 3 minutes. Set aside to cool slightly, then strain into a small bowl using a fine-mesh sieve.

2 Whisk the egg yolks, granulated sugar, and cornstarch together in a large bowl. Pour in the warm cream mixture, whisking constantly. Pour the combined mixture back into the saucepan and cook over low heat for 6 to 8 minutes, stirring continuously, until the custard thickens. Pour into a bowl and place a piece of plastic wrap directly on top of the custard to keep it from forming a skin. Refrigerate until ready to use.

3 Preheat the oven to 350°F. Spray a 6-cup oven-safe baking dish with gluten-free nonstick spray. Place the baking dish on a baking sheet.

4 To make the topping: In a large bowl, whisk together the brown sugar, oat flour, potato starch, tapioca starch, cinnamon, baking powder, xanthan gum, and salt. Add the egg and stir to mix well. Using wet fingers, incorporate the rolled oats. Pour the clarified butter over the oat mixture and blend with your fingers until well incorporated.

5 To make the apples: In a large bowl, mix together the apples, granulated sugar, potato starch, and cinnamon (this does not need to macerate). Place the apple mixture in the prepared dish. Crumble the topping over the apples in a nice even layer.

6 Bake for about 40 minutes, until the apples are tender and the topping is golden. Let sit for 20 to 30 minutes, until the juices congeal, and serve warm with the cardamom custard.

Note: Leftovers will keep in the refrigerator for about 4 days. Rewarm in a 300°F oven for 15 to 20 minutes.

blueberry crisp

You can be playful with this recipe. It will work with almost any berry or any combination of berries. Blueberries typically don't lose much juice in macerating. If you are using other kinds of berries, especially strawberries, just be sure to macerate the berries for a while (30 minutes) and remove some of the excess juice. Sometimes I save the juices from the macerated fruit, cook them down in a small nonstick skillet until reduced by about half (5 or 7 minutes; keep an eye on it), and serve the warm syrup over the crisp at room temperature.

Gluten-free nonstick spray

TOPPING

142 grams (¾ cup) firmly packed brown sugar

45 grams (½ cup) gluten-free oat flour

36 grams (¼ cup) potato starch

26 grams (¼ cup) tapioca starch

2 teaspoons ground cinnamon

1¼ teaspoons double-acting baking powder

½ teaspoon xanthan gum

½ teaspoon fine salt

1 egg

101 grams (1 cup) rolled oats or 100 grams (1 cup) quinoa flakes

⅓ cup melted clarified butter or coconut oil

BLUEBERRIES

28 to 30 ounces (5¼ cups) frozen blueberries

87 grams (½ cup) granulated sugar

36 grams (¼ cup) potato starch

1 Preheat the oven to 350°F. Spray a 6-cup oven-safe baking dish with gluten-free nonstick spray. Place the baking dish on a baking sheet.

2 To make the topping: In a large bowl, whisk together the brown sugar, oat flour, potato starch, tapioca starch, cinnamon, baking powder, xanthan gum, and salt. Add the egg and stir to mix well (the mixture will be wet and sticky). Using wet fingers, incorporate the rolled oats. Pour the clarified butter over the oat mixture and blend with your fingers until the butter is well incorporated.

3 To make the blueberries: In a small bowl, mix together the blueberries, granulated sugar, and potato starch until well combined. Place the blueberries in the bottom of the prepared dish. Crumble the topping over the blueberries in a nice even layer.

4 Bake for 30 minutes, or until the blueberries are tender and the topping is golden. Let sit for 20 to 30 minutes, until the juices congeal, and then serve.

Note: Leftovers will keep in the refrigerator for about 4 days. Rewarm in a 300°F oven for 15 to 20 minutes.

vegan strawberry and rhubarb crisp

MAKES 8 SERVINGS

You can use this same vegan crisp topping on any berry. Just be sure to macerate the berries for a while and remove some of the excess juice. If rhubarb is not in season, feel free to use any other berry by weight. You can also use frozen rhubarb (don't thaw it first), but it will require a little extra baking time, about 5 minutes.

¼ cup orange juice

2 Tablespoons flaxseed meal

Gluten-free nonstick spray

FRUIT

16 ounces (3 cups) strawberries, stemmed and quartered

2 stalks rhubarb, each 12 to 14 inches and cut into 1-inch chunks

87 grams (½ cup) granulated sugar

36 grams (¼ cup) potato starch

1 teaspoon ground cardamom

VEGAN CRISP TOPPING

142 grams (¾ cup) firmly packed brown sugar

45 grams (½ cup) gluten-free oat flour

36 grams (¼ cup) potato starch

26 grams (¼ cup) tapioca starch

2 teaspoons ground cinnamon

1¼ teaspoons double-acting baking powder

½ teaspoon xanthan gum

½ teaspoon fine salt

202 grams (2 cups) rolled oats or 200 grams (2 cups) quinoa flakes

⅓ cup melted coconut oil

1 In a small mixing bowl, whisk together the orange juice and flaxseed meal. Set aside to hydrate while you prepare the fruit and topping.

2 Preheat the oven to 350°F. Spray a 6-cup oven-safe baking dish with gluten-free nonstick spray. Place the baking dish on a baking sheet.

3 To make the fruit: In a large bowl, combine the strawberries, rhubarb, and granulated sugar and mix until well incorporated. Let this sit to macerate while you make the topping.

4 To make the vegan crisp topping: In a large bowl, whisk together the brown sugar, oat flour, potato starch, tapioca starch, cinnamon, baking powder, xanthan gum, and salt. Add the hydrated flaxseed meal and stir to mix well (the mixture will be wet and sticky). Using wet fingers, incorporate the rolled oats. Pour the coconut oil over the oat mixture and blend with your fingers until the oil is well incorporated.

5 Drain off the juice that has accumulated around the fruit, add the potato starch and cardamom, and mix together until well incorporated. Place the fruit mixture in the prepared dish. Crumble the topping loosely over the top of the fruit in a nice even layer.

6 Bake for about 40 minutes, until the fruit is tender and the topping is golden. Let the crisp sit for 15 to 20 minutes before serving. The juices need a chance to thicken.

Note: Leftovers will keep in the refrigerator for about 4 days. Rewarm in a 300°F oven for 15 to 20 minutes.

apple and raspberry cobbler

MAKES 8 SERVINGS

Gluten-free nonstick spray

FRUIT

3 Granny Smith apples, cored, peeled, and sliced ¼ inch thick

6 ounces (1 cup) raspberries, fresh or frozen

88 grams (½ cup) granulated sugar

36 grams (¼ cup) potato starch

1 Tablespoon lemon zest (from 1 lemon)

TOPPING

60 grams (½ cup) sorghum flour

45 grams (½ cup) almond flour or gluten free oat flour

34 grams (¼ cup) sweet rice flour

24 grams (3 Tablespoons) potato starch

2 Tablespoons granulated sugar

1 teaspoon double-acting baking powder

½ teaspoon xanthan gum

¼ teaspoon baking soda

¼ teaspoon fine salt

4 Tablespoons (½ stick) cold unsalted butter or Earth Balance Vegan Buttery Sticks, cut into 8 slices

¼ cup slivered almonds

¼ cup buttermilk (see note, page 26)

1 egg

2 teaspoons almond extract

1 Tablespoon turbinado sugar, to finish

This recipe is great for a casual evening at home. If you want to dress it up for a dinner party, try making individual servings in oven-safe ramekins. It always seems a little more special when you get an individual dessert. Serve it plain, with ice cream, or with plain or Flavored Whipped Cream (page 256).

1 Preheat the oven to 350°F. Spray a 6-cup oven-safe baking dish with gluten-free nonstick spray. Place the baking dish on a baking sheet.

2 To make the fruit: Place the apples, raspberries, granulated sugar, potato starch, and lemon zest in the baking dish and mix together until well incorporated (this does not need to macerate).

3 To make the topping: In a food processor, pulse together the sorghum flour, almond flour, sweet rice flour, potato starch, granulated sugar, baking powder, xanthan gum, baking soda, and salt until well combined. Scatter the butter pieces over the top of the dry ingredients and pulse until the mixture is crumbly and resembles coarse meal. Transfer the flour mixture to a mixing bowl and mix in the slivered almonds. (You can do the recipe up to this point and refrigerate, covered, overnight. Add the liquid ingredients in the morning and proceed as directed.)

4 In a small bowl, whisk together the buttermilk, egg, and almond extract. Add the buttermilk mixture to the dry ingredients and mix with a rubber scraper until the dough starts to come together.

5 Dollop the topping over the fruit mixture and smooth with dampened hands. Sprinkle the turbinado sugar over the topping. Bake for 35 to 40 minutes. Individual baked servings usually take about 30 minutes to bake, depending on the size of the vessel. Remove from the oven to a wire cooling rack. Let sit for about 10 minutes, until the juices congeal, and then serve.

Note: Leftovers will keep in the refrigerator for about 4 days. Rewarm in a 300°F oven for 15 to 20 minutes.

summer fruit cobbler

MAKES 8 SERVINGS

Gluten-free nonstick spray

FRUIT

1 pound stone fruit, each pitted and cut into quarters

½ pound cherries, fresh or frozen, pitted and cut in half

132 grams (¾ cup) granulated sugar

36 grams (¼ cup) potato starch

1 Tablespoon lemon zest (from 1 lemon)

TOPPING

60 grams (½ cup) sorghum flour

45 grams (½ cup) almond flour or gluten-free oat flour

34 grams (¼ cup) sweet rice flour

24 grams (3 Tablespoons) potato starch

2 Tablespoons granulated sugar

1 teaspoon double-acting baking powder

½ teaspoon xanthan gum

¼ teaspoon baking soda

¼ teaspoon fine salt

4 Tablespoons (½ stick) cold unsalted butter or Earth Balance Vegan Buttery Sticks, cut into 8 slices

¼ cup sliced almonds

¼ cup buttermilk (see note, page 26)

1 egg

2 teaspoons almond extract

1 Tablespoon turbinado sugar, to finish

You can use any combination of stone fruits in this recipe. Just be sure to macerate the fruit for a while and remove some of the excess juice. I would encourage you to weigh your fruit at the market or at home. This way you can use any combination of stone fruit that you may want. The weight will give you the best success with this recipe.

1 Preheat the oven to 350°F. Spray a 6-cup oven-safe baking dish with gluten-free nonstick spray. Place the baking dish on a baking sheet.

2 To make the fruit: In a large bowl, combine the stone fruit, cherries, and granulated sugar and mix until well incorporated. Let this sit to macerate while you make the topping.

3 To make the topping: In a food processor, pulse together the sorghum flour, almond flour, sweet rice flour, potato starch, granulated sugar, baking powder, xanthan gum, baking soda, and salt until well combined. Scatter butter pieces over the top of the dry ingredients and pulse until the mixture is crumbly and resembles coarse meal. Transfer the flour mixture to a mixing bowl and mix in the sliced almonds. (You can do the recipe up to this point and refrigerate, covered, overnight. Add the liquid ingredients in the morning and proceed as directed.)

4 In a small bowl, whisk together the buttermilk, egg, and almond extract. Add the buttermilk mixture to the dry ingredients and mix with a rubber scraper until the dough starts to come together.

5 Drain off the juice that has accumulated around the fruit and place the fruit in the prepared dish. Add the potato starch and lemon zest and mix together until well incorporated.

6 Dollop the topping over the fruit mixture and smooth with dampened hands. Sprinkle the turbinado sugar over the topping. Bake for 35 to 40 minutes. Remove from the oven to a wire cooling rack. Let sit for 20 to 30 minutes, until the juices congeal, and then serve.

Note: Leftovers will keep in the refrigerator for about 4 days. Rewarm in a 300°F oven for 15 to 20 minutes.

plum cobbler with pine nut topping

MAKES 8 SERVINGS

You can substitute any stone fruits in this recipe. Just be sure to macerate the fruit for a while and remove some of the excess juice. When buying fruit, it is best to adhere to the weight given in the recipe.

Gluten-free nonstick spray

FRUIT

2 pounds plums pitted and cut into ½-inch wedges

132 grams (¾ cup) granulated sugar

36 grams (¼ cup) potato starch

1 Tablespoon lemon zest (from 1 lemon)

TOPPING

60 grams (½ cup) sorghum flour

45 grams (½ cup) almond flour or gluten-free oat flour

34 grams (¼ cup) sweet rice flour

24 grams (3 Tablespoons) potato starch

2 Tablespoons granulated sugar

1 teaspoon double-acting baking powder

½ teaspoon xanthan gum

¼ teaspoon baking soda

¼ teaspoon fine salt

4 Tablespoons (½ stick) cold unsalted butter or Earth Balance Vegan Buttery Sticks, cut into 8 slices

½ cup pine nuts, toasted

¼ cup buttermilk (see note, page 26)

1 egg

2 teaspoons vanilla extract

1 Tablespoon turbinado sugar, to finish

1 Preheat the oven to 350°F. Spray a 2-cup oven-safe baking dish with gluten-free nonstick spray. Place the baking dish on a baking sheet.

2 To make the fruit: In a large bowl, combine the plums and granulated sugar and mix until well incorporated. Let this sit to macerate while you make the topping.

3 To make the topping: In a food processor, pulse together the sorghum flour, almond flour, sweet rice flour, potato starch, granulated sugar, baking powder, xanthan gum, baking soda, and salt until well combined. Scatter the butter pieces over the top of the dry ingredients and pulse until the mixture is crumbly and resembles coarse meal. Transfer the flour mixture to a mixing bowl and mix in the pine nuts. (You can do the recipe to this point and refrigerate, covered, overnight. Add the liquid ingredients in the morning and proceed as directed.)

4 In a small bowl, whisk together the buttermilk, egg, and vanilla. Add the buttermilk mixture to the dry ingredients and mix with a rubber scraper until the dough starts to come together.

5 Pour off half of the juices that have accumulated in the bowl with the plums, add the potato starch and lemon zest, and mix thoroughly. Spoon the plums into the prepared baking dish.

6 Dollop the topping over the fruit in an even layer and smooth with dampened hands. Sprinkle the turbinado sugar over the topping and bake for 10 to 15 minutes. Remove from the oven to a wire cooling rack. Let sit for 20 to 30 minutes, until the juices congeal, and then serve.

Note: Leftovers will keep in the refrigerator for about 4 days. Rewarm in a 300°F oven for 15 to 20 minutes.

YEASTED BREADS & ROLLS

TIPS FOR SUCCESS

It was through much trial and error and eventual success that I was able to learn the tips and tricks I am sharing with you on handling gluten-free baking with yeast.

Without gluten strands, yeast dough has a tough time holding onto the gases created in the "rise" of the bread—the bread rarely achieves the beautiful domed top that we see in wheat bread. Sometimes a bread can come out of the oven looking glorious but then sinks as it cools. In my other baking, I found that the leavenings other than yeast did a much better job of expanding the baked goods. My banana bread uses baking soda and baking powder, and I always have a beautiful dome and crumb. I gave up the fight and, for a time, I made my bread with just baking powder and no yeast. That recipe is just so incredibly easy (see my Weeknight Bread on page 239).

I found that the loaves with baking powder were much prettier, but I missed the yeasty flavor. My breakthrough came when I lowered my expectations of the yeast and started adding baking soda into the mix. Baking powder is not the right answer for yeasted bread because baking powder starts to work immediately. Because we need to let the dough rise in the pan for 50 minutes, the baking powder loses its effectiveness during that long rest. Baking soda was the better choice because it does its job with the heat of the oven and the gases that are released later in the baking process. This means that an additional lift happens toward the end of the baking. Now all my breads contain both baking soda and yeast. This new generation of loaves has beautiful domes, a tender crumb, and a complex yeasty flavor.

Here are some of my most important tips for baking gluten-free yeasted breads.

WATER TEMPERATURE IS IMPORTANT. When I call for warm water in the recipes that follow, that means 90° to 95°F. Don't use boiling water, which is too hot and can kill the yeast. The general rule of thumb is that if it is too hot for your fingers, it is too hot for the yeast.

USE SMALLER PANS FOR SMALLER LOAVES. Gluten-free bread works best when it does not exceed the size of a 1½-pound loaf. That means that the recipe should have no more than 3 to 3½ cups of flour and 1¼ to 2 cups of liquid. Remember that surface tension is always working against us in gluten-free baking, so invest in two 8½ by 4½-inch loaf pans and bake all of your loaves in these pans.

SPRAY YOUR PAN. Spray the pan with a light coating of gluten-free nonstick canola or coconut oil. I also spray the top of the loaf or brush it with olive oil before I place it in the oven. This allows the surface to remain pliable and expand while it bakes. Spraying the top also acts as a binder if you are sprinkling seeds, nuts, or salt on it.

SMOOTH THE SURFACE OF YOUR BATTER. Push the batter evenly into your pan and spend some time smoothing the surface. You want to make it slightly dome-shaped in the middle (refer to the tutorial on page 218). Gluten-free dough is not as forgiving as dough made with wheat flour. If you put it in the pan all lumpy and bumpy, your finished loaf will also be lumpy and bumpy.

ALWAYS VENT YOUR DOUGH. I use a sharp paring knife to make a small incision along the entire length of the loaf. Make sure it is ½ inch in depth (see the tutorial on page 218). The venting allows steam to escape—your loaf can expand freely toward the top of the pan.

THE DOUGH SHOULD RISE JUST TO THE TOP OF THE PAN. Let the dough rise in a draft-free area, such as the top of the refrigerator, the clothes washer, or a turned-off oven. This will happen in 50 to 60 minutes. The dough should look tight and smooth when you put it in the oven. There have been times when I have let the dough rise for too long, and it starts to look flabby and deflated (see page 218 for an example). Don't worry! There is a fix. Place the dough back in the stand mixer bowl with the paddle attachment in place, add 1 teaspoon of baking powder, and give it a good mix for 2 minutes. Respray the loaf pan, place the dough in the pan, then reshape, and re-vent. Place in the oven immediately and bake for the required time.

DO NOT OPEN THE OVEN. Do not be tempted to open the oven door. Gluten-free dough is very moody. It needs to bake uninhibited by drafts. It is fine to tent a piece of foil big enough to cover the loaf lightly over the pan. It should not be pressed down to seal off the loaf pan. Spray a light nonstick cooking spray on the side facing the loaf to ensure that the bread batter will not stick to the foil.

TAKE THE BREAD'S TEMPERATURE. Once the time for baking is up, tip the loaf out of the pan and take the temperature to be sure that you don't have a soggy interior; the internal temperature should be between 205° and 210°F. Place your thermometer into the side of the loaf and toward the middle. If it is not up to temperature, simply place the loaf on a parchment hammock (no pan), return it to the oven, and continue to bake for another 5 minutes; then check the temperature again.

REMOVE BREAD FROM THE PAN. Once the loaf is baked, remove the bread from the pan as soon as possible. The longer gluten-free bread sits in a loaf pan, the more it will steam and get soggy. I simply set the loaf pan on its side, let the bread slide forward, and then sit the bread back upright out of the pan. This style of bread needs to release its steam for a good long while for optimal texture. Let it sit out for several hours on a wire cooling rack.

FREEZE YOUR BREAD. I always slice my loaves of bread once they are completely cooled. I place the entire loaf of slices in a resealable bag or other tightly sealed container and freeze. I use the bread directly from the freezer. A few minutes in the toaster thaws it for a sandwich. The bread does not really keep very well outside of the freezer.

1. This photo shows dough that is smoothed and vented. **2.** The second photo shows what overproofed bread looks like. In the chapter opener, I refer to it as flabby and I give a fix for rescuing the bread (see page 217).

All of the bread recipes in this book, except the brioche recipes, can be made into dinner rolls. It is just a matter of using your muffin pan instead of the loaf pan. All of the recipes will make 12 dinner rolls if you are using a standard 12-cup muffin pan. I like to start by weighing the full amount of mixed dough and dividing the dough by 12. Dinner rolls will rise in 34 to 40 minutes. Bake them at 350°F for 25 to 30 minutes. The internal temperature will be 205° to 210°F. Follow the instructions for bread for cooling, freezing, and storing the dinner rolls.

Method #1 – Roll the portioned dough into a tight ball and place in muffin cup; let rise. **Method #2** – Divide each portion of dough into 3 equal-sized balls and place all three in a standard muffin cup; let rise. **Method #3** – Roll each portion into a tight ball and cut into three horizontal slices. Dip each slice in melted butter or clarified butter and place all three slices back together in the same configuration into a standard muffin cup; let rise.

master bread with four variations

The master recipe has multiple variations, and beyond the ones I've provided, the flavor possibilities are endless. In the morning, I like toast and tea, and the currant-cinnamon version of this bread is my favorite. The savory variations of this bread are great served as dinner rolls with a soup or stew. (See page 218–219 for the dinner roll instructions.) The vegetable purees in this book are interchangeable. Just be sure to substitute by weight.

Gluten-free nonstick spray

174 grams (1¼ cups) potato starch

144 grams (1 cup plus
2 Tablespoons) sorghum flour

82 grams (¾ cup) tapioca starch

2 Tablespoons psyllium husk powder

2 Tablespoons whole-grain teff (optional)

1 Tablespoon firmly packed brown sugar

2¼ teaspoons (one ¼-ounce package) instant yeast

1 teaspoon fine salt, plus more to finish

½ teaspoon baking soda

11 fluid ounces (1¼ cups plus 2 Tablespoons) warm water

2 Tablespoons melted and slightly cooled clarified butter, coconut oil, canola oil, or olive oil, plus more to finish

133 grams (½ cup) sweet potato puree (see page 28)

1 Spray an 8½ by 4½-inch loaf pan with gluten-free nonstick spray.

2 In the bowl of a stand mixer fitted with the paddle attachment, whisk together the potato starch, sorghum flour, tapioca starch, psyllium husk powder, teff (if using), brown sugar, yeast, salt, and baking soda until well incorporated.

3 In a 2-cup liquid measuring cup, combine the water and clarified butter.

4 Add the water-butter mixture and the sweet potato puree to the mixing bowl and mix on very low speed until the mixture comes together into a smooth, dense batter, 20 to 30 seconds. It is at this point that you can add by hand, or with a very low speed on your mixer, any of the mix-ins listed in the variations below.

5 While the batter is still in the mixing bowl, push it together with a rubber spatula until it approximates the length and width of the loaf pan. Slide the dough gently into the prepared loaf pan. With a dampened rubber spatula, press the dough down into the corners of the pan and smooth the top. Slide the spatula along each of the long sides, creating a domed center. This removes air pockets and prevents holes from forming in the finished loaf. Brush the top with clarified butter. Using a very sharp paring knife, make a ½-inch-deep cut down the length of the loaf, 6 to 7 inches long. Sprinkle lightly with salt (see the how-to photos on page 218).

6 Set the loaf pan aside in a warm place to rise for about 50 minutes and preheat the oven to 350°F. The dough should rise to the top edge of the loaf pan. Set a timer and check on it. If the loaf overproofs, it will not rise properly and dome in the oven (read about rescuing overproofed loaves on page 217).

7 Bake for 75 to 80 minutes, until the internal temperature reaches 205° to 210°F on an instant read thermometer and the loaf has a slight hollow sound when you tap on the top of it.

8 Transfer the loaf pan to a wire cooling rack and immediately tip the pan onto its side, letting the bread slide out of the pan. Carefully sit the loaf upright—this releases the steam and keeps the bread from getting soggy on the bottom. Cool to room temperature before serving, about 1 hour.

Note: Store leftovers in the freezer. To freeze, let the bread cool to room temperature, then slice. Store the slices in a resealable bag in the freezer for 3 weeks. Toast the bread directly from the freezer, or let it defrost before using.

Variations

Bacon-Gouda Bread: Finely chop two slices of crisp cooked thick-cut bacon and add it along with ½ cup grated aged Gouda to the dough in step 4. Bake as directed.

Currant-Cinnamon Bread: Add ½ cup currants and 2 teaspoons ground cinnamon to the dough in step 4. Bake as directed.

Seeded Loaf: Add 2 Tablespoons poppy seeds, 2 Tablespoons sesame seeds, 2 teaspoons nigella seeds, and 1 teaspoon onion salt or garlic salt to the dough in step 4. Bake as directed.

Maple-Oatmeal Bread: Add ½ cup rolled oats and 1 teaspoon maple extract to the dough in step 4. Bake as directed.

sandwich bread

This is sandwich bread in its truest form: a perfect blank canvas for any and all sandwich creations. After it cools, slice it and freeze it in a resealable bag. Just thaw slices for a few minutes in the toaster before using.

Gluten-free nonstick spray

174 grams (1¼ cups) potato starch

144 grams (1 cup plus 2 Tablespoons) sorghum flour

82 grams (¾ cup) tapioca starch

2 Tablespoons psyllium husk powder

1 Tablespoon firmly packed brown sugar

2¼ teaspoons (one ¼-ounce package) instant yeast

1 teaspoon fine salt, plus more to finish

½ teaspoon baking soda

10 fluid ounces (1¼ cups) warm water

2 Tablespoons melted and slightly cooled clarified butter, coconut oil, canola oil, or olive oil, plus more to finish

133 grams (½ cup) mashed potatoes (see page 28)

1 Spray an 8½ by 4½-inch loaf pan with gluten-free nonstick spray.

2 In the bowl of a stand mixer fitted with the paddle attachment, whisk together the potato starch, sorghum flour, tapioca starch, psyllium husk powder, brown sugar, yeast, salt, and baking soda.

3 In a 2-cup liquid measuring cup, combine the water and clarified butter.

4 Add the water-butter mixture and the mashed potatoes to the mixing bowl and mix on very low speed until the mixture comes together into a smooth, dense batter, 20 to 30 seconds.

5 While the batter is still in the mixing bowl, push it together with a rubber spatula until it approximates the length and width of the loaf pan. Slide the dough gently into the prepared loaf pan. With a dampened spatula, press the dough down into the corners of the pan and smooth the top. Slide the spatula along each of the long sides, creating a domed center. This removes air pockets and prevents holes from forming in the finished loaf. Brush the top with clarified butter. Using a very sharp paring knife, make a ½-inch-deep cut down the length of the loaf, 6 to 7 inches long. Sprinkle lightly with salt (see the how-to photos on page 218).

6 Set the loaf pan aside in a warm place to rise for about 50 minutes and preheat the oven to 350°F. The dough should rise to the top edge of the loaf pan. Set a timer and check on it. If the loaf overproofs, it will not rise properly and dome in the oven (read about rescuing overproofed loaves on page 217).

7 Bake for 75 to 80 minutes, until the internal temperature reaches 205° to 210°F on an instant-read thermometer and the loaf has a slight hollow sound when you tap on the top of it.

8 Transfer the loaf to a wire cooling rack and immediately tip the pan onto its side, letting the bread slide out of the pan. Carefully sit the loaf upright—this releases the steam and keeps the bread from getting soggy on the bottom. Cool to room temperature before serving, about 1 hour.

Note: Store leftovers in the freezer. To freeze, let the bread cool to room temperature, then slice. Store the slices in a resealable bag in the freezer for 3 weeks. Toast the bread directly from the freezer, or let it defrost before using.

sourdough bread

MAKES ONE 8½ BY 4½-INCH LOAF

My secret to adding the familiar sour tang of a starter comes from kombucha. In the past, I have made a gluten-free sourdough starter from scratch, but it needs to be kept in the refrigerator and fed every week. Kombucha makes the whole process a lot easier. The sour flavor comes through without being overly acidic. My favorite kombucha is GT's Kombucha, original flavor, organic and raw.

Gluten-free nonstick spray

174 grams (1¼ cups) potato starch

144 grams (1 cup plus 2 Tablespoons) sorghum flour

82 grams (¾ cup) tapioca starch

2 Tablespoons psyllium husk powder

2 Tablespoons firmly packed brown sugar

2¼ teaspoons (one ¼-ounce package) instant yeast

1 teaspoon fine salt, plus more to finish

½ teaspoon baking soda

11 fluid ounces (1¼ cups plus 2 Tablespoons) unflavored kombucha

2 Tablespoons melted and slightly cooled clarified butter, coconut oil, canola oil, or olive oil, plus more to finish

133 grams (½ cup) mashed potatoes (see page 28)

1 Spray an 8½ by 4½-inch loaf pan with gluten-free nonstick spray.

2 In the bowl of a stand mixer fitted with the paddle attachment, whisk together the potato starch, sorghum flour, tapioca starch, psyllium husk powder, brown sugar, yeast, salt, and baking soda.

3 In a 2-cup liquid measuring cup, combine the kombucha and clarified butter.

4 Add the kombucha-butter mixture and the mashed potatoes to the mixing bowl and mix on very low speed until the mixture comes together into a smooth, dense batter, 20 to 30 seconds.

5 While the batter is still in the mixing bowl, push it together with a rubber spatula until it approximates the length and width of the loaf pan. Slide the dough gently into the prepared loaf pan. With a dampened spatula, press the dough down into the corners of the pan and smooth the top. Slide the spatula along each of the long sides, creating a domed center. This removes air pockets and prevents holes from forming in the finished loaf. Brush the top with clarified butter. Using a very sharp paring knife, make a ½-inch-deep cut down the length of the loaf, 6 to 7 inches long. Sprinkle lightly with salt (see the how-to photos on page 218).

6 Set the loaf pan aside in a warm place to rise for about 50 minutes and preheat the oven to 350°F. The dough should rise to the top edge of the loaf pan. Set a timer and check on it. If the loaf overproofs, it will not rise properly and dome in the oven (read about rescuing overproofed loaves on page 217).

continued

sourdough bread, continued

7 Bake for 80 to 85 minutes, until the internal temperature reaches 205° to 210°F on an instant-read thermometer and the loaf has a slight hollow sound when you tap on the top of it.

8 Transfer the loaf to a wire cooling rack and immediately tip the pan onto its side, letting the bread slide out of the pan. Carefully sit the loaf upright—this releases the steam and keeps the bread from getting soggy on the bottom. Cool to room temperature before serving, about 1 hour.

Note: Store leftovers in the freezer. To freeze, let the bread cool to room temperature, then slice. Store the slices in a resealable bag in the freezer for 3 weeks. Toast the bread directly from the freezer, or let it defrost before using.

pumpkin bread with olives, parmesan, and rosemary

MAKES ONE 9 BY 5-INCH LOAF

This recipe makes the biggest loaf in this chapter because of the extra goodies that are in the finished bread. You can still use the 8¹/₂ by 4¹/₂-inch loaf pan that I recommend you use for all of the other breads, but if you have a 9 by 5-inch loaf pan, you can use that as well. If you are not a fan of olives, just leave them out. Any aged cheese will work. I love to make this recipe with grated aged Gouda and without the olives as dinner rolls (see page 219) to have with a winter stew or soup.

Gluten-free nonstick spray

174 grams (1¼ cups) potato starch

144 grams (1 cup plus 2 Tablespoons) sorghum flour

82 grams (¾ cup) tapioca starch

2 Tablespoons psyllium husk powder

2 Tablespoons whole-grain teff (optional)

1 Tablespoon firmly packed brown sugar

2¼ teaspoons (one ¼-ounce package) instant yeast

1 teaspoon fine salt, plus more to finish

½ teaspoon baking soda

11 fluid ounces (1¼ cups plus 2 Tablespoons) warm water

2 Tablespoons melted and slightly cooled clarified butter, coconut oil, canola oil, or olive oil, plus more to finish

133 grams (½ cup) pumpkin puree

5 ounces (½ cup) dry-cured olives or green olives, pitted and halved

70 grams (¾ cup) grated Parmesan

1 Tablespoon fresh rosemary, minced

1 Spray a 9 by 5-inch loaf pan with gluten-free nonstick spray.

2 In the bowl of a stand mixer fitted with the paddle attachment, whisk together the potato starch, sorghum flour, tapioca starch, psyllium husk powder, teff (if using), brown sugar, yeast, salt, and baking soda.

3 In a 2-cup liquid measuring cup, combine the water and clarified butter.

4 Add the water-butter mixture and the pumpkin puree to the mixing bowl and mix on very low speed until the mixture comes together into a smooth, dense batter, 20 to 30 seconds. Add the olives, Parmesan, and rosemary and mix on a very low speed until the ingredients are fully incorporated.

5 While the batter is still in the mixing bowl, push it together with a rubber spatula until it approximates the length and width of the loaf pan. Slide the dough gently into the prepared loaf pan. With a dampened spatula, press the dough down into the corners of the pan and smooth the top. Slide the spatula along each of the long sides, creating a domed center. This removes air pockets and prevents holes from forming in the finished loaf. Brush the top with clarified butter. Using a very sharp paring knife, make a ¹/₂-inch-deep cut down the length of the loaf, 6 to 7 inches long. Sprinkle lightly with salt (see the how-to photos on page 218).

continued

6 Set the loaf pan aside in a warm place to rise for about 50 minutes and preheat the oven to 350°F. The dough should rise to the top edge of the loaf pan. Set a timer and check on it. If the loaf overproofs, it will not rise properly and dome in the oven (read about rescuing overproofed loaves on page 217).

7 Bake for 75 to 80 minutes, until the internal temperature reaches 205° to 210°F on an instant-read thermometer and the loaf has a slight hollow sound when you tap on the top of it.

8 Transfer the loaf to a wire cooling rack and immediately tip the pan onto its side, letting the bread slide out of the pan. Carefully sit the loaf upright—this releases the steam and keeps the bread from getting soggy on the bottom. Cool to room temperature before serving, about 1 hour.

Note: Store leftovers in the freezer. To freeze, let the bread cool to room temperature, then slice. Store the slices in a resealable bag in the freezer for 3 weeks. Toast the bread directly from the freezer, or let it defrost before using.

pumpernickel (brown) bread

MAKES ONE 8½ BY 4½-INCH LOAF

Pumpernickel is a brown bread with a complex flavor mix of molasses, cocoa powder, and caraway. Not everyone likes caraway, so I would suggest that you taste the seed before adding it. My version leaves out the rye flour, which is a gluten grain, but you won't be able to tell the difference from the real deli rye bread. For extra interest and texture, add ½ cup of roasted unsalted sunflower seeds. This bread is great toasted and spread with orange marmalade for breakfast, but it also adapts well to your favorite pressed sandwich for lunch or dinner.

Gluten-free nonstick spray

174 grams (1¼ cups) potato starch

144 grams (1 cup plus 2 Tablespoons) sorghum flour

82 grams (¾ cup) tapioca starch

2 Tablespoons psyllium husk powder

2 Tablespoons unsweetened cocoa powder

2 Tablespoons firmly packed brown sugar

1 Tablespoon orange zest (from 1 navel orange) (optional)

2¼ teaspoons (one ¼-ounce package) instant yeast

1 teaspoon caraway seeds (optional)

1 teaspoon fine salt

½ teaspoon baking soda

9 fluid ounces (1 cup plus 2 Tablespoons) warm water

2 Tablespoons melted and slightly cooled clarified butter, coconut oil, canola oil, or olive oil, plus more to finish

133 grams (½ cup) sweet potato puree (see page 28)

85 grams (¼ cup) molasses

1 Spray an 8½ by 4½-inch loaf pan with gluten-free nonstick spray.

2 In the bowl of a stand mixer fitted with the paddle attachment, whisk together the potato starch, sorghum flour, tapioca starch, psyllium husk powder, cocoa powder, brown sugar, orange zest (if using), yeast, caraway seeds (if using), salt, and baking soda.

3 In a 2-cup liquid measuring cup, combine the water and clarified butter.

4 In a 1-cup measuring cup, combine the sweet potato puree and the molasses.

5 Add the water-butter mixture and the sweet potato puree–molasses mixture to the bowl and mix on very low speed until the mixture comes together into a smooth, dense batter, 20 to 30 seconds.

6 While the batter is still in the mixing bowl, push it together with a rubber spatula until it approximates the length and width of the loaf pan. Slide the dough gently into the prepared loaf pan. With a dampened spatula, press the dough down into the corners of the pan and smooth the top. Slide the spatula along each of the long sides, creating a domed center. This removes air pockets and prevents holes from forming in the finished loaf. Brush the top with clarified butter. Using a very sharp paring knife, make a ½-inch-deep cut down the length of the loaf, 6 to 7 inches long. Sprinkle lightly with salt (see the how-to photos on page 218).

continued

pumpernickel (brown) bread, continued

7 Set the loaf pan aside in a warm place to rise for about 50 minutes and preheat the oven to 350°F. The dough should rise to the top edge of the loaf pan. Set a timer and check on it. If the loaf overproofs, it will not rise properly and dome in the oven (read about rescuing overproofed loaves on page 217).

8 Bake for 70 to 75 minutes, until the internal temperature reaches 205° to 210°F on an instant-read thermometer and the loaf has a slight hollow sound when you tap on top of it.

9 Transfer the loaf to a wire cooling rack and immediately tip the pan onto its side and let the bread slide out of the pan. Carefully sit the loaf upright—this releases the steam and keeps the bread from getting soggy. Cool to room temperature before serving, about 1 hour.

Note: Store leftovers in the freezer. To freeze, let the bread cool to room temperature, then slice. Store the slices in a resealable bag in the freezer for 3 weeks. Toast the bread directly from the freezer, or let it defrost before using.

brioche

MAKES 6 TO 8 SERVINGS

Brioche is a soft, cakey egg- and butter-filled bread. My version uses far less butter and eggs than other recipes. Because this bread does not contain gluten strands, it does not hold onto the amount of butter and egg that is contained in a traditional brioche. I also did away with the long rise of the traditional brioche. My version is a lot easier to make, yet the flavor still comes through. Be sure to use the tube pan that I recommend (refer to the tutorial on page 236).

Gluten-free nonstick spray

160 grams (1⅓ cups) sorghum flour

72 grams (½ cup) potato starch

58 grams (⅓ cup) granulated sugar

52 grams (½ cup) tapioca starch

1½ teaspoons xanthan gum

2¼ teaspoons (one ¼-ounce package) instant yeast

½ teaspoon baking soda

½ teaspoon fine salt

⅔ cup milk or dairy-free milk, room temperature

3 Tablespoons melted and slightly cooled clarified butter or coconut oil

2 eggs plus 2 egg yolks, room temperature

1 Spray a 6-cup tube pan or Bundt pan with gluten-free nonstick spray.

2 In the bowl of a stand mixer fitted with the paddle attachment, whisk together the sorghum flour, potato starch, granulated sugar, tapioca starch, xanthan gum, yeast, baking soda, and salt.

3 In a 2-cup liquid measuring cup, combine the milk and clarified butter.

4 Add the milk-butter mixture, eggs, and egg yolks to the bowl. Mix on very low speed until the mixture comes together into a smooth batter, about 1 minute. Increase to high speed and mix for 30 seconds more to incorporate some air.

5 Transfer the dough to the prepared pan. With a dampened spatula, press the dough down into the corners of the pan and smooth the top. This removes air pockets and prevents holes from forming in the finished loaf.

6 Set the pan aside at room temperature until the dough has doubled in size, 50 to 60 minutes. Do not let the dough rise above the edge of the pan. While the dough is rising, preheat the oven to 350°F.

7 Once the dough has doubled in size, bake for 20 to 22 minutes, until the internal temperature reaches 205° to 210°F on an instant-read thermometer and the loaf has a slight hollow sound when you tap on top of it.

continued

8 Remove the pan from the oven and let the bread cool in the pan for 10 minutes. Place a wire cooling rack over the top of the pan and invert the bread onto the cooling rack. Cool to room temperature before serving, about 60 minutes.

Note: Store leftovers in the freezer. To freeze, let the bread cool to room temperature, then slice. Store the slices in a resealable bag in the freezer for 3 weeks. Toast the bread directly from the freezer, or let it defrost before using.

Variation

Cinnamon Brioche: To the dry ingredients in step 2, add 1 Tablespoon cinnamon. Continue as indicated in the recipe.

1. The consistency of the brioche dough will be more like a stiff batter, unlike typical brioche dough. **2.** This is the finished proofing height, about ⅔ full. As the brioche bakes, it will rise to the edge of the pan.

chocolate brioche

MAKES 6 TO 8 SERVINGS

This brioche is good eaten plain, but it can also be the star of your favorite bread pudding recipe. Cut it into cubes and use it just as you would any brioche. The only difference is that you shouldn't soak the bread in the egg mixture for very long. Unlike gluten bread, it can lose its texture.

Gluten-free nonstick spray

176 grams (1 cup) granulated sugar

120 grams (1 cup) sorghum flour

72 grams (½ cup) potato starch

52 grams (½ cup) tapioca starch

27 grams (⅓ cup) unsweetened cocoa powder

2¼ teaspoons (one ¼-ounce package) instant yeast

1½ teaspoons xanthan gum

½ teaspoon espresso powder

½ teaspoon baking soda

½ teaspoon fine salt

⅔ cup milk or dairy-free milk, room temperature

3 Tablespoons melted and slightly cooled clarified butter or coconut oil

2 eggs plus 2 egg yolks, room temperature

1 Spray a 6-cup tube pan or Bundt pan with gluten-free nonstick spray.

2 In the bowl of a stand mixer fitted with the paddle attachment, whisk together the granulated sugar, sorghum flour, potato starch, tapioca starch, cocoa powder, yeast, xanthan gum, espresso powder, baking soda, and salt.

3 In a 2-cup liquid measuring cup, whisk together the milk and butter.

4 Add the milk-butter mixture, eggs, and egg yolks to the mixing bowl. Mix on very low speed until the mixture comes together into a smooth batter, about 1 minute. Increase to high speed and mix for 30 seconds more to incorporate some air.

5 Transfer the dough to the prepared pan. With a dampened spatula, press the dough down into the corners of the pan and smooth the top. This removes air pockets and prevents holes from forming in the finished loaf. Set aside for 50 to 60 minutes. The dough will double in size; do not let it rise above the edge of the pan. While the dough is rising, preheat the oven to 350°F.

6 Once the dough has doubled in size, bake for 20 to 22 minutes, until the internal temperature reaches 205° to 210°F on an instant-read thermometer and the loaf has a slight hollow sound when you tap on top of it.

7 Remove the pan from the oven and let the bread cool in the pan for 10 minutes. Place a wire cooling rack over the top of the pan and invert the bread onto the cooling rack. Cool for 20 to 30 minutes and serve.

Note: Store leftovers in the freezer. To freeze, let the bread cool to room temperature, then slice. Store the slices in a resealable bag in the freezer for 3 weeks. Toast the bread directly from the freezer, or let it defrost before using.

weeknight bread

MAKES ONE 8½ BY 4½-INCH LOAF

This is my everyday bread—it is so easy and flavorful, and there is no waiting around for the yeast to activate and rise. I developed this recipe for my good friend Jaime Cid. He is not gluten-intolerant but he does love moist, flavorful bread. This is the bread that I bake for company when I am serving my soup or stew "one-pot wonders." I also like to bake this loaf when I have been invited for dinner. Bringing this bread will ensure that I can have bread with my meal. Try using your favorite gluten-free beer instead of the water called for in the recipe. I think dark gluten-free ale gives the best depth of flavor.

Gluten-free nonstick spray

120 grams (1 cup) sorghum flour

90 grams (½ cup) gluten-free oat flour

72 grams (¾ cup) potato starch

52 grams (½ cup) tapioca starch

½ cup roasted, unsalted sunflower seeds or roasted, unsalted pumpkin seeds, plus more to finish

2 Tablespoons psyllium husk powder

2 Tablespoons firmly packed brown sugar

2 Tablespoons whole-grain teff (optional)

1 teaspoon fine salt, plus more to finish

14 fluid ounces (1¾ cups) water, or 6 fluid ounces (¾ cup) gluten-free beer and 8 fluid ounces (1 cup) water

2 Tablespoons melted and slightly cooled clarified butter, coconut oil, canola oil, or olive oil, plus more to finish

1 Tablespoon double-acting baking powder

1 Preheat the oven to 350°F. Spray an 8½ by 4½-inch loaf pan with gluten-free nonstick spray.

2 In the bowl of a stand mixer fitted with the paddle attachment, whisk together the sorghum flour, oat flour, potato starch, tapioca starch, sunflower seeds, psyllium husk powder, brown sugar, teff (if using), and salt.

3 In a 2-cup liquid measuring cup, combine the water and clarified butter.

4 Add the water-butter mixture to the dry ingredients. Mix on low speed until the mixture comes together into a smooth batter, about 1 minute. Let the batter sit in the mixer at room temperature for about 10 minutes.

5 Add the baking powder. Mix on very low speed until fully incorporated, about 30 seconds. If the dough starts to stiffen and climb up the bowl, stop the mixer and use a rubber spatula to scrape down the sides of the bowl.

continued

6 While the batter is still in the mixing bowl, push it together with a rubber spatula until it approximates the length and width of the loaf pan. Slide the dough gently into the prepared loaf pan. With a dampened spatula, press the dough down into the corners of the pan and smooth the top. Slide the spatula along each of the long sides, creating a domed center. This removes air pockets and prevents holes from forming in the finished loaf. Brush the top with clarified butter. Using a very sharp paring knife, make a ½-inch-deep cut down the length of the loaf, 6 to 7 inches long. Sprinkle lightly with salt (see the how-to photos on page 218).

7 Bake for 65 to 70 minutes, until the internal temperature reaches 205° to 210°F on an instant-read thermometer and the loaf has a slight hollow sound when you tap on top of it.

8 Transfer the loaf to a wire cooling rack and immediately tip the pan onto its side and let the bread slide out of the pan. Carefully sit the loaf upright—this releases the steam and keeps the bread from getting soggy on the bottom. Cool to room temperature before serving, about 1 hour.

Note: Store leftovers in the freezer. To freeze, let the bread cool to room temperature, then slice. Store the slices in a resealable bag in the freezer for 3 weeks. Toast the bread directly from the freezer, or let it defrost before using.

FROSTINGS, GLAZES & TOPPINGS

I decided to put all of the frostings, glazes, and garnishes in one chapter and let you pick and choose. I will usually give you some guidance in the headnote to each individual recipe. I would like to point out that I have devised the glazes to be used with the Bundt cakes, muffins, quick breads, and scones. The layer cakes require the frosting recipes that yield 4 cups of frosting. Follow your palate and be creative. There are no rules!

If you are going with the vegan options, make sure to use the full-fat canned coconut milk (instead of the heavy cream) and the Earth Balance Vegan Buttery Sticks. The coconut cream at the top of the can should be blended into the coconut milk before it is added. This can be accomplished by warming the entire contents of the can until it is easy to blend. Let the coconut milk cool to room temperature before adding it to the frosting. You can use any of the alternative milks in place of the full-fat cow's milk.

Note: Always sift powdered sugar. Simply place a sieve over a mixing bowl and, using a wooden spoon, stir the sugar and push it through the sieve. This will help achieve smooth, lump-free frostings and glazes.

simple vanilla glaze

This is my simple go-to recipe for any of the Bundt cakes, muffins, quick breads, scones, and even some cookie recipes, such as the Ginger Cookies (page 130).

MAKES ⅓ CUP, ENOUGH FOR 1 LOAF, 12 MUFFINS, 8 SCONES, OR 1 BUNDT CAKE

117 grams (1¼ cups) confectioners' sugar, plus more as needed

2 Tablespoons milk or dairy-free milk, plus more as needed

1 teaspoon vanilla extract or 1 vanilla bean, pod split in half lengthwise and seeds scraped

1 Using a fine-mesh sieve set over a bowl, sift the confectioners' sugar. Add the milk and vanilla and mix with a spoon. If the frosting is too thick, beat in more milk, 1 teaspoon at a time. If the frosting becomes too thin, blend in a small amount of confectioners' sugar (1 Tablespoon). Blend until smooth.

2 Drizzle the baked good using a spoon. The glaze will set up really fast if the drizzled baked good is placed in the refrigerator for 10 minutes.

Note: The glaze can be stored in an airtight container in the refrigerator for up to 2 weeks. Allow it to come to room temperature before using or reheat gently in the microwave for 30 seconds, or until it reaches a drizzling consistency.

citrus glaze

Use this glaze for the Poached Lemon Cake (page 110). Switch out the lemon zest for orange zest and use it on the Poached Orange Cake with Pecans (page 109). You can also use it on any of the Bundt cakes, muffins, quick breads, or scones. Use a Microplane fine grater to create the zest.

MAKES ⅓ CUP, ENOUGH FOR 1 LOAF, 12 MUFFINS, 8 SCONES, OR 1 BUNDT CAKE

117 grams (1¼ cups) confectioners' sugar, plus more as needed

2 Tablespoons freshly squeezed orange juice or lemon juice (from 1 orange or lemon), plus more as needed

2 teaspoons orange zest or lemon zest (from 1 orange or lemon)

1 Using a fine-mesh sieve set over a bowl, sift the confectioners' sugar. Add the juice and the zest and mix with a spoon. If the frosting is too thick, blend in more juice, 1 teaspoon at a time. If the frosting becomes too thin, blend in a small amount of confectioners' sugar (1 Tablespoon). Blend until smooth.

2 Drizzle the baked good using a spoon. The glaze will set up really fast if the drizzled baked good is placed in the refrigerator for 10 minutes.

Note: The glaze can be stored in an airtight container in the refrigerator for up to 2 weeks. Allow it to come to room temperature before using or reheat gently in the microwave for 30 seconds, or until it reaches a drizzling consistency.

coffee glaze

I love this glaze with the Roasted Banana Cake (page 77), the Olive Oil and Cherry Bundt Cake (page 90), the New York–Style Coffee Cake (page 83), or the Vegan Pumpkin Cake (page 80).

MAKES ⅓ CUP, ENOUGH FOR 1 LOAF, 12 MUFFINS, 8 SCONES, OR 1 BUNDT CAKE

117 grams (1¼ cups) confectioners' sugar, plus more as needed

2 Tablespoons strongly brewed coffee, or 1 teaspoon instant coffee granules diluted in 1 Tablespoon hot water, plus more as needed

1 teaspoon coffee extract (optional)

1 Using a fine-mesh sieve set over a bowl, sift the confectioners' sugar. Add the coffee and the coffee extract (if using) and mix with a spoon. If the frosting is too thick, beat in more coffee, 1 teaspoon at a time. If the frosting becomes too thin, blend in a small amount of confectioners' sugar (1 Tablespoon). Blend until smooth.

2 Drizzle the baked good using a spoon. The glaze will set up really fast if the drizzled baked good is placed in the refrigerator for 10 minutes.

Note: The glaze can be stored in an airtight container in the refrigerator for up to 2 weeks. Allow it to come to room temperature before using or reheat gently in the microwave for 30 seconds, or until it reaches a drizzling consistency.

maple glaze

I really like this glaze over the Roasted Banana Cake (page 77). It can also be used to top any of the scones. I think it is especially good over the Cinnamon and Praline Pecan Scones (page 57).

MAKES ⅓ CUP, ENOUGH FOR 1 LOAF, 12 MUFFINS, 8 SCONES, OR 1 BUNDT CAKE

47 grams (½ cup) confectioners' sugar, plus more as needed

1 Tablespoon melted and cooled clarified butter or coconut oil

2 Tablespoons maple syrup, plus more as needed

1 teaspoon maple extract (optional)

1 Using a fine-mesh sieve set over a bowl, sift the confectioners' sugar. To the sugar add the clarified butter, maple syrup, and maple extract (if using) and mix with a spoon. If the frosting is too thick, beat in more maple syrup, 1 teaspoon at a time. If the frosting becomes too thin, blend in a small amount of confectioners' sugar (1 Tablespoon). Blend until smooth.

2 Drizzle the baked good using a spoon. The glaze will set up really fast if the drizzled baked good is placed in the refrigerator for 10 minutes.

Note: The glaze can be stored in an airtight container in the refrigerator for up to 2 weeks. Allow it to come to room temperature before using or reheat gently in the microwave for 30 seconds, or until it reaches a drizzling consistency.

cream cheese glaze

This is another all-purpose glaze that you can use on any of the quick breads or muffins. I think it goes really well with the carrot quick bread or muffins (page 44). It is like having carrot cake for breakfast. It is also great on any of the Bundt cakes.

MAKES 1 CUP, MORE THAN ENOUGH FOR 1 LOAF, 12 MUFFINS, 8 SCONES, OR 1 BUNDT CAKE

94 grams (1 cup) confectioners' sugar, sifted

4 ounces regular or vegan cream cheese, softened to room temperature

3 Tablespoons milk or dairy-free milk

2 teaspoons vanilla extract

Pinch of fine salt

1 In a small bowl, combine the confectioners' sugar, cream cheese, 1 Tablespoon of the milk, the vanilla, and salt and mix with a spoon or a stand mixer. Blend well and continue to add milk until you reach the desired consistency. Place the glaze in the refrigerator for 30 minutes to set up a bit. Drizzle quick bread or muffins with the glaze.

Note: The glaze can be stored in an airtight container in the refrigerator for up to 5 days. Allow it to come to room temperature before using or reheat gently in the microwave, for 30 seconds, or until it reaches a drizzling consistency.

streusel topping

This can be used in combination with any of the quick breads or muffins. It should be made prior to making the batter. After you have filled the loaf pan or the muffin tins, you can simply scatter the streusel lightly over the top and bake as directed. I love the textural change that it provides. After baking, you can add any of the glazes for an extra-special touch. Don't feel compelled to use all of the streusel. It will keep in an airtight container in the freezer for several months.

MAKES ENOUGH FOR 1 LOAF OR 12 MUFFINS

63 grams (⅓ cup) firmly packed brown sugar

30 grams (¼ cup) sorghum flour

18 grams (2 Tablespoons) potato starch

13 grams (2 Tablespoons) tapioca starch

2 teaspoons ground cinnamon

½ teaspoon xanthan gum

½ cup pecans, coarsely chopped (optional)

3 Tablespoons melted and slightly cooled clarified butter or coconut oil

1 In a bowl, whisk together the brown sugar, sorghum flour, potato starch, tapioca starch, cinnamon, xanthan gum, and pecans (if using). Pour the clarified butter into the dry ingredients and stir with a fork until all of the dry ingredients are moistened. Continue to process with the fork or your fingers until you achieve a crumbly consistency.

2 After placing the batter in the loaf pan or muffin pan, sprinkle the streusel topping over it evenly and lightly. Don't press down. Bake as directed for each individual loaf or muffins.

vegan caramel sauce

This is good on everything. I especially love it on banana quick bread or muffins. Sometimes I spread it on my morning toast. Sometimes I stand in front of the refrigerator and eat it by the spoonful. My secret is out!

MAKES 1 CUP, ENOUGH FOR 1 LOAF, 12 MUFFINS, OR A FILLING FOR A LAYER CAKE

72 grams (¼ cup) cashew butter

¼ cup maple syrup

2 Tablespoons melted coconut oil

4 pitted dates

1 teaspoon vanilla extract

Pinch of fine salt

1 Place the cashew butter, maple syrup, coconut oil, dates, vanilla, and salt in a small blender or food processor and puree until smooth.

2 Transfer the caramel to a glass jar and place it in the refrigerator to chill and stiffen up. If you would like the caramel to be spreadable, let it sit at room temperature for 30 minutes to 1 hour. Store leftover caramel in the refrigerator.

coconut caramel sauce (vegan) plain, coffee, or bourbon flavored

You can use this sauce with all of my vegan cakes, but it is also good with the Ginger Cake (page 89). In fact, this caramel is so good that I often cook it a little longer and use it on the Roasted Banana Cake (page 77).

MAKES ½ CUP, MORE THAN ENOUGH FOR 1 LOAF, 12 MUFFINS, 8 SCONES, OR 1 BUNDT CAKE

1 can (14 ounces) full-fat unsweetened coconut milk, chilled

¼ cup water

1 Tablespoon light corn syrup

88 grams (½ cup) granulated sugar

2 Tablespoons water, bourbon, or espresso (or 2 Tablespoons hot water plus 1 teaspoon espresso powder), cooled

1 teaspoon vanilla extract

⅛ teaspoon fine salt

1 Open the can of coconut milk and scrape the coconut cream from the top as best you can. In a small bowl placed on a scale, weigh the coconut cream and add coconut milk to bring the amount to 120 grams. Place the bowl of coconut milk back in the refrigerator (it is best to use it cold). Reserve the rest of the can for another use.

2 Put the water in a small saucepan with the corn syrup. Measure the granulated sugar and place it in a shallow mound in the center of the saucepan. Over medium-high heat, bring to a boil, without stirring, until the sugar starts to turn brown (you will begin to see dark spots after 8 to 10 minutes). Once the sugar has reached this stage, give the pan a swirl or two to incorporate the brown spots. The caramel should be an even orange-brown.

3 Remove the pan from the heat (I usually place the pan in an empty sink), very carefully add the 2 Tablespoons water, and whisk until it stops bubbling. Return the pan to medium heat and whisk out any sugary lumps. Add the coconut cream from the refrigerator and whisk vigorously until smooth. Continue to whisk for 4 to 5 minutes: 4 minutes will achieve a drizzle consistency (you are looking for what is called the "thread stage," which will read 230° to 234°F on an instant-read thermometer) and 5 minutes will achieve a spreadable consistency (the "firm-ball stage," 242° to 249°F). Reduce the heat to low and add the vanilla and salt. Remove from the heat.

4 Let the sauce cool completely, then transfer to an airtight container. Store in the refrigerator for up to a month. You can reheat the sauce in a saucepan over very gentle heat or in the microwave for 2 minutes at 50 percent power.

Note: You won't really know the consistency of the caramel until it has been refrigerated for a time. If it is too thin, you can pour it into a small saucepan over medium heat and bring to a boil. Cook for another 2 minutes. If the caramel is too stiff, heat it gently in the microwave (1 minute at 50 percent power) or in a saucepan (on low heat) on the stove. Add 1 Tablespoon light corn syrup and stir until well incorporated.

pumpkin butter

Sometimes I like to serve this with the Ginger Cake (page 89) or the Holiday Fruitcake (page 102). I think it works best to slice the cake first and add a dollop of pumpkin butter along with a dollop of fresh whipped cream on the cut side. I sometimes make this pumpkin butter just for my morning toast and tea.

MAKES 2 CUPS

1 (15-ounce) can pumpkin puree

190 grams (1 cup) firmly packed brown sugar

2 teaspoons ground ginger

2 teaspoons ground cinnamon

1 teaspoon vanilla extract

½ teaspoon fine salt

¼ teaspoon ground cardamom

¼ teaspoon ground nutmeg

1 In a medium bowl, place the pumpkin puree, brown sugar, ginger, cinnamon, vanilla, salt, cardamom, and nutmeg. Mix with a rubber spatula or whisk until well incorporated.

2 Transfer the pumpkin mixture to a heavy 2- to 3-quart saucepan. Bring to a sputtering simmer over medium heat. Cook, stirring constantly, until it is thick and shiny, about 5 minutes. This step is crucial for taking the canned flavor out of the pumpkin and blooming the spices.

3 Pour the mixture back into the mixing bowl and let it cool until warm to the touch. The pumpkin butter can be refrigerated and used later. You can store it in an airtight container in the refrigerator for several weeks.

ginger jam

This jam is excellent served with any of the Bundt cakes or as a topping for the Roasted Banana Cake (page 77) or the Ginger Cake (page 89). You can also just spread it on toast.

MAKES ½ CUP

113 grams (about 1 cup) candied ginger (not candy with ginger flavor), cut into ¼-inch dice

½ cup water

44 grams (¼ cup) granulated sugar

3 Tablespoons freshly squeezed lemon juice (from 1 to 2 lemons)

2 Tablespoons unsalted butter or Earth Balance Vegan Buttery Sticks

2 Tablespoons cold water

1 In a saucepan, place the candied ginger, ½ cup water, granulated sugar, and lemon juice. Boil the mixture for 5 to 7 minutes, until the ginger softens and the sugar dissolves.

2 Remove the pan from the heat and drop in the butter. Let the mixture cool for about 20 minutes.

3 Transfer the mixture to a small blender or a small cup that can be used with an immersion blender and add the cold water. Blend the mixture until it is smooth and creamy. Check the texture, making sure that it is blended to a silky puree, keeping in mind that it will thicken up in the refrigerator.

4 Scoop the mixture into a glass jar with a lid. It will keep in the refrigerator for several weeks.

simple chocolate frosting

This frosting yields enough to fill and cover one 8-inch layer cake. Halve the recipe to yield enough for 12 cupcakes.

MAKES 2 CUPS, ENOUGH FOR AN 8-INCH CAKE

352 grams (3¾ cups) confectioners' sugar

81 grams (½ cup) unsweetened cocoa powder

½ cup (1 stick) unsalted butter or Earth Balance Vegan Buttery Sticks, softened

2 teaspoons vanilla extract

1 cup heavy cream or full-fat canned coconut milk, plus more as needed

1 In the bowl of a stand mixer fitted with the paddle attachment, blend together the confectioners' sugar and cocoa powder. On low speed, beat in the butter until the mixture is crumbly. Beat in the vanilla and then gradually add the cream to make a spreadable frosting. Do not add the cream all at once; add it gradually until you achieve the desired consistency.

Note: Store in the refrigerator in an airtight container for up to 1 month. Bring back to room temperature and whip briefly in the stand mixer or with a hand mixer, until it returns to its fluffy frosting state, before using.

maple frosting

Maple is always a big hit with me. Sometimes I just divide this recipe in half and use it on my Roasted Banana Cake (page 77). It is also good on the Orange and Almond Butter Layer Cake (page 95).

MAKES 3 CUPS, ENOUGH TO FILL AND FROST ONE 8- OR 9-INCH LAYER CAKE

1½ cups unsalted butter (3 sticks) or Earth Balance Vegan Buttery Sticks, softened

2 Tablespoons firmly packed brown sugar

3 Tablespoons heavy cream or full-fat canned coconut milk, plus more as needed

2 teaspoons maple extract

2 teaspoons vanilla extract

¼ teaspoon fine salt

329 grams (3½ cups) confectioners' sugar

1 In the bowl of a stand mixer fitted with the paddle attachment, blend the butter, brown sugar, cream, maple extract, vanilla, and salt on medium speed until smooth, 1 to 2 minutes. Reduce the mixer speed to low, slowly add the confectioners' sugar, and whip until the frosting is smooth, 1 to 2 minutes. If the frosting is too dense, add another teaspoon of cream. Increase the speed to medium high and whip the frosting until it is light and fluffy, 3 to 5 minutes.

Note: Store in the refrigerator in an airtight container for up to 1 month. Bring back to room temperature and whip briefly in the stand mixer or with a hand mixer, until it returns to its fluffy frosting state, before using.

almond frosting

I use this frosting recipe most often with my Orange and Almond Butter Layer Cake (page 95) but you can also use it to frost the Classic Chocolate Layer Cake (page 85).

MAKES 3 CUPS, ENOUGH TO FILL AND FROST ONE
8- OR 9-INCH LAYER CAKE

1½ cups unsalted butter (3 sticks) or Earth Balance Vegan Buttery Sticks, softened

3 Tablespoons heavy cream or full-fat canned coconut milk, plus more as needed

2 teaspoons almond extract

1 teaspoon vanilla extract

¼ teaspoon fine salt

329 grams (3½ cups) confectioners' sugar

1 In the bowl of a stand mixer fitted with the paddle attachment, blend the butter, cream, almond extract, vanilla, and salt on medium speed until smooth, 1 to 2 minutes. Reduce the speed to low, slowly add the confectioners' sugar, and whip until the frosting is smooth, 1 to 2 minutes. If the frosting is too dense, add another teaspoon of cream. Increase the speed to medium high and whip the frosting until it is light and fluffy, 3 to 5 minutes.

Note: Store in the refrigerator in an airtight container for up to 1 month. Bring back to room temperature and whip briefly in the stand mixer or with a hand mixer, until it returns to its fluffy frosting state, before using.

coffee frosting

I use this frosting recipe most often with my Classic Chocolate Layer Cake (page 85). Mocha madness!

MAKES 3 CUPS, ENOUGH TO FILL AND FROST ONE
8- OR 9-INCH LAYER CAKE

1½ cups unsalted butter (3 sticks) or Earth Balance Vegan Buttery Sticks, softened

3 Tablespoons heavy cream or full-fat canned coconut milk, plus more as needed

2 Tablespoons instant espresso or instant coffee granules

1 Tablespoon vanilla extract

¼ teaspoon fine salt

329 grams (3½ cups) confectioners' sugar

1 In the bowl of a stand mixer fitted with the paddle attachment, blend the butter, cream, instant espresso, vanilla, and salt on medium speed until smooth, 1 to 2 minutes. Reduce the speed to low, slowly add the confectioners' sugar, and whip until the frosting is smooth, 1 to 2 minutes. If the frosting is too dense, add another teaspoon of cream. Increase the speed to medium high and whip the frosting until it is light and fluffy, 3 to 5 minutes.

Note: Store in the refrigerator in an airtight container for up to 1 month. Bring back to room temperature and whip briefly in the stand mixer or with a hand mixer, until it returns to its fluffy frosting state, before using.

cream cheese vanilla bean frosting

This frosting is such a huge component of my Carrot Layer Cake (page 105)—you can't have carrot cake without cream cheese frosting.

MAKES 3 CUPS, ENOUGH TO FILL AND FROST ONE 6 OR 9 INCH LAYER CAKE

1 pound regular or vegan cream cheese, softened but still cool

10 Tablespoons (1¼ sticks) unsalted butter or Earth Balance Vegan Buttery Sticks, room temperature

2 Tablespoons full-fat sour cream or vegan sour cream

1 teaspoon vanilla extract

1 vanilla bean, pod split in half lengthwise and seeds scraped

188 grams (2 cups) confectioners' sugar, sifted

Milk or heavy cream, as needed

1 In the bowl of a stand mixer fitted with the paddle attachment, mix the cream cheese, butter, and sour cream. Add the vanilla and the seeds from the vanilla bean. Blend the mixture until it is smooth and even. On very low speed, mix in the confectioners' sugar until the frosting is smooth and creamy. If the frosting is too thick, beat in 1 teaspoon of milk. If the frosting becomes too thin, beat in a small amount of confectioners' sugar. It is best to frost your cake while the frosting is still at room temperature.

Note: Store in the refrigerator in an airtight container for up to 1 month. Bring back to room temperature and whip briefly in the stand mixer or with a hand mixer, until it returns to its fluffy frosting state, before using.

chocolate glaze

This is good with the Roasted Banana Cake (page 77) as well as the Olive Oil and Cherry Bundt Cake (page 90). The corn syrup helps the glaze from getting too drippy.

MAKES 1 CUP, MORE THAN ENOUGH FOR 1 LOAF, 12 MUFFINS, 8 SCONES, OR 1 BUNDT CAKE

6 Tablespoons unsalted butter or Earth Balance Vegan Buttery Sticks, softened

4 ounces (about ¾ cup) semisweet chocolate, coarsely chopped

2 teaspoons light corn syrup

1 To make on the stovetop: Combine the butter, chocolate, and corn syrup in a bowl over a double boiler. Stir until nearly all of the chocolate is melted; there can still be a few visible pieces. Remove the bowl from the heat and stir slowly until the chocolate is completely melted and the glaze is smooth.

2 To make in the microwave: Combine the butter, chocolate, and corn syrup in a microwave-safe bowl and melt in the microwave on medium power for about 2 minutes. You may need to return the glaze to the microwave for another minute at medium power. Stir the mixture until completely smooth; do not whisk or beat.

3 To use as a poured glaze, allow the glaze to cool to 90°F, or let it set up completely until it is the consistency of canned chocolate fudge icing, and spread on a cake with a spatula.

Note: Store for up to 1 month in an airtight container. Bring to room temperature before using.

chocolate ganache

I use this recipe to fill my Classic Chocolate Layer Cake (page 85) and then I make a batch of the Simple Chocolate Frosting (page 250) for the top and sides. This combo is so chocolaty that chocolate lovers feel that they have died and gone to heaven.

MAKES 1 CUP, ENOUGH TO FILL AN 8- OR
9-INCH LAYER CAKE

¾ cup heavy cream or full-fat canned coconut milk

5 ounces (about 1 cup) semisweet chocolate, chopped into small pieces

1 Tablespoon hazelnut liqueur, such as Frangelico, or any chocolate liqueur

1 In a saucepan, bring the cream to a simmer. Reduce the heat to very low, add the chocolate, and stir until the chocolate melts. Remove from the heat and add the liqueur. Pour the ganache into a small bowl and chill for about an hour, until it has thickened to a spreadable consistency.

Note: If you are not using the ganache right away, refrigerate it for up to 1 month. When ready to use, let it sit at room temperature for 15 to 20 minutes, until it comes back to a spreadable consistency.

caramel sauce

This is a good all-purpose caramel sauce for the Chocolate Ganache Tart (page 184) or the Brownies (page 133). I also like to swirl this caramel sauce into my whipped cream topping for the Coconut Cream Pie (page 197). If you want a vegan caramel sauce, try the Coconut Caramel Sauce on page 248.

MAKES 1¼ CUPS

1 cup heavy cream

1 Tablespoon light corn syrup

95 grams (½ cup) firmly packed brown sugar

Pinch of fine salt

1 teaspoon vanilla extract

1 Put the cream in a small heavy saucepan. Whisk in the corn syrup, brown sugar, and salt and bring to a boil. Turn the heat down to medium and continue to boil for 15 minutes, whisking every few minutes.

2 When the glaze has come together into a smooth, thick caramel, remove from the heat and stir in the vanilla. You are looking for what is called the soft-ball stage, which will read 234° to 240°F on your instant-read thermometer.

Note: Store the sauce in the refrigerator for up to 1 month. When ready to use, gently reheat in a small pot over low heat, and then mix gently with a whisk to re-emulsify.

vanilla buttercream frosting

This is a nice all-purpose buttercream frosting for all of my cakes. You can switch it up by leaving out the vanilla and adding 2 Tablespoons of lemon or orange zest. I use this frosting for the Lemon Layer Cake (page 92) and the Orange and Almond Butter Layer Cake (page 95).

MAKES 3 CUPS, ENOUGH TO FILL AND FROST ONE 8- OR 9-INCH LAYER CAKE

1½ cups (3 sticks) unsalted butter or Earth Balance Vegan Buttery Sticks, softened

3 Tablespoons heavy cream or full-fat canned coconut milk, plus more as needed

1 Tablespoon vanilla extract or 1 vanilla bean, pod split in half lengthwise and seeds scraped

¼ teaspoon fine salt

329 grams (3½ cups) confectioners' sugar

1 In the bowl of a stand mixer fitted with the paddle attachment, blend the butter, cream, vanilla, and salt on medium speed until smooth, 1 to 2 minutes. Reduce the speed to low, slowly add the confectioners' sugar, and whip until the frosting is smooth, 1 to 2 minutes. If the frosting is too dense, add another teaspoon of cream. Increase the speed to medium high and whip the frosting until it is light and fluffy, 1 to 2 minutes.

Note: Store in the refrigerator in an airtight container for up to 1 month. Bring back to room temperature and whip briefly in the stand mixer or with a hand mixer, until it returns to its fluffy frosting state, before using.

candied carrot curls

I know these look really fussy (see page 104), but I promise you they are not. Carrot curls really elevate a carrot cake and make it worthy of a special occasion. Save up your takeout Chinese chopsticks—you will need about 20 of them.

MAKES 20 CURLS, ENOUGH FOR ONE CARROT LAYER CAKE

Gluten-free nonstick spray

2 large carrots

1 cup water

1 cup granulated sugar, plus more for finishing (optional)

1 Preheat the oven to 225°F. Line a baking sheet with parchment paper and lightly spray with gluten-free nonstick spray. Using a vegetable peeler, peel long strips from the carrots. (Strips will get wider as you get closer to the core of the carrot. The wider strips work best.)

2 Bring the water and granulated sugar to a boil in a large heavy saucepan over medium-high heat. Add the carrot strips and reduce the heat to medium-low. Simmer the carrot strips for 2 minutes. Drain in a wire-mesh strainer and let cool for about 5 minutes.

3 Working quickly, wrap each carrot strip around a chopstick (you will need about 20 chopsticks). Fashion the carrot strip in a spiral by starting from the fat end of the chopstick and going upward to the skinny end (like a candy cane). Place the wrapped chopsticks back on the baking sheet, leaving several inches between each one. Sprinkle with granulated sugar, if desired.

continued

candied carrot curls, continued

4 Bake for 20 minutes. As the carrot strips bake, they will begin to look translucent. Remove the baking sheet from the oven and let the curls sit at room temperature until completely dry (about 30 minutes). Carefully remove the curls from each chopstick and place them on a folded piece of paper within an airtight container.

Note: Don't make the carrot curls more than a day ahead. Depending on the humidity in your area, they can lose their crunch. You can dry them out again by placing them on a baking sheet and heating them in a 225°F oven for 10 minutes.

candied pecans

I found this recipe in a magazine years ago. It was such a revelation and so tasty that I have been using it ever since. It works with any nut you prefer. I often like the simplicity of a cake that is frosted and decorated with some well-placed candied nuts. You can make the candied pecans ahead, let them dry out for a day, and then chop them coarsely as a garnish for any of the cakes or use them whole. Your favorite glaze or frosting will help them to adhere to the cake.

MAKES APPROX. 1 CUP

¼ pound whole pecans, walnuts, hazelnuts, or almonds

2 Tablespoons honey

1 Preheat the oven to 310°F.

2 Add the pecans and honey to a small oven-safe sauté pan and place in the oven. After 5 minutes, stir the pecans to evenly coat them with the now-melted honey. After another 5 minutes, stir again. After a final 5 minutes, remove the pan from the oven and empty the nuts out onto parchment paper, making sure to separate the nuts so they don't stick together as they cool.

flavored whipped cream

Whipped cream is always a welcome addition to any dessert. You can make it plain, but I would encourage you to try some of the variations. My colleague and friend Kristene Loayza taught me how to transform my whipped cream into a softer and more billowy presentation by adding a small amount of crème fraîche. It will make your desserts camera-ready. Wink, wink!

MAKES 2 CUPS

basic vanilla

1 cup heavy cream

3 Tablespoons confectioners' sugar

2 teaspoons vanilla extract or 1 vanilla bean, pod split in half lengthwise and seeds scraped

3 to 4 Tablespoons crème fraîche

orange

1 cup heavy cream

3 Tablespoons undiluted orange juice concentrate, thawed

2 Tablespoons confectioners' sugar

3 to 4 Tablespoons crème fraîche

mocha

1 cup heavy cream combined with 2 teaspoons instant coffee granules (let sit for 5 minutes and then stir and add to mixer)

¼ cup confectioners' sugar

1 Tablespoon unsweetened cocoa powder

3 to 4 Tablespoons crème fraîche

almond or hazelnut

1 cup heavy cream

2 Tablespoons confectioners' sugar

2 Tablespoons Amaretto (almond) or Frangelico (hazelnut) liqueur

3 to 4 Tablespoons crème fraîche

ginger

1 cup heavy cream

2 Tablespoons confectioners' sugar

2 Tablespoons very finely minced crystallized ginger

1 teaspoon finely grated fresh ginger

3 to 4 Tablespoons crème fraîche

1 In the bowl of a stand mixer fitted with the whip attachment, whip the cream on medium-high speed until the trails of the whip stay visible in the cream (4 to 5 minutes). Add the confectioners' sugar and flavorings and continue to whip until soft hills and valleys begin to form (1 minute). Remove the bowl from the mixer and fold in the crème fraîche gently with a big spoon or rubber spatula until the mixture becomes soft and billowy.

Note: Be careful not to overbeat or you will make sweetened flavored butter. You can rescue overbeaten (curdled) whipped cream by removing the bowl from the mixer, adding 1 to 2 Tablespoons of cold heavy cream, and mixing with a big spoon or rubber spatula until the cream is well incorporated. It will return to soft and billowy.

resources

The following listing includes sources for the ingredients and tools that I have found to be essential for successful gluten-free baking. I have tried so many options and these are tried and true.

INGREDIENTS

Flours, Starches, and Gums

As I mentioned in the introduction to this book, all of my recipes were tested with Bob's Red Mill (bobsredmill.com) flours. They are readily available, and best of all, the flours are organic and milled fine. Milling is so important for the final baked good. Finely milled flour will ensure a baked good with a silky mouthfeel. I am sure that we have all had gluten-free baked goods that were gritty and unpleasant. To avoid that, begin your baking with Bob's Red Mill. I also use Bob's xanthan gum.

Another fantastic company that I love, Authentic Foods (authenticfoods.com), also carries superfine-grind flours that are unbeatable. The downside is that while most of their products are GMO-free, they are not organic.

All of the flours that I use in this book can be ordered through Amazon.com. It is worth the Amazon Prime membership to be able to order all of your flours and get free shipping. The delivery costs on flours would be difficult to bear otherwise. Be sure to check your local health food market or the natural food aisle in your favorite grocery store as well.

The only time I veer away from Bob's Red Mill for flour is with Mochiko sweet rice flour from Koda Farms (kodafarms.com). It is absolutely the best, especially for my piecrusts. It has a powdery fine texture that allows the starches to be more readily available. It gives my piecrust the best workability. Don't skimp with sweet rice flour—go with Koda.

Additionally, I have discovered that Now brand (nowfoods.com) is the best psyllium husk powder because it is milled into a fine powder from a reputable source. You can order it from their website or from Amazon.com, or check with your local health food store.

Applesauce

I don't always have time to make apple puree (see page 30). It is perfectly fine to substitute in a high-quality applesauce. It should be dense and made without water added. Some national brands are thin and watery. This will definitely affect your baking. What you are looking for is a dense, well-blended (not chunky) applesauce with no additives. These are my favorite brands: Santa Cruz (santacruzorganic.com), Whole Foods 365 (wholefoodsmarket.com), North Coast (northcoast.organic), and Trader Joe's (traderjoes.com) unsweetened applesauce.

Double-Acting Baking Powder

Once a single-action product, such as baking soda, is exposed to moisture, it reacts one time. A double-action product, such as baking powder, reacts once when it is exposed to moisture and then again when exposed to heat. Sometimes I include both baking soda and baking powder to ensure additional lift both at the beginning of baking and again at the end. This is especially important in gluten-free baking, when we don't have the gluten formation that is capable of holding more of the gas that is produced with leavening. My favorite brand is Clabber Girl (clabbergirl.com), but you can use any double-acting gluten-free brand.

Baking Spray

My favorite brand is Spectrum High Heat Canola Spray Oil (available through Amazon.com or at grocery or health food stores). It has a fine-spray nozzle and does its job so beautifully. Gluten-free baked goods have a tendency to stick to bakeware more readily than baked goods made with gluten. This is *not* due to the amount of sugar. I believe it has something to do with gluten acting as a barrier. Gluten-free baked goods tend to be a little stickier as a result and can really present a problem when it comes time to get them out of the pan. Clarified butter works really well but it needs to be put on in a nice even layer, which is hard to achieve. Coconut oil is also great, but it needs to be in a container with a fine-mist spray. I have never found olive oil sprays to be that effective.

Butter and Alternatives

I tend to use a lot of clarified butter in my baked goods. It is lactose-free and still has the rich butter flavor. Making your own clarified butter is easy (see my tutorial on page 25) but there are many brands of clarified butter on the market; my favorite is made by Organic Valley (organicvalley.coop).

After clarified butter, my next favorite fat throughout this book is coconut oil (Nutiva Brand is my favorite, but there are a lot of good ones out there). Measure it by melting it first and then cooling it. Always measure it in a liquid measuring cup.

When it comes to a butter alternative for piecrusts and frostings, I really only have one answer—Earth Balance (earthbalancenatural.com)! All of their fats are nonhydrogenated. The buttery sticks are packaged just like regular butter, in $^1/_2$-cup sticks. This allows you to use them in the same way as butter. I like the one that is soy free, but you be the judge. This brand is widely available in grocery stores.

Cocoa Powder and Chocolate

I use Scharffen Berger's unsweetened cocoa powder, chocolate chips, and chocolate bars (scharffenberger.com). My other favorite brand is Guittard (guittard.com). Both are premium brands, and they are going to cost a little more than other national brands. My view is that if you are going to the trouble of baking, go the extra distance and use the good stuff. It is best to weigh chocolate whether it is powder, bars, or chips. Chips vary in size, and chopped chocolate will fill a cup with huge discrepancies depending on how coarse you chop it. Follow the weights that I give in each recipe and avoid the pitfalls.

Canned Coconut Milk

I don't really have a favorite brand—just be sure that the coconut milk is 100 percent coconut milk. Some brands add water and even coconut water. When I call for coconut milk, use the full-fat coconut milk. I think it is also important that it be organic. Coconut cream will always rise to the top of the can. To use coconut milk to its best advantage, make sure the coconut cream is incorporated into the coconut milk. I achieve this by emptying the contents of the can into a microwave-safe bowl or a saucepan. Gently heat the mixture over a low temperature on the stove or in the microwave for 1 minute at 50 percent power, and whisk until well blended. Let cool before using.

Flavorings and Extracts

Here is another area where I refuse to scrimp. Flavor is so key to successful baked goods. Remember, you are also fighting the expectation that gluten-free will taste dietetic, dry, and flavorless. Flavorganics (flavorganics.com) has a full line of really great extracts. All of them are organic and pure (no fake flavors). When it comes to vanilla, I do love using the seeds of a vanilla bean. However, vanilla beans are very expensive. The next best thing is vanilla bean paste. My favorite is Nielsen-Massey's Madagascar bourbon vanilla bean paste (nielsenmassey.com). It is also expensive but not as pricey as vanilla beans. I use it in the same quantity as vanilla extract. It imparts a beautiful depth and complexity with the added bonus of the flecks of vanilla bean seeds. Both brands are widely available online as well as at most grocery stores, kitchen supply shops, and cake decorating shops.

Royal Icing

When it comes to royal icing and decorating cutout cookies, Wilton (wilton.com) is the benchmark for both tools and tutorials. Wilton carries everything for the advanced baker as well as for the novice. If you're just beginning, I suggest you keep it really simple. Wilton makes royal icing already in a tube with a piping tip (this is what we used for my gingerbread men on page 120). The icing comes in a variety of colors and in both gel and opaque. You can find the tubes in most grocery stores in the baking aisle, or you can go online and order it directly.

Salt

I stipulate fine salt throughout the book. I am referring to the size of the particles. A coarse salt will measure differently than a fine grind. All my recipes use fine-grind salt.

Sour Cream Alternatives

There are so many more flavorful dairy alternatives nowadays. When it comes to sour cream, I like Tofutti brand (tofutti.com) sour cream and cream cheese. I have tested the Tofutti sour cream in all of my cake recipes that call for regular sour cream. Whole Foods and many other health food stores usually carry these products.

Brown Sugar

I always keep dark brown sugar in my pantry. I find that brown sugar promotes better browning in baked goods and has slightly more nutrients than white sugar. The difference between light and dark brown sugar is simply the amount of molasses that each contains. Light brown sugar has less molasses per total volume of sugar (about 3.5 percent) while dark brown sugar has more (6.5 percent). You can easily see the difference in their makeup using just your eyeballs: dark brown sugar is darker in color and looks more like molasses. You can taste it, too: dark brown sugar has a slightly more complex flavor that people often characterize as being similar to caramel or toffee. Dark brown sugar weighs more, contains more moisture, and is more acidic than light brown sugar. It also draws in more moisture through the process of baking. All of my recipes were devised using dark brown sugar, but you can also use light brown sugar.

Other Sugars

Feel free to substitute sugars as you see fit. There are so many to choose from. Just be mindful of the fact that I only tested with dark brown sugar, light brown sugar, and white granulated sugar. Some of the other sugars do not dissolve as readily, especially turbinado. That is why I use turbinado as a textural enhancement in cobblers, crisps, ginger cookies, and so on. Coconut sugar has a really complex flavor that I love but it also takes a while to break down in baked goods plus it can leave a gritty texture. On the other end of the spectrum, superfine-grind sugar is not ideal either. The smaller particles don't always have enough texture for the

creaming method that I use throughout this book. Aeration and structure are built when you cream the butter and sugar together in the mixer and add the eggs one at a time.

Vegetable Purees

I generally make my own vegetable purees (see the recipes on page 28) but sometimes I am short on time and I don't feel like fussing. My favorite brand and the one that works best with my recipes is the Farmer's Market brand (farmersmarketfoods.com). They make organic butternut squash, pumpkin, and sweet potato purees. You can usually find this brand at Whole Foods (wholefoodsmarket.com). Whatever brand you choose, just be sure that water has not been added. I have been caught off-guard and ended up with some failed baked goods due to too much water in the puree.

Yeast

Active dry yeast and instant (or rapid-rise) yeast are the two most common yeasts available to us as home bakers. The two yeasts can be used interchangeably in recipes, but active dry yeast needs to be dissolved in water before using, while instant yeast can be mixed right into the dough. I like the immediacy of instant yeast, and so it is the only yeast I use throughout this book. My favorite brand is SAF Red Label—the red label is for lower-sugar-content baked goods. It is the only yeast you will need for this book. You can order it through Amazon.com or King Arthur Flour (kingarthurflour.com). I also use Fleischmann's RapidRise Instant Yeast. Fleischmann's is premeasured in individual packets and can be found in most grocery stores.

TOOLS

Bins and Jars

Storage bins are so important to my baking. I like plastic bins that can be tightly sealed and have a large enough opening for refilling and dispensing flour, nuts, and grains. The glass ones are pretty, but they are heavy and breakable. I label both on the lid and the front of each bin using painters' tape or a thick permanent marker. When you are working with so many flours, it is easy to confuse them. I buy my flours in bulk and store them in the closet, where it is cool, until I need to refill the bins. The best place to find these handy organizers is Bed Bath & Beyond (bedbathandbeyond.com) and the Container Store (containerstore.com).

Cake Strips

Cake strips are a great tool for baking flat layer cakes (see the tutorial on page 75). They help the layers bake more evenly. They are widely available online as well as at kitchen and baking supply shops.

Instant-Read Thermometer

It is important to take the temperature of your baked bread; otherwise there is no way to know if it is cooked to the middle. There are a lot of great thermometers out there. You don't need a really expensive one. However, if you do want to invest in what I consider the best one on the market, I would have you choose a Thermapen (thermoworks.com).

Oven Thermometer

As I advised in the introduction, get a good instant-read thermometer and use it to evaluate how the temperature dial on your stove correlates to your actual oven temperature. It is best to buy thermometers from a high-end kitchen store. The ones that are sold in grocery stores tend to give out quickly. I usually put one in the front of my oven (hanging off the lower baking rack) and another one at the back of the oven on the same rack as the rack I use for baked goods. I know this sounds excessive, but this gives you the best read on your oven.

Rolling Pin with Spacers

I love the invention of spacers. The food stylist in me that wants everything to be precise. If you are a confident pie roller, you may not need this tool. However, an even thickness will ensure even browning and beautiful pies and cutout cookies. Sur La Table (surlatable.com) and Williams Sonoma (williams-sonoma.com) both carry these tools.

Scale

I have had my Escali (escali.com) for the entire time I have been developing gluten-free recipes (more than seventeen years). It has been a trooper. I bought another brand to have on hand and it is already retired after only five years. I say go with Escali—you can find it at many retail stores and online.

Silicone Pastry Mat

My favorite one is made by Sur La Table (surlatable.com). It has a nice sticky surface that holds up with hand washing (don't put it in the dishwasher). I also love the concentric circles that are printed on the mat and allow you to see the circumference of your pie dough, even through the parchment.

acknowledgments

There is no such thing as a fearless leader. I needed an army of talented individuals to make this book possible. There are so many people to thank, from my early days of teaching baking classes all the way through to having my book published. First and foremost, I thank my mother, Phyllis Wesche. My mother's faith and belief in me has always been a great source of strength. Over the years we have transitioned from being mother and son to becoming the best of friends. A boy always needs his mom. My mother is the first person I turn to when things go wrong or right. I love her so very much.

My stepdad, LeRoy Wesche, has always led by example and has taught me how to remain engaged with life. As I have watched him grow older, I have found his strength, vitality, and striving to learn and remain fit in body, mind, and spirit to be truly an inspiration.

My grandmother, Louise Blake: I learned to cook standing on a chair next to Grandma. She loved to entertain and see her family and friends together sharing food and fun. It was never fussy, just good food that always seemed to magically appear from thin air. I now understand that she must have worked so hard when nobody was around. Grandma was absolutely my best friend growing up. I know that I speak for everyone in the family when I say that she was the beating heart at the center of the entire family. I miss her terribly, but I also know that she is with me every day.

When I was first beginning my exploration of gluten-free baking, some friends told me about the Gluten-Free Grocery Store. I stopped in and met the owner, Topher Delaney. Topher was always so generous and supportive. Her energy and enthusiasm were dizzying. She was the first person to suggest that I teach, and she offered up her store for me to test my skills. I discovered that I had such a passion for passing on the information, never mind that I am an introvert. Topher did not take no for an answer. She put a bread-baking machine in my arms and told me that she wanted me to teach a Gluten-Free Bread in the Bread Machine class in a few weeks. I did what she told me, and look at me now!

Shortly after that, I heard about a new inn in Napa that was going to be a gluten-free facility. The first time I visited the Inn on Randolph, it was a construction zone. At the center of this mess was the dynamic Karen Lynch. She believed in me unconditionally and asked me to lead my first gluten-free weekend shortly after the inn was scheduled to open. I led a total of six weekend retreats over the course of several years. Teaching was so rewarding, and I really felt called upon to stay on this mission. The full-weekend format allowed me to "go deep," and at the end of each weekend, I felt so empowered. It was so great to see the students leave feeling empowered as well. I would also like to thank Louise Boas, who was the chef at the Inn on Randolph. Louise imbued the kitchen with warmth and love.

Thanks also to Mary Claire Draeger DeSoto of Draeger's Grocery Stores in the Bay Area. Mary Claire had the foresight to have a gluten-free section in each of her grocery stores. This was before a gluten-free section was commonplace. She also allowed me to teach in the grocery store. Along the way, food photographer Annabelle Breakey offered up her studio for me to teach in. Annabelle mentored me in so many ways, both as a food stylist and as a cooking professional. Thanks, Annabelle—you always made work fun! I would also like to thank my colleague and friend Karen Shinto. Karen is a fellow food stylist and recipe developer. I assisted her for fourteen years. She taught me precision and a fierce work ethic. We share a naughty sense of humor and so many good times. I love you, Karen.

I knew that I broke through with my teaching when I was asked by Jodi Liano of San Francisco Cooking School to teach each new crop of baking students a four-hour course in allergen-free baking. It is always such a privilege to share this information with people who are learning to master the pastry arts. I know that all of my students have gone out into the world "baking" a difference for allergy sufferers. Thank you, Jodi, for giving allergen-free equal time. Thank you to the talented pastry chefs at SF Cooking School, Nicole Plue and Jessica Sullivan, who see that allergen-free is now a matter of hospitality and that the students should leave with a working knowledge of allergens and how to work around them.

A special shout-out to Erika Lenkert, the editor of *Gluten-Free Forever* magazine. It was a career highlight to be included in the pages of her magazine. Thank you, Erika, for giving the gluten-free community a beautiful food magazine.

I would like to thank all of the talented people at Ten Speed Press—Julie Bennett, Emma Campion, Ashley Lima, Jane Chinn, David Hawk, Windy Dorresteyn, my patient and hardworking editor, Emma Rudolph, and my copy editor, Nancy Bailey. This cookbook was made possible because one person, Kara Plikaitis, believed in me enough to sell Ten Speed on having me do a cookbook. Thank you, Kara! Making you laugh is one of life's great joys. I would also like to thank the book's photographer, Kelly Puleio. Thank you for bringing your full beautiful self to this project. You make food SEXY! Thank you, Claire Mack and David Gantz. Your collection of props and beautiful studio elevated this project beyond what I could have hoped for. I would also like to thank my team of wonder women: my assistants, Kristene Loayza and Natalie Drobny, and my project manager, Sheri Codiana. The careful attention to detail was astounding! I love you, ladies.

Thanks also to Jessica Milanes. I first met Jessica as one of my students at San Francisco Cooking School. She became my intern on this cookbook. She has been my editor, recipe tester, assistant food stylist, sounding board, and hand model. You have been invaluable, Jessica. You are such a superstar hard worker. Thank you!!! The only reason that this book got written is because of your support and talent.

I would also like to thank my chosen family here in San Francisco. You all are such an inspiration to me. We are living our lives together, sharing wondrous food, wondrous celebration, wondrous laughs, and wondrous fun! Thanks to all of you. You are the wind beneath my wings—Shahla Cano (my Persian sister), Jaime Cid, Kirk Livingston (my brothers from another mother), Maribelle Cid (my second mom—the louder, more audacious one), Neil Levine (your generosity is quiet and steady), Kathleen Marshall, John Goldsmith, Larry Bates, Brent Seward, Gabriel (Gabo) Whitler-Zendejas (mi angelito), Drew Ward, Jim Ward, and Eric See. I love you all.

A special thank you to Rebecca Katz. I loved being your food stylist on *Clean Soups*. We hit it off immediately, and now it is privilege to call you a friend. Your mentorship on this book has meant everything to me. As far as I am concerned, you are the Meryl Streep of cookbooks and my best-supporting actress. LOL!

Finally, I would like to thank all of my past students, friends, and colleagues who worked on testing my recipes for this book. You all gave such careful attention to detail. I am humbled and blessed. Thank you.

Nancy Blake

Melissa Bohnstedt

Letty Flohr

Amy Fothergill

Kerry Franzetta

Rachae Jensen

Kathleen Marshall

Maureen Martin

John Edward McGee

Mathew Nathan

Maria Navla

Elizabeth Nordt

Kim Rice

Betsy Stromberg

about the author

Jeffrey Larsen is a food stylist, recipe developer, pastry chef, and baking/cooking instructor specializing in allergen-free baking and cooking. He has developed products and recipes for Nutiva, Hidden Valley Ranch, and Just, Inc. As a food stylist, Jeffrey has worked on a number of cookbooks, cooking magazines, and advertising campaigns. His allergen-free journey began when he started developing recipes for his gluten-intolerant mother in 2002. In helping his mother, Jeffrey gave himself a head start when he discovered that he is also gluten-intolerant. Jeffrey is based in San Francisco, but he also has ties to Denver, New York, and Los Angeles.

www.jeffreylarsen.com

index

Published in the United States by Ten Speed Press, an imprint of the
Crown Publishing Group, a division of Penguin Random House LLC, New York.

www.crownpublishing.com
www.tenspeed.com

Ten Speed Press and the Ten Speed Press colophon are registered trademarks
of Penguin Random House LLC.

Library of Congress Cataloging-in-Publication Data
Names: Larsen, Jeffrey, 1962– author. | Puleio, Kelly, photographer.
Title: Gluten-free baking at home : 102 foolprof recipes
  for delicious breads, cakes, cookies, and more / Jeffrey Larsen ;
photographs by Kelly Puleio.
Description: First edition. | New York : Ten Speed Press, [2019] | Includes
  bibliographical references and index. |
Identifiers: LCCN 2018060697 (print) | LCCN 2019000223 (ebook) | ISBN
  9780399582806 (eBook) | ISBN 9780399582790 (hardcover : alk. paper)
Subjects: LCSH: Bread. | Cookies. | Pies. | Baking. | Gluten-free
  diet–Recipes. | LCGFT: Cookbooks.
Classification: LCC TX765 (ebook) | LCC TX765 .L33 2019 (print) | DDC
  641.5/639311–dc23
LC record available at https://lccn.loc.gov/2018060697

Hardcover ISBN: 978-0-399-58279-0
eBook ISBN: 9780-0-399-58280-6

Printed in China

Design by Ashley Lima
Food styling by Jeffrey Larsen
Food styling assistance by Natalie Drobny, Jessica Milanes, and Kristene Loayza
Prop styling by Claire Mack

10 9 8 7 6 5 4 3 2 1

First Edition